ISBN 978-1-330-22846-3
PIBN 10058081

This book is a reproduction of an important historical work. Forgotten Books uses
state-of-the-art technology to digitally reconstruct the work, preserving the original format
whilst repairing imperfections present in the aged copy. In rare cases, an imperfection in
the original, such as a blemish or missing page, may be replicated in our edition. We do,
however, repair the vast majority of imperfections successfully; any imperfections that
remain are intentionally left to preserve the state of such historical works.

1 MONTH OF
FREE
READING

at

www.ForgottenBooks.com

By purchasing this book you are eligible for one month membership to ForgottenBooks.com, giving you unlimited access to our entire collection of over 1,000,000 titles via our web site and mobile apps.

To claim your free month visit: www.forgottenbooks.com/free58081

English
Français
Deutsche
Italiano
Español
Português

www.forgottenbooks.com

Mythology Photography **Fiction**
Fishing Christianity **Art** Cooking
Essays Buddhism Freemasonry
Medicine **Biology** Music **Ancient**
Egypt Evolution Carpentry Physics
Dance Geology **Mathematics** Fitness
Shakespeare **Folklore** Yoga Marketing
Confidence Immortality Biographies
Poetry **Psychology** Witchcraft
Electronics Chemistry History **Law**
Accounting **Philosophy** Anthropology
Alchemy Drama Quantum Mechanics
Atheism Sexual Health **Ancient History**
Entrepreneurship Languages Sport
Paleontology Needlework Islam
Metaphysics Investment Archaeology
Parenting Statistics Criminology
Motivational

THE ALDINE EDITION
OF THE BRITISH
POETS

THE POETICAL WORKS OF WILLIAM WORDSWORTH

VOL. II

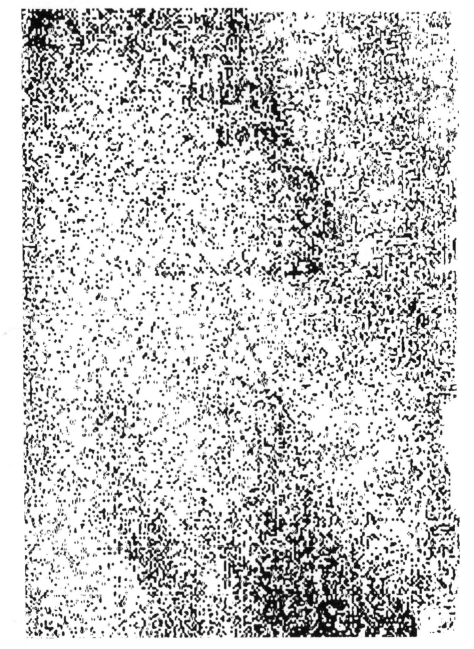

THE POETICAL WORKS OF

WILLIAM WORDSWORTH

EDITED WITH MEMOIR BY

EDWARD DOWDEN

IN SEVEN VOLUMES

VOL. II

LONDON

GEORGE BELL & SONS, YORK ST., COVENT GARDEN

NEW YORK: 112, FOURTH AVENUE

1892

CHISWICK PRESS :—C. WHITTINGHAM AND CO., TOOKS COURT
CHANCERY LANE.

Eu.

CONTENTS.

VOL. II.

POEMS OF THE IMAGINATION.

POEMS.

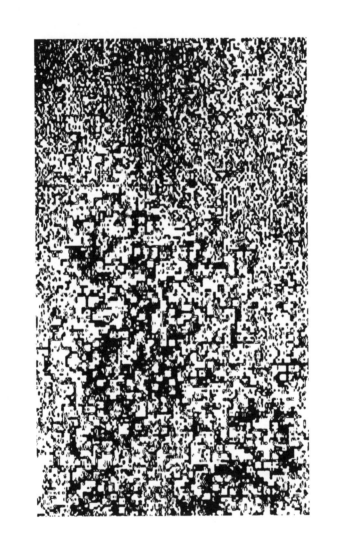

POEMS OF THE FANCY.

I.

A MORNING EXERCISE.

FANCY, who leads the pastimes of the glad,
Full oft is pleased a wayward dart to throw;
Sending sad shadows after things not sad,
Peopling the harmless fields with signs of woe:
Beneath her sway, a simple forest cry   5
Becomes an echo of man's misery.

　　Blithe ravens croak of death; and when the
　　　　owl
Tries his two voices for a favourite strain—
Tu-whit—Tu-whoo! the unsuspecting fowl
Forebodes mishap or seems but to complain;   10
Fancy, intent to harass and annoy,
Can thus pervert the evidence of joy.

　　Through border wilds where naked Indians
　　　　stray,
Myriads of notes attest her subtle skill;   14
A feathered task-master cries, "WORK AWAY!"
And in thy iteration, "WHIP POOR WILL!"[1]
Is heard the spirit of a toil-worn slave,
Lashed out of life, not quiet in the grave.

　[1] See Waterton's "Wanderings in South America."

What wonder? at her bidding, ancient lays
Steeped in dire grief the voice of Philomel; 20
And that fleet messenger of summer days,
The Swallow, twittered subject to like spell;
But ne'er could Fancy bend the buoyant Lark
To melancholy service—hark! O hark!

The daisy sleeps upon the dewy lawn,   25
Not lifting yet the head that evening bowed;
But *He* is risen, a later star of dawn,
Glittering and twinkling near yon rosy cloud;
Bright gem instinct with music, vocal spark;
The happiest bird that sprang out of the Ark! 30

Hail, blest above all kinds!—Supremely
      skilled
Restless with fixed to balance, high with low,
Thou leav'st the halcyon free her hopes to build
On such forbearance as the deep may show;
Perpetual flight, unchecked by earthly ties, 35
Leav'st to the wandering bird of Paradise.

Faithful, though swift as lightning, the meek
      dove;
Yet more hath Nature reconciled in thee;
So constant with thy downward eye of love,
Yet, in aërial singleness, so free;   40
So humble, yet so ready to rejoice
In power of wing and never-wearied voice.

To the last point of vision, and beyond,
Mount, daring warbler!—that love-prompted
      strain,
('Twixt thee and thine a never-failing bond), 45
Thrills not the less the bosom of the plain:
Yet might'st thou seem, proud privilege! to sing
All independent of the leafy spring.

How would it please old Ocean to partake,
With sailors longing for a breeze in vain, 50
The harmony thy notes most gladly make
Where earth resembles most his own domain!
Urania's self might welcome with pleased ear
These matins mounting towards her native
    sphere.

Chanter by heaven attracted, whom no bars
To daylight known deter from that pursuit, 56
'Tis well that some sage instinct, when the stars
Come forth at evening, keeps Thee still and
    mute;
For not an eyelid could to sleep incline 59
Wert thou among them, singing as they shine!

                        1828.

II.

A FLOWER GARDEN.

AT COLEORTON HALL, LEICESTERSHIRE.

TELL me, ye Zephyrs! that unfold,
While fluttering o'er this gay Recess,
Pinions that fanned the teeming mould
Of Eden's blissful wilderness,
Did only softly-stealing hours
There close the peaceful lives of flowers?

Say, when the *moving* creatures saw
All kinds commingled without fear,
Prevailed a like indulgent law
For the still growths that prosper here? 10
Did wanton fawn and kid forbear
The half-blown rose, the lily spare?

Or peeped they often from their beds,
And prematurely disappeared,
Devoured like pleasure ere it spreads   15
A bosom to the sun endeared?
If such their harsh untimely doom,
It falls not *here* on bud or bloom.

All summer-long the happy Eve
Of this fair Spot her flowers may bind,   20
Nor e'er, with ruffled fancy, grieve,
From the next glance she casts, to find
That love for little things by Fate
Is rendered vain as love for great.

Yet, where the guardian fence is wound,   25
So subtly are our eyes beguiled,
We see not nor suspect a bound,
No more than in some forest wild;
The sight is free as air—or crost
Only by art in nature lost.   30

And though the jealous turf refuse
By random footsteps to be prest,
And feed on never-sullied dews,
Ye, gentle breezes from the west,
With all the ministers of hope   35
Are tempted to this sunny slope!

And hither throngs of birds resort;
Some, inmates lodged in shady nests,
Some, perched on stems of stately port
That nod to welcome transient guests;   40
While hare and leveret, seen at play,
Appear not more shut out than they.

Apt emblem (for reproof of pride)
This delicate Enclosure shows

Of modest kindness, that would hide   45
The firm protection she bestows;
Of manners, like its viewless fence,
Ensuring peace to innocence.

Thus spake the moral Muse—her wing
Abruptly spreading to depart,   50
She left that farewell offering,
Memento for some docile heart;
That may respect the good old age
When Fancy was Truth's willing Page;
And Truth would skim the flowery glade, 55
Though entering but as Fancy's Shade.

                                        1824.

III.

A WHIRL-BLAST from behind the hill
Rushed o'er the wood with startling sound;
Then—all at once the air was still,
And showers of hailstones pattered round.
Where leafless oaks towered high above,   5
I sat within an undergrove
Of tallest hollies, tall and green;
A fairer bower was never seen.
From year to year the spacious floor
With withered leaves is covered o'er,   10
And all the year the bower is green.
But see! where'er the hailstones drop
The withered leaves all skip and hop;
There 's not a breeze—no breath of air—
Yet here, and there, and every where   15
Along the floor, beneath the shade
By those embowering hollies made,
The leaves in myriads jump and spring,

As if with pipes and music rare
Some Robin Good-fellow were there,   20
And all those leaves in festive glee,
Were dancing to the minstrelsy.

1798.

IV.

THE WATERFALL AND THE EGLANTINE.

I.

"BEGONE, thou fond presumptuous Elf,"
Exclaimed an angry Voice,
"Nor dare to thrust thy foolish self
Between me and my choice!"
A small Cascade fresh swoln with snows   5
Thus threatened a poor Briar-rose,
That, all bespattered with his foam,
And dancing high and dancing low,
Was living, as a child might know,
In an unhappy home.   10

II.

"Dost thou presume my course to block?
Off, off! or, puny Thing!
I'll hurl thee headlong with the rock
To which thy fibres cling."
The Flood was tyrannous and strong;   15
The patient Briar suffered long,
Nor did he utter groan or sigh,
Hoping the danger would be past;
But, seeing no relief, at last
He ventured to reply.   20

III.

"Ah!" said the Briar, "blame me not;
Why should we dwell in strife?
We who in this sequestered spot
Once lived a happy life!
You stirred me on my rocky bed—   25
What pleasure through my veins you spread
The summer long, from day to day,
My leaves you freshened and bedewed;
Nor was it common gratitude
That did your cares repay.   30

IV.

When spring came on with bud and bell,
Among these rocks did I
Before you hang my wreaths to tell
That gentle days were nigh!
And in the sultry summer hours   35
I sheltered you with leaves and flowers;
And in my leaves—now shed and gone,
The linnet lodged, and for us two
Chanted his pretty songs, when you
Had little voice or none.   40

V.

But now proud thoughts are in your breast—
What grief is mine you see,
Ah! would you think, even yet how blest
Together we might be!
Though of both leaf and flower bereft,   45
Some ornaments to me are left—
Rich store of scarlet hips is mine,
With which I, in my humble way,
Would deck you many a winter day,
A happy Eglantine!"   50

VI.

What more he said I cannot tell,
The Torrent down the rocky dell
Came thundering loud and fast;
I listened, nor aught else could hear;
The Briar quaked—and much I fear   55
Those accents were his last.

1800.

V.

THE OAK AND THE BROOM.

A PASTORAL.

I.

His simple truths did Andrew glean
Beside the babbling rills;
A careful student he had been
Among the woods and hills.
One winter's night, when through the trees   5
The wind was roaring, on his knees
His youngest born did Andrew hold:
And while the rest, a ruddy quire,
Were seated round their blazing fire,
This Tale the Shepherd told.   10

II.

"I saw a crag, a lofty stone
As ever tempest beat!
Out of its head an Oak had grown,
A Broom out of its feet.
The time was March, a cheerful noon—   15
The thaw-wind, with the breath of June,
Breathed gently from the warm south-west:
When, in a voice sedate with age,
This Oak, a giant and a sage,
His neighbour thus addressed:—   20

III.

'Eight weary weeks, through rock and clay,
Along this mountain's edge,
The Frost hath wrought both night and day,
Wedge driving after wedge.
Look up! and think, above your head   25
What trouble, surely, will be bred;
Last night I heard a crash—'tis true,
The splinters took another road—
I see them yonder—what a load
For such a Thing as you!   30

IV.

You are preparing as before,
To deck your slender shape;
And yet, just three years back—no more—
You had a strange escape:
Down from yon cliff a fragment broke;   35
It thundered down, with fire and smoke,
And hitherward pursued its way;
This ponderous block was caught by me,
And o'er your head, as you may see,
'Tis hanging to this day!   40

V.

If breeze or bird to this rough steep
Your kind's first seed did bear;
The breeze had better been asleep,
The bird caught in a snare:
For you and your green twigs decoy   45
The little witless shepherd-boy
To come and slumber in your bower;
And trust me, on some sultry noon,
Both you and he, Heaven knows how soon!
Will perish in one hour.   50

VI.

From me this friendly warning take '—
The Broom began to doze,
And thus, to keep herself awake,
Did gently interpose:
'My thanks for your discourse are due;   55
That more than what you say is true
I know, and I have known it long;
Frail is the bond by which we hold
Our being, whether young or old,
Wise, foolish, weak, or strong.   60

VII.

Disasters, do the best we can,
Will reach both great and small;
And he is oft the wisest man,
Who is not wise at all.
For me, why should I wish to roam?   65
This spot is my paternal home,
It is my pleasant heritage;
My father many a happy year
Spread here his careless blossoms, here
Attained a good old age.   70

VIII.

Even such as his may be my lot.
What cause have I to haunt
My heart with terrors? Am I not
In truth a favoured plant!
On me such bounty Summer pours,   75
That I am covered o'er with flowers;
And when the Frost is in the sky,
My branches are so fresh and gay
That you might look at me and say,
This Plant can never die.   80

IX.

The butterfly, all green and gold,
To me hath often flown,
Here in my blossoms to behold
Wings lovely as his own.
When grass is chill with rain or dew, 85
Beneath my shade the mother-ewe
Lies with her infant lamb; I see
The love they to each other make,
And the sweet joy which they partake,
It is a joy to me.' 90

X.

Her voice was blithe, her heart was light;
The Broom might have pursued
Her speech, until the stars of night
Their journey had renewed;
But in the branches of the oak 95
Two ravens now began to croak
Their nuptial song, a gladsome air;
And to her own green bower the breeze
That instant brought two stripling bees
To rest, or murmur there. 100

XI.

One night, my Children! from the north
There came a furious blast;
At break of day I ventured forth,
And near the cliff I passed.
The storm had fallen upon the Oak, 105
And struck him with a mighty stroke,
And whirled, and whirled him far away;
And, in one hospitable cleft,
The little careless Broom was left
To live for many a day." 110

1800.

VI.

TO A SEXTON.

LET thy wheel-barrow alone—
Wherefore, Sexton, piling still
In thy bone-house bone on bone?
'Tis already like a hill
In a field of battle made,
Where three thousand skulls are laid ;
These died in peace each with the other,—
Father, sister, friend, and brother.

Mark the spot to which I point !
From this platform, eight feet square,   10
Take not even a finger-joint:
Andrew's whole fire-side is there.
Here, alone, before thine eyes,
Simon's sickly daughter lies,
From weakness now and pain defended,   15
Whom he twenty winters tended.

Look but at the gardener's pride—
How he glories, when he sees
Roses, lilies, side by side,
Violets in families !   20
By the heart of Man, his tears,
By his hopes and by his fears,
Thou, too heedless, art the Warden
Of a far superior garden.

Thus then, each to other dear,   25
Let them all in quiet lie,
Andrew there, and Susan here,
Neighbours in mortality,

And should I live through sun and rain
Seven widowed years without my Jane,   30
O Sexton, do not then remove her,
Let one grave hold the Loved and Lover!

1799.

VII.

TO THE DAISY.

> "Her[1] divine skill taught me this,
> That from every thing I saw
> I could some instruction draw,
> And raise pleasure to the height
> Through the meanest object's sight.
> By the murmur of a spring,
> Or the least bough's rustelling;
> By a Daisy whose leaves spread
> Shut when Titan goes to bed;
> Or a shady bush or tree;
> She could more infuse in me
> Than all Nature's beauties can
> In some other wiser man."
>
> G. WITHER.

In youth from rock to rock I went,
From hill to hill in discontent
Of pleasure high and turbulent,
   Most pleased when most uneasy;
But now my own delights I make,—
My thirst at every rill can slake,
And gladly Nature's love partake
   Of Thee, sweet Daisy!

Thee Winter in the garland wears
That thinly decks his few grey hairs;   10
Spring parts the clouds with softest airs,
   That she may sun thee;

[1] His Muse.

Whole Summer-fields are thine by right;
And Autumn, melancholy Wight!
Doth in thy crimson head delight   15
   When rains are on thee.

In shoals and bands, a morrice train,
Thou greet'st the traveller in the lane;
Pleased at his greeting thee again;
   Yet nothing daunted,   20
Nor grieved if thou be set at nought:
And oft alone in nooks remote
We meet thee, like a pleasant thought,
   When such are wanted.

Be violets in their secret mews   25
The flowers the wanton Zephyrs choose;
Proud be the rose, with rains and dews
   Her head impearling,
Thou liv'st with less ambitious aim,
Yet hast not gone without thy fame;   30
Thou art indeed by many a claim
   The Poet's darling.

If to a rock from rains he fly,
Or, some bright day of April sky,
Imprisoned by hot sunshine lie   35
   Near the green holly,
And wearily at length should fare;
He needs but look about, and there
Thou art!—a friend at hand, to scare
   His melancholy.   40

A hundred times, by rock or bower,
Ere thus I have lain couched an hour,
Have I derived from thy sweet power
   Some apprehension;

Some steady love; some brief delight;   45
Some memory that had taken flight;
Some chime of fancy wrong or right;
    Or stray invention.

If stately passions in me burn,
And one chance look to Thee should turn, 50
I drink out of an humbler urn
    A lowlier pleasure;
The homely sympathy that heeds
The common life our nature breeds;
A wisdom fitted to the needs   55
    Of hearts at leisure.

Fresh-smitten by the morning ray,
When thou art up, alert and gay,
Then, cheerful Flower! my spirits play
    With kindred gladness :   60
And when, at dusk, by dews opprest
Thou sink'st, the image of thy rest
Hath often eased my pensive breast
    Of careful sadness.

And all day long I number yet,   65
All seasons through, another debt,
Which I, wherever thou art met,
    To thee am owing;
An instinct call it, a blind sense;
A happy, genial influence,   70
Coming one knows not how, nor whence,
    Nor whither going.

Child of the Year! that round dost run
Thy pleasant course,—when day's begun
As ready to salute the sun   75
    As lark or leveret,

II.   C

Thy long-lost praise thou shalt regain;
Nor be less dear to future men
Than in old time;—thou not in vain
　　Art Nature's favourite.[1]　　　　　　　　80

　　　　　　　　　　　　　　　　1802.

VIII.

TO THE SAME FLOWER.

WITH little here to do or see
Of things that in the great world be,
Daisy! again I talk to thee,
　　For thou art worthy,
Thou unassuming Common-place
Of Nature, with that homely face,
And yet with something of a grace
　　Which love makes for thee!

Oft on the dappled turf at ease
I sit, and play with similes,　　　　　　10
Loose types of things through all degrees,
　　Thoughts of thy raising:
And many a fond and idle name
I give to thee, for praise or blame,
As is the humour of the game,　　　　　15
　　While I am gazing.

A nun demure of lowly port;
Or sprightly maiden, of Love's court,
In thy simplicity the sport
　　Of all temptations?　　　　　　　20

---

[1] See, in Chaucer and the elder Poets, the honours
formerly paid to this flower.

A queen in crown of rubies drest;
A starveling in a scanty vest;
Are all, as seems to suit thee best,
    Thy appellations.

A little Cyclops with one eye   25
Staring to threaten and defy,
That thought comes next—and instantly
    The freak is over,
The shape will vanish—and behold
A silver shield with boss of gold,   30
That spreads itself, some faery bold
    In fight to cover!

I see thee glittering from afar—
And then thou art a pretty star;
Not quite so fair as many are   35
    In heaven above thee!
Yet like a star, with glittering crest,
Self-poised in air thou seem'st to rest;—
May peace come never to his nest,
    Who shall reprove thee!   40

Bright *Flower!* for by that name at last,
When all my reveries are past,
I call thee, and to that cleave fast,
    Sweet silent creature!
That breath'st with me in sun and air,   45
Do thou, as thou art wont, repair
My heart with gladness, and a share
    Of thy meek nature!

                                        1802.

IX.

THE GREEN LINNET.

BENEATH these fruit-tree boughs that shed
Their snow-white blossoms on my head,
With brightest sunshine round me spread
   Of spring's unclouded weather,
In this sequestered nook how sweet
To sit upon my orchard-seat!
And birds and flowers once more to greet,
   My last year's friends together.

One have I marked, the happiest guest
In all this covert of the blest: 10
Hail to Thee, far above the rest
   In joy of voice and pinion!
Thou, Linnet! in thy green array,
Presiding Spirit here to-day,
Dost lead the revels of the May;   15
   And this is thy dominion.

While birds, and butterflies, and flowers,
Make all one band of paramours,
Thou, ranging up and down the bowers,
   Art sole in thy employment: 20
A Life, a Presence like the Air,
Scattering thy gladness without care,
Too blest with any one to pair;
   Thyself thy own enjoyment.

Amid yon tuft of hazel trees,   25
That twinkle to the gusty breeze,
Behold him perched in ecstasies,
   Yet seeming still to hover;

There! where the flutter of his wings
Upon his back and body flings 30
Shadows and sunny glimmerings,
   That cover him all over.

My dazzled sight he oft deceives,
A Brother of the dancing leaves;
Then flits, and from the cottage eaves 35
   Pours forth his song in gushes;
As if by that exulting strain
He mocked and treated with disdain
The voiceless Form he chose to feign,
   While fluttering in the bushes. 40

                    1803.

I.

TO A SKY-LARK.

Up with me! up with me into the clouds!
   For thy song, Lark, is strong;
Up with me, up with me into the clouds!
   Singing, singing,
With clouds and sky about thee ringing, 5
   Lift me, guide me, till I find
That spot which seems so to thy mind!

I have walked through wildernesses dreary,
And to-day my heart is weary;
Had I now the wings of a Faery, 10
Up to thee would I fly.
There is madness about thee, and joy divine
   In that song of thine;
Lift me, guide me, high and high
To thy banqueting-place in the sky. 15

Joyous as morning,
Thou art laughing and scorning;
Thou hast a nest for thy love and thy rest,
And, though little troubled with sloth,
Drunken Lark! thou would'st be loth   20
To be such a traveller as I.
Happy, happy Liver,
With a soul as strong as a mountain river
Pouring out praise to the almighty Giver,
Joy and jollity be with us both!   25

Alas! my journey, rugged and uneven,
Through prickly moors or dusty ways must
    wind;
But hearing thee, or others of thy kind,
As full of gladness and as free of heaven,
I, with my fate contented, will plod on,   30
And hope for higher raptures, when life's day
    is done.

1805.

XI.

TO THE SMALL CELANDINE.[1]

PANSIES, lilies, kingcups, daisies,
Let them live upon their praises;
Long as there 's a sun that sets,
Primroses will have their glory;
Long as there are violets,
They will have a place in story:
There 's a flower that shall be mine,
'Tis the little Celandine.

[1] Common Pilewort.

Eyes of some men travel far
For the finding of a star;   10
Up and down the heavens they go,
Men that keep a mighty rout!
I'm as great as they, I trow,
Since the day I found thee out,
Little Flower—I'll make a stir,   15
Like a sage astronomer.

Modest, yet withal an Elf
Bold, and lavish of thyself;
Since we needs must first have met
I have seen thee, high and low,   20
Thirty years or more, and yet
'Twas a face I did not know;
Thou hast now, go where I may,
Fifty greetings in a day.

Ere a leaf is on a bush,   25
In the time before the thrush
Has a thought about her nest,
Thou wilt come with half a call,
Spreading out thy glossy breast
Like a careless Prodigal;   30
Telling tales about the sun,
When we've little warmth, or none.

Poets, vain men in their mood!
Travel with the multitude:
Never heed them; I aver   35
That they all are wanton wooers;
But the thrifty cottager,
Who stirs little out of doors,
Joys to spy thee near her home;
Spring is coming, Thou art come!   40

Comfort have thou of thy merit,
Kindly, unassuming Spirit!
Careless of thy neighbourhood,
Thou dost show thy pleasant face
On the moor, and in the wood,   45
In the lane ;—there's not a place,
Howsoever mean it be,
But 'tis good enough for thee.

Ill befall the yellow flowers,
Children of the flaring hours!   50
Buttercups, that will be seen,
Whether we will see or no ;
Others, too, of lofty mien ;
They have done as worldlings do,
Taken praise that should be thine,   55
Little, humble Celandine.

Prophet of delight and mirth,
Ill-requited upon earth ;
Herald of a mighty band,
Of a joyous train ensuing,   60
Serving at my heart's command,
Tasks that are no tasks renewing,
I will sing, as doth behove,
Hymns in praise of what I love!
                    April 30, 1802.

XII.

TO THE SAME FLOWER.

PLEASURES newly found are sweet
When they lie about our feet:
February last, my heart
First at sight of thee was glad;
All unheard of as thou art,
Thou must needs, I think, have had,
Celandine! and long ago,
Praise of which I nothing know.

I have not a doubt but he,
Whosoe'er the man might be,   10
Who the first with pointed rays
(Workman worthy to be sainted)
Set the sign-board in a blaze,
When the rising sun he painted,
Took the fancy from a glance   15
At thy glittering countenance.

Soon as gentle breezes bring
News of winter's vanishing,
And the children build their bowers,
Sticking 'kerchief-plots of mould   20
All about with full-blown flowers,
Thick as sheep in shepherd's fold!
With the proudest thou art there,
Mantling in the tiny square.

Often have I sighed to measure   25
By myself a lonely pleasure,
Sighed to think I read a book

Only read, perhaps, by me;
Yet I long could overlook
Thy bright coronet and Thee,   30
And thy arch and wily ways,
And thy store of other praise.

Blithe of heart, from week to week
Thou dost play at hide-and-seek;
While the patient primrose sits   35
Like a beggar in the cold,
Thou, a flower of wiser wits,
Slip'st into thy sheltering hold;
Liveliest of the vernal train
When ye all are out again.   40

Drawn by what peculiar spell,
By what charm of sight or smell,
Does the dim-eyed curious Bee,
Labouring for her waxen cells,
Fondly settle upon Thee   45
Prized above all buds and bells
Opening daily at thy side,
By the season multiplied?

Thou art not beyond the moon,
But a thing " beneath our shoon:"   50
Let the bold Discoverer thrid
In his bark the polar sea;
Rear who will a pyramid;
Praise it is enough for me,
If there be but three or four   55
Who will love my little Flower.

May 1, 1802.

XIII.

THE SEVEN SISTERS;

OR,

THE SOLITUDE OF BINNORIE.

SEVEN Daughters had Lord Archibald,
All children of one mother:
You could not say in one short day
What love they bore each other.
A garland of seven lilies wrought!
Seven Sisters that together dwell;
But he, bold Knight as ever fought,
Their Father, took of them no thought,
He loved the wars so well.
Sing, mournfully, oh! mournfully.   10
The solitude of Binnorie!

II.

Fresh blows the wind, a western wind,
And from the shores of Erin,
Across the wave, a Rover brave
To Binnorie is steering: 15
Right onward to the Scottish strand
The gallant ship is borne;
The warriors leap upon the land,
And hark! the Leader of the band
Hath blown his bugle horn.   20
Sing, mournfully, oh! mournfully,
The solitude of Binnorie.

III.

Beside a grotto of their own,
With boughs above them closing,

The Seven are laid, and in the shade   25
They lie like fawns reposing.
But now, upstarting with affright
At noise of man and steed,
Away they fly to left, to right—
Of your fair household, Father-knight,   30
Methinks you take small heed!
Sing, mournfully, oh! mournfully,
The solitude of Binnorie.

IV.

Away the seven fair Campbells fly,
And over hill and hollow,   35
With menace proud, and insult loud,
The youthful Rovers follow.
Cried they, " Your Father loves to roam :
Enough for him to find
The empty house when he comes home;   40
For us your yellow ringlets comb,
For us be fair and kind !"
Sing, mournfully, oh! mournfully,
The solitude of Binnorie.

V.

Some close behind, some side by side,   45
Like clouds in stormy weather;
They run, and cry, " Nay, let us die,
And let us die together."
A lake was near; the shore was steep;
There never foot had been;   50
They ran, and with a desperate leap
Together plunged into the deep,
Nor ever more were seen.
Sing, mournfully, oh! mournfully,
The solitude of Binnorie.   55

VI.

The stream that flows out of the lake,
As through the glen it rambles,
Repeats a moan o'er moss and stone,
For those seven lovely Campbells.
Seven little Islands, green and bare,   60
Have risen from out the deep:
The fishers say those sisters fair
By faeries all are buried there,
And there together sleep.
Sing, mournfully, oh! mournfully,   65
The solitude of Binnorie.

1800.

XIV.

WHO fancied what a pretty sight
This Rock would be if edged around
With living snow-drops? circlet bright!
How glorious to this orchard-ground!
Who loved the little Rock, and set
Upon its head this coronet?

Was it the humour of a child?
Or rather of some gentle maid,
Whose brows, the day that she was styled
The shepherd-queen, were thus arrayed?   10
Of man mature, or matron sage?
Or old man toying with his age?

I asked—'twas whispered; The device
To each and all might well belong:
It is the Spirit of Paradise   15
That prompts such work, a Spirit strong,
That gives to all the self-same bent
Where life is wise and innocent.

1803.

XV.

THE REDBREAST CHASING THE BUTTERFLY.

ART thou the bird whom Man loves best,
The pious bird with the scarlet breast,
    Our little English Robin ;
The bird that comes about our doors
When Autumn-winds are sobbing ?
Art thou the Peter of Norway Boors ?
    Their Thomas in Finland,
    And Russia far inland ?
The bird that by some name or other
All men who know thee call their brother,   10
The darling of children and men ?
Could Father Adam[1] open his eyes
And see this sight beneath the skies,
He 'd wish to close them again.
—If the Butterfly knew but his friend,   15
Hither his flight he would bend ;
And find his way to me,
Under the branches of the tree :
In and out, he darts about ;
Can this be the bird, to man so good,   20
That, after their bewildering,
Covered with leaves the little children,
    So painfully in the wood ?

What ailed thee, Robin, that thou could'st
    pursue

[1] See "Paradise Lost," Book XI., where Adam points out to Eve the ominous sign of the Eagle chasing "two Birds of gayest plume," and the gentle Hart and Hind pursued by their enemy.

> A beautiful creature,   25
> That is gentle by nature?
> Beneath the summer sky
> From flower to flower let him fly;
> 'Tis all that he wishes to do.
> The cheerer Thou of our in-door sadness,   30
> He is the friend of our summer gladness:
> What hinders, then, that ye should be
> Playmates in the sunny weather,
> And fly about in the air together!
> His beautiful wings in crimson are drest,   35
> A crimson as bright as thine own:
> Would'st thou be happy in thy nest,
> O pious Bird! whom man loves best,
> Love him, or leave him alone!

April 18, 1802.

XVI.

SONG FOR THE SPINNING WHEEL.

FOUNDED UPON A BELIEF PREVALENT AMONG
THE PASTORAL VALES OF WESTMORELAND.

> SWIFTLY turn the murmuring wheel!
> Night has brought the welcome hour,
> When the weary fingers feel
> Help, as if from faery power;
> Dewy night o'ershades the ground;   5
> Turn the swift wheel round and round!
>
> Now, beneath the starry sky,
> Couch the widely-scattered sheep;—
> Ply the pleasant labour, ply!
> For the spindle, while they sleep,   10

Runs with speed more smooth and fine,
Gathering up a trustier line.

Short-lived likings may be bred
By a glance from fickle eyes ;
But true love is like the thread   15
Which the kindly wool supplies,
When the flocks are all at rest
Sleeping on the mountain's breast.

                                   1812.

XVII.

HINT FROM THE MOUNTAINS

FOR CERTAIN POLITICAL PRETENDERS.

" WHO but hails the sight with pleasure
When the wings of genius rise,
Their ability to measure
        With great enterprise ;
But in man was ne'er such daring   5
As yon Hawk exhibits, pairing
His brave spirit with the war in
        The stormy skies !

Mark him, how his power he uses,
Lays it by, at will resumes !   10
Mark, ere for his haunt he chooses
        Clouds and utter glooms !
There he wheels in downward mazes ;
Sunward now his flight he raises,
Catches fire, as seems, and blazes   15
        With uninjured plumes !"—

" Stranger, 'tis no act of courage
Which aloft thou dost discern;
No bold *bird* gone forth to forage
'Mid the tempest stern;   20
But such mockery as the nations
See, when public perturbations
Lift men from their native stations,
    Like yon TUFT OF FERN;

Such it is; the aspiring creature   25
Soaring on undaunted wing,
(So you fancied) is by nature
    A dull helpless thing,
Dry and withered, light and yellow;—
That to be the tempest's fellow!   30
Wait—and you shall see how hollow
    Its endeavouring!"

                  1817.

XVIII.

ON SEEING A NEEDLECASE IN THE FORM OF A HARP.

THE WORK OF E. M. S.

FROWNS are on every Muse's face,
    Reproaches from their lips are sent,
That mimicry should thus disgrace
    The noble Instrument.

A very Harp in all but size!
    Needles for strings in apt gradation!
Minerva's self would stigmatize
    The unclassic profanation.

II.   D

Even her *own* needle that subdued
    Arachne's rival spirit,   10
Though wrought in Vulcan's happiest mood,
    Such honour could not merit.

And this too from the Laureate's Child,
    A living lord of melody!
How will her Sire be reconciled   15
    To the refined indignity?

I spake, when whispered a low voice,
    "Bard! moderate your ire;
Spirits of all degrees rejoice
    In presence of the lyre.   20

The Minstrels of Pygmean bands,
    Dwarf Genii, moonlight-loving Fays,
Have shells to fit their tiny hands
    And suit their slender lays.

Some, still more delicate of ear,   25
    Have lutes (believe my words)
Whose framework is of gossamer,
    While sunbeams are the chords.

Gay Sylphs this miniature will court,
    Made vocal by their brushing wings,   30
And sullen Gnomes will learn to sport
    Around its polished strings;

Whence strains to love-sick maiden dear,
    While in her lonely bower she tries
To cheat the thought she cannot cheer,   35
    By fanciful embroideries.

Trust, angry Bard! a knowing Sprite,
  Nor think the Harp her lot deplores ;
Though 'mid the stars the Lyre shine bright,
  Love *stoops* as fondly as he soars."   40

                    1827.

XIX.

TO A LADY,

IN ANSWER TO A REQUEST THAT I WOULD
WRITE HER A POEM UPON SOME DRAWINGS
THAT SHE HAD MADE OF FLOWERS IN THE
ISLAND OF MADEIRA.

FAIR Lady! can I sing of flowers
  That in Madeira bloom and fade,
I who ne'er sate within their bowers,
  Nor through their sunny lawns have strayed?
How they in sprightly dance are worn   5
  By Shepherd-groom or May-day queen,
Or holy festal pomps adorn,
  These eyes have never seen.

Yet tho' to me the pencil's art
  No like remembrances can give,   10
Your portraits still may reach the heart
  And there for gentle pleasure live;
While Fancy ranging with free scope
  Shall on some lovely Alien set
A name with us endeared to hope,   15
  To peace, or fond regret.

Still as we look with nicer care,
  Some new resemblance we may trace,

A *Heart's-ease* will perhaps be there,
   A *Speedwell* may not want its place.   20
And so may we, with charmèd mind
   Beholding what your skill has wrought,
Another *Star-of-Bethlehem* find,
   A new *Forget-me-not.*

From earth to heaven with motion fleet   25
   From heaven to earth our thoughts will pass,
A *Holy-thistle* here we meet
   And there a *Shepherd's weather-glass;*
And haply some familiar name
   Shall grace the fairest, sweetest, plant   30
Whose presence cheers the drooping frame
   Of English Emigrant.

Gazing she feels its power beguile
   Sad thoughts, and breathes with easier breath;
Alas! that meek that tender smile   35
   Is but a harbinger of death:
And pointing with a feeble hand
   She says, in faint words by sighs broken,
Bear for me to my native land
   This precious Flower, true love's last token. 40
                    1845. (?)

XX.

   Glad sight wherever new with old
   Is joined through some dear homeborn tie;
   The life of all that we behold
   Depends upon that mystery.
   Vain is the glory of the sky,
   The beauty vain of field and grove,
   Unless, while with admiring eye
   We gaze, we also learn to love.
                    1845. (?)

XXI.

THE CONTRAST.

THE PARROT AND THE WREN.

I.

WITHIN her gilded cage confined
I saw a dazzling Belle,
A Parrot of that famous kind
Whose name is NON-PAREIL.

Like beads of glossy jet her eyes ;   5
And, smoothed by Nature's skill,
With pearl or gleaming agate vies
Her finely-curvèd bill..

Her plumy mantle's living hues,
In mass opposed to mass,   10
Outshine the splendour that imbues
The robes of pictured glass.

And, sooth to say, an apter Mate
Did never tempt the choice
Of feathered Thing most delicate   15
In figure and in voice.

But, exiled from Australian bowers,
And singleness her lot,
She trills her song with tutored powers,
Or mocks each casual note.   20

No more of pity for regrets
With which she may have striven !
Now but in wantonness she frets,
Or spite, if cause be given ;

Arch, volatile, a sportive bird   25
By social glee inspired;
Ambitious to be seen or heard,
And pleased to be admired!

II.

THIS moss-lined shed, green, soft, and dry,
Harbours a self-contented Wren,   30
Not shunning man's abode, though shy,
Almost as thought itself, of human ken.

Strange places, coverts unendeared,
She never tried; the very nest
In which this Child of Spring was reared   35
Is warmed thro' winter by her feathery breast.

To the bleak winds she sometimes gives
A slender unexpected strain;
Proof that the hermitess still lives,
Though she appear not, and be sought in vain. 40

Say, Dora! tell me, by yon placid moon,
If called to choose between the favoured pair,
Which would you be,—the bird of the saloon,
By lady-fingers tended with nice care,
Caressed, applauded, upon dainties fed,   45
Or Nature's DARKLING of this mossy shed?
                                        1825.

XXII.

THE DANISH BOY.

A FRAGMENT.

I.

BETWEEN two sister moorland rills
There is a spot that seems to lie
Sacred to flowerets of the hills,
And sacred to the sky.
And in this smooth and open dell
There is a tempest-stricken tree;
A corner-stone by lightning cut,
The last stone of a lonely hut;
And in this dell you see
A thing no storm can e'er destroy,　　　10
The shadow of a Danish Boy.

II.

In clouds above, the lark is heard,
But drops not here to earth for rest;
Within this lonesome nook the bird
Did never build her nest.　　　15
No beast, no bird, hath here his home;
Bees, wafted on the breezy air,
Pass high above those fragrant bells
To other flowers:—to other dells
Their burdens do they bear;　　　20
The Danish Boy walks here alone:
The lovely dell is all his own.

III.

A Spirit of noon-day is he;
Yet seems a form of flesh and blood;

Nor piping shepherd shall he be,   25
Nor herd-boy of the wood.
A regal vest of fur he wears,
In colour like a raven's wing;
It fears not rain, nor wind, nor dew;
But in the storm 'tis fresh and blue   30
As budding pines in spring;
His helmet has a vernal grace,
Fresh as the bloom upon his face.

IV.

A harp is from his shoulder slung;
Resting the harp upon his knee,   35
To words of a forgotten tongue
He suits its melody.
Of flocks upon the neighbouring hill
He is the darling and the joy;
And often, when no cause appears,   40
The mountain-ponies prick their ears,
—They hear the Danish Boy,
While in the dell he sings alone
Beside the tree and corner-stone.

V.

There sits he; in his face you spy   45
No trace of a ferocious air,
Nor ever was a cloudless sky
So steady or so fair.
The lovely Danish Boy is blest
And happy in his flowery cove: 50
From bloody deeds his thoughts are far;
And yet he warbles songs of war,
That seem like songs of love,
For calm and gentle is his mien;
Like a dead Boy he is serene.   55

1799.

XXIII.

SONG

FOR THE WANDERING JEW.

THOUGH the torrents from their fountains
Roar down many a craggy steep,
Yet they find among the mountains
Resting-places calm and deep.

Clouds that love through air to hasten,   5
Ere the storm its fury stills,
Helmet-like themselves will fasten
On the heads of towering hills.

What if through the frozen centre
Of the Alps the Chamois bound,   10
Yet he has a home to enter
In some nook of chosen ground:

And the Sea-horse, though the ocean
Yield him no domestic cave,
Slumbers without sense of motion,   15
Couched upon the rocking wave.

If on windy days the Raven
Gambol like a dancing skiff,
Not the less she loves her haven
In the bosom of the cliff.   20

The fleet Ostrich, till day closes,
Vagrant over desert sands,
Brooding on her eggs reposes
When chill night that care demands.

Day and night my toils redouble,   25
Never nearer to the goal;
Night and day, I feel the trouble
Of the Wanderer in my soul.

                                        1800.

XXIV.

STRAY PLEASURES.

"—— Pleasure is spread through the earth
In stray gifts to be claimed by whoever shall find."

By their floating mill,
    That lies dead and still,
Behold yon Prisoners three,
The Miller with two Dames, on the breast of
        the Thames!
The platform is small, but gives room for them
        all;   5
And they're dancing merrily.

From the shore come the notes
    To their mill where it floats,
To their house and their mill tethered fast:
To the small wooden isle where, their work to
        beguile,   10
They from morning to even take whatever is
        given;—
And many a blithe day they have past.

In sight of the spires,
    All alive with the fires
Of the sun going down to his rest,   15
In the broad open eye of the solitary sky,
They dance,—there are three, as jocund as free,
While they dance on the calm river's breast.

Man and Maidens wheel,
They themselves make the reel,   20
And their music's a prey which they seize;
It plays not for them,—what matter? 'tis theirs;
And if they had care, it has scattered their cares
While they dance, crying, "Long as ye please!"

They dance not for me,   25
Yet mine is their glee!
Thus pleasure is spread through the earth
In stray gifts to be claimed by whoever shall
    find;
Thus a rich loving-kindness, redundantly kind,
Moves all nature to gladness and mirth.   30

The showers of the spring
Rouse the birds, and they sing;
If the wind do but stir for his proper delight,
Each leaf, that and this, his neighbour will kiss;
Each wave, one and t'other, speeds after his
    brother;   35
They are happy, for that is their right!

1806.

XXV.

THE PILGRIM'S DREAM;

OR, THE STAR AND THE GLOW-WORM.

A PILGRIM, when the summer day
Had closed upon his weary way,
A lodging begged beneath a castle's roof;
But him the haughty Warder spurned;

And from the gate the Pilgrim turned,
To seek such covert as the field
Or heath-besprinkled copse might yield,
Or lofty wood, shower-proof.

He paced along; and pensively,
Halting beneath a shady tree,   10
Whose moss-grown root might serve for couch
        or seat,
Fixed on a Star his upward eye;
Then from the tenant of the sky
He turned, and watched with kindred look
A Glow-worm, in a dusky nook,   15
Apparent at his feet.

The murmur of a neighbouring stream
Induced a soft and slumbrous dream,
A pregnant dream, within whose shadowy
        bounds
He recognised the earth-born Star,   20
And *That* which glittered from afar;
And (strange to witness!) from the frame
Of the ethereal Orb there came
Intelligible sounds.

Much did it taunt the humble Light   25
That now, when day was fled, and night
Hushed the dark earth, fast closing weary eyes,
A very reptile could presume
To show her taper in the gloom,
As if in rivalship with One   30
Who sate a ruler on his throne
Erected in the skies.

" Exalted Star!" the Worm replied,
" Abate this unbecoming pride,

Or with a less uneasy lustre shine;   35
Thou shrink'st as momently thy rays
Are mastered by the breathing haze;
While neither mist, nor thickest cloud
That shapes in heaven its murky shroud,
Hath power to injure mine.   40

But not for this do I aspire
To match the spark of local fire,
That at my will burns on the dewy lawn,
With thy acknowledged glories;—No!
Yet, thus upbraided, I may show   45
What favours do attend me here,
Till, like thyself, I disappear
Before the purple dawn."

When this in modest guise was said,
Across the welkin seemed to spread   50
A boding sound—for aught but sleep unfit!
Hills quaked, the rivers backward ran;
That Star, so proud of late, looked wan;
And reeled with visionary stir
In the blue depth, like Lucifer   55
Cast headlong to the pit!

Fire raged: and, when the spangled floor
Of ancient ether was no more,
New heavens succeeded, by the dream brought
          forth:
And all the happy Souls that rode   60
Transfigured through that fresh abode
Had heretofore, in humble trust,
Shone meekly 'mid their native dust,
The Glow-worms of the earth!

This knowledge, from an Angel's voice   65
Proceeding, made the heart rejoice
Of Him who slept upon the open lea :
Waking at morn he murmured not ;
And, till life's journey closed, the spot
Was to the Pilgrim's soul endeared,   70
Where by that dream he had been cheered
Beneath that shady tree.

1818.

XXVI.

THE POET AND THE CAGED

TURTLEDOVE.

As often as I murmur here
    My half-formed melodies,
Straight from her osier mansion near
    The Turtledove replies :
Though silent as a leaf before,
    The captive promptly coos ;
Is it to teach her own soft lore,
    Or second my weak Muse ?

I rather think the gentle Dove
    Is murmuring a reproof,   10
Displeased that I from lays of love
    Have dared to keep aloof ;
That I, a Bard of hill and dale,
    Have carolled, fancy free,
As if nor dove nor nightingale   15
    Had heart or voice for me.

If such thy meaning, O forbear,
    Sweet Bird ! to do me wrong ;

Love, blessed Love, is everywhere
   The spirit of my song: 20
'Mid grove, and by the calm fireside,
   Love animates my lyre—
That coo again!—'t is not to chide,
   I feel, but to inspire.

                      1830.

XXVII.

A WREN'S NEST.

AMONG the dwellings framed by birds
   In field or forest with nice care,
Is none that with the little Wren's
   In snugness may compare.

No door the tenement requires,
   And seldom needs a laboured roof;
Yet is it to the fiercest sun
   Impervious, and storm-proof.

So warm, so beautiful withal,
   In perfect fitness for its aim,   10
That to the Kind by special grace
   Their instinct surely came.

And when for their abodes they seek
   An opportune recess,
The hermit has no finer eye   15
   For shadowy quietness.

These find, 'mid ivied abbey-walls,
   A canopy in some still nook;
Others are pent-housed by a brae
   That overhangs a brook.   20

There to the brooding bird her mate
    Warbles by fits his low clear song;
And by the busy streamlet both
    Are sung to all day long.

Or in sequestered lanes they build,   25
    Where, till the flitting bird's return,
Her eggs within the nest repose,
    Like relics in an urn.

But still, where general choice is good,
    There is a better and a best;   30
And, among fairest objects, some
    Are fairer than the rest;

This, one of those small builders proved
    In a green covert, where, from out
The forehead of a pollard oak,   35
    The leafy antlers sprout;

For She who planned the mossy lodge,
    Mistrusting her evasive skill,
Had to a Primrose looked for aid
    Her wishes to fulfil.   40

High on the trunk's projecting brow,
    And fixed an infant's span above
The budding flowers, peeped forth the nest
    The prettiest of the grove!

The treasure proudly did I show   45
    To some whose minds without disdain
Can turn to little things; but once
    Looked up for it in vain:

'Tis gone—a ruthless spoiler's prey,
　Who heeds not beauty, love, or song,　50
'Tis gone! (so seemed it) and we grieved
　Indignant at the wrong.

Just three days after, passing by
　In clearer light the moss-built cell
I saw, espied its shaded mouth;　55
　And felt that all was well.

The Primrose for a veil had spread
　The largest of her upright leaves;
And thus, for purposes benign,
　A simple flower deceives.　60

Concealed from friends who might disturb
　Thy quiet with no ill intent,
Secure from evil eyes and hands
　On barbarous plunder bent,

Rest, Mother-bird! and when thy young　65
　Take flight, and thou art free to roam,
When withered is the guardian Flower,
　And empty thy late home,

Think how ye prospered, thou and thine,
　Amid the unviolated grove　70
Housed near the growing Primrose-tuft
　In foresight, or in love.

　　　　　　　　　1833.

XXVIII.

LOVE LIES BLEEDING.

You call it, "Love lies bleeding,"—so you may,
Though the red Flower, not prostrate, only
    droops,
As we have seen it here from day to day,
From month to month, life passing not away:
A flower how rich in sadness! Even thus
    stoops,   5
(Sentient by Grecian sculpture's marvellous
    power),
Thus leans, with hanging brow and body bent
Earthward in uncomplaining languishment,
The dying Gladiator.   So, sad Flower!
('Tis Fancy guides me willing to be led,   10
Though by a slender thread,)
So drooped Adonis, bathed in sanguine dew
Of his death-wound, when he from innocent air
The gentlest breath of resignation drew;
While Venus in a passion of despair   15
Rent, weeping over him, her golden hair
Spangled with drops of that celestial shower.
She suffered, as Immortals sometimes do;
But pangs more lasting far *that* Lover knew
Who first, weighed down by scorn, in some lone
    bower   20
Did press this semblance of unpitied smart
Into the service of his constant heart,
His own dejection, downcast Flower! could
    share
With thine, and gave the mournful name which
    thou wilt ever bear.

                                    1845. (?)

XXIX.

COMPANION TO THE FOREGOING.

NEVER enlivened with the liveliest ray
That fosters growth or checks or cheers decay,
Nor by the heaviest rain-drops more deprest,
This Flower, that first appeared as summer's
    guest,
Preserves her beauty 'mid autumnal leaves,   5
And to her mournful habits fondly cleaves.
When files of stateliest plants have ceased to
    bloom,
One after one submitting to their doom,
When her coevals each and all are fled,
What keeps her thus reclined upon her lone-
    some bed?   10

    The old mythologists, more impressed than we
Of this late day by character in tree
Or herb that claimed peculiar sympathy,
Or by the silent lapse of fountain clear,
Or with the language of the viewless air   15
By bird or beast made vocal, sought a cause
To solve the mystery, not in Nature's laws
But in Man's fortunes. Hence a thousand
    tales
Sung to the plaintive lyre in Grecian vales.
Nor doubt that something of their spirit swayed
The fancy-stricken Youth or heart-sick Maid, 21
Who, while each stood companionless and eyed
This undeparting Flower in crimson dyed,
Thought of a wound which death is slow to cure,
A fate that has endured and will endure,   25
And, patience coveting yet passion feeding,
Called the dejected Lingerer *Love lies Bleeding.*
                 1845. (?)

XXX.

RURAL ILLUSIONS.

Sylph was it ? or a Bird more bright
   Than those of fabulous stock ?
A second darted by ;—and lo !
   Another of the flock,
Through sunshine flitting from the bough   5
   To nestle in the rock.
Transient deception ! a gay freak
   Of April's mimicries !
Those brilliant strangers, hailed with joy
   Among the budding trees,   10
Proved last year's leaves, pushed from the spray
   To frolic on the breeze.

Maternal Flora ! show thy face,
   And let thy hand be seen,
Thy hand here sprinkling tiny flowers,   15
   That, as they touch the green,
Take root (so seems it) and look up
   In honour of their Queen.
Yet, sooth, those little starry specks,
   That not in vain aspired   20
To be confounded with live growths,
   Most dainty, most admired,
Were only blossoms dropped from twigs
   Of their own offspring tired.

Not such the World's illusive shows ;   25
   Her wingless flutterings,
Her blossoms which, though shed, outbrave
   The floweret as it springs,

For the undeceived, smile as they may,
  Are melancholy things: 30
But gentle Nature plays her part
  With ever-varying wiles,
And transient feignings with plain truth
  So well she reconciles,
That those fond Idlers most are pleased   35
  Whom oftenest she beguiles.

                                1832.

XXXI.

THE KITTEN AND FALLING LEAVES.

THAT way look, my Infant, lo!
What a pretty baby-show!
See the Kitten on the wall,
Sporting with the leaves that fall,
Withered leaves—one—two—and three—   5
From the lofty elder-tree!
Through the calm and frosty air
Of this morning bright and fair,
Eddying round and round they sink
Softly, slowly: one might think,   10
From the motions that are made,
Every little leaf conveyed
Sylph or Faery hither tending,—
To this lower world descending,
Each invisible and mute,   15
In his wavering parachute.
——But the Kitten, how she starts,
Crouches, stretches, paws, and darts!
First at one, and then its fellow,
Just as light and just as yellow;   20
There are many now—now one—
Now they stop and there are none:

What intenseness of desire
In her upward eye of fire!
With a tiger-leap half-way   25
Now she meets the coming prey,
Lets it go as fast, and then
Has it in her power again:
Now she works with three or four,
Like an Indian conjurer;   30
Quick as he in feats of art,
Far beyond in joy of heart.
Were her antics played in the eye
Of a thousand standers-by,
Clapping hands with shout and stare,   35
What would little Tabby care
For the plaudits of the crowd?
Over happy to be proud,
Over wealthy in the treasure
Of her own exceeding pleasure!   40

'Tis a pretty baby-treat;
Nor, I deem, for me unmeet;
Here, for neither Babe nor me,
Other playmate can I see.
Of the countless living things,   45
That with stir of feet and wings
(In the sun or under shade,
Upon bough or grassy blade)
And with busy revellings,
Chirp and song, and murmurings,   50
Made this orchard's narrow space,
And this vale, so blithe a place;
Multitudes are swept away
Never more to breathe the day:
Some are sleeping; some in bands   55
Travelled into distant lands;
Others slunk to moor and wood,
Far from human neighbourhood;

And among the Kinds that keep
With us closer fellowship,   60
With us openly abide,
All have laid their mirth aside.

   Where is he that giddy Sprite,
Blue-cap, with his colours bright,
Who was blest as bird could be,   65
Feeding in the apple-tree ;
Made such wanton spoil and rout,
Turning blossoms inside out ;
Hung—head pointing towards the ground—
Fluttered, perched, into a round   70
Bound himself, and then unbound ;
Lithest, gaudiest Harlequin !
Prettiest tumbler ever seen !
Light of heart and light of limb ;
What is now become of Him ?   75
Lambs, that through the mountains went
Frisking, bleating merriment,
When the year was in its prime,
They are sobered by this time.
If you look to vale or hill,   80
If you listen, all is still,
Save a little neighbouring rill,
That from out the rocky ground
Strikes a solitary sound.
Vainly glitter hill and plain,   85
And the air is calm in vain ;
Vainly Morning spreads the lure
Of a sky serene and pure ;
Creature none can she decoy
Into open sign of joy :   90
Is it that they have a fear
Of the dreary season near ?
Or that other pleasures be
Sweeter even than gaiety ?

Yet whate'er enjoyments dwell   95
In the impenetrable cell
Of the silent heart which Nature
Furnishes to every creature;
Whatsoe'er we feel and know
Too sedate for outward show,   100
Such a light of gladness breaks,
Pretty Kitten! from thy freaks,—
Spreads with such a living grace
O'er my little Dora's face;
Yes, the sight so stirs and charms   105
Thee, Baby, laughing in my arms,
That almost I could repine
That your transports are not mine,
That I do not wholly fare
Even as ye do, thoughtless pair!   110
And I will have my careless season
Spite of melancholy reason,
Will walk through life in such a way
That, when time brings on decay,
Now and then I may possess   115
Hours of perfect gladsomeness.
—Pleased by any random toy;
By a kitten's busy joy,
Or an infant's laughing eye
Sharing in the ecstasy;   120
I would fare like that or this,
Find my wisdom in my bliss;
Keep the sprightly soul awake,
And have faculties to take,
Even from things by sorrow wrought, 125
Matter for a jocund thought,
Spite of care, and spite of grief,
To gambol with Life's falling Leaf.

                              1804.

XXXII.

ADDRESS TO MY INFANT DAUGHTER, DORA,

ON BEING REMINDED THAT SHE WAS A MONTH OLD THAT DAY, SEPTEMBER 16.

————Hast thou then survived—
Mild Offspring of infirm humanity,
Meek Infant! among all forlornest things
The most forlorn—one life of that bright star,
The second glory of the Heavens?—Thou hast;
Already hast survived that great decay, 6
That transformation through the wide earth
  felt,
And by all nations. In that Being's sight
From whom the Race of human kind proceed,
A thousand years are but as yesterday; 10
And one day's narrow circuit is to Him
Not less capacious than a thousand years.
But what is time? What outward glory?
  Neither
A measure is of Thee, whose claims extend
Through "heaven's eternal year."—Yet hail to
  Thee, 15
Frail, feeble, Monthling!—by that name, me-
  thinks,
Thy scanty breathing-time is portioned out
Not idly.—Hadst thou been of Indian birth,
Couched on a casual bed of moss and leaves,
And rudely canopied by leafy boughs, 20
Or to the churlish elements exposed
On the blank plains,—the coldness of the night,
Or the night's darkness, or its cheerful face

Of beauty, by the changing moon adorned,
Would, with imperious admonition, then   25
Have scored thine age, and punctually timed
Thine infant history, on the minds of those
Who might have wandered with thee.—Mother's
    love,
Nor less than mother's love in other breasts,
Will, among us warm-clad and warmly housed,
Do for thee what the finger of the heavens   31
Doth all too often harshly execute
For thy unblest coevals, amid wilds
Where fancy hath small liberty to grace
The affections, to exalt them or refine ;   35
And the maternal sympathy itself,
Though strong, is, in the main, a joyless tie
Of naked instinct, wound about the heart.
Happier, far happier is thy lot and ours !
Even now—to solemnize thy helpless state, 40
And to enliven in the mind's regard
Thy passive beauty—parallels have risen,
Resemblances, or contrasts, that connect,
Within the region of a father's thoughts,
Thee and thy mate and sister of the sky.   45
And first ;—thy sinless progress, through a
    world
By sorrow darkened and by care disturbed,
Apt likeness bears to hers, through gathered
    clouds
Moving untouched in silver purity,   49
And cheering oft-times their reluctant gloom.
Fair are ye both, and both are free from stain :
But thou, how leisurely thou fill'st thy horn
With brightness ! leaving her to post along,
And range about, disquieted in change,
And still impatient of the shape she wears. 55
Once up, once down the hill, one journey, Bab,
That will suffice thee ; and it seems that now

Thou hast fore-knowledge that such task is
    thine;
Thou travellest so contentedly, and sleep'st
In such a heedless peace. Alas! full soon 60
Hath this conception, grateful to behold,
Changed countenance, like an object sullied o'er
By breathing mist; and thine appears to be
A mournful labour, while to her is given
Hope, and a renovation without end.   65
—That smile forbids the thought; for on thy
    face
Smiles are beginning, like the beams of dawn,
To shoot and circulate; smiles have there been
    seen;
Tranquil assurances that Heaven supports
The feeble motions of thy life, and cheers 70
Thy loneliness: or shall those smiles be called
Feelers of love, put forth as if to explore
This untried world, and to prepare thy way
Through a strait passage intricate and dim?
Such are they; and the same are tokens, signs, 75
Which, when the appointed season hath arrived,
Joy, as her holiest language, shall adopt;
And Reason's godlike Power be proud to own.

                    1804.

XXXIII.

THE WAGGONER.

" In Cairo's crowded streets
The impatient Merchant, wondering, waits in vain,
And Mecca saddens at the long delay."
                                        THOMSON.

TO CHARLES LAMB, ESQ.

MY DEAR FRIEND,
        When I sent you, a few weeks ago, the " Tale
of Peter Bell," you asked " why ' The Waggoner ' was
not added ?"—To say the truth,—from the higher
tone of imagination, and the deeper touches of passion
aimed at in the former, I apprehended this little
Piece could not accompany it without disadvantage.
In the year 1806, if I am not mistaken, " The
Waggoner " was read to you in manuscript, and, as
you have remembered it for so long a time, I am the
more encouraged to hope that, since the localities
on which the Poem partly depends did not prevent
its being interesting to you, it may prove acceptable
to others.   Being therefore in some measure the
cause of its present appearance, you must allow me
the gratification of inscribing it to you ; in acknow-
ledgment of the pleasure I have derived from your
Writings, and of the high esteem with which
        I am very truly yours,
        WILLIAM WORDSWORTH.

RYDAL MOUNT, *May* 20, 1819.

CANTO FIRST.

'TIS spent—this burning day of June !
Soft darkness o'er its latest gleams is stealing ;
The buzzing dor-hawk, round and round, is
        wheeling,—
That solitary bird

Is all that can be heard   5
In silence deeper far than that of deepest noon!

Confiding Glow-worms, 'tis a night
Propitious to your earth-born light!
But where the scattered stars are seen
In hazy straits the clouds between,   10
Each, in his station twinkling not,
Seems changed into a pallid spot.
The mountains against heaven's grave weight
Rise up, and grow to wondrous height.
The air, as in a lion's den,   15
Is close and hot;—and now and then
Comes a tired and sultry breeze
With a haunting and a panting,
Like the stifling of disease;
But the dews allay the heat,   20
And the silence makes it sweet.

Hush, there is some one on the stir!
'Tis Benjamin the Waggoner;
Who long hath trod this toilsome way,
Companion of the night and day.   25
That far-off tinkling's drowsy cheer,
Mixed with a faint yet grating sound
In a moment lost and found,
The Wain announces—by whose side
Along the banks of Rydal Mere   30
He paces on, a trusty Guide,—
Listen! you can scarcely hear!
Hither he his course is bending;—
Now he leaves the lower ground,
And up the craggy hill ascending   35
Many a stop and stay he makes,
Many a breathing-fit he takes;—
Steep the way and wearisome,
Yet all the while his whip is dumb!

The Horses have worked with right good-
    will,   40
And so have gained the top of the hill;
He was patient, they were strong,
And now they smoothly glide along,
Recovering breath, and pleased to win
The praises of mild Benjamin.   45
Heaven shield him from mishap and snare!
But why so early with this prayer?
Is it for threatenings in the sky?
Or for some other danger nigh?
No; none is near him yet, though he   50
Be one of much infirmity;
For at the bottom of the brow,
Where once the DOVE and OLIVE-BOUGH
Offered a greeting of good ale
To all who entered Grasmere Vale;   55
And called on him who must depart
To leave it with a jovial heart;
There, where the DOVE and OLIVE-BOUGH
Once hung, a Poet harbours now,
A simple water-drinking Bard;   60
Why need our Hero then (though frail
His best resolves) be on his guard?
He marches by, secure and bold;
Yet, while he thinks on times of old,
It seems that all looks wondrous cold;   65
He shrugs his shoulders, shakes his head,
And, for the honest folk within,
It is a doubt with Benjamin
Whether they be alive or dead!

Here is no danger,—none at all!   70
Beyond his wish he walks secure;
But pass a mile—and *then* for trial,—
Then for the pride of self-denial;
If he resist that tempting door,

Which with such friendly voice will call;   75
If he resist those casement panes,
And that bright gleam which thence will fall
Upon his Leaders' bells and manes,
Inviting him with cheerful lure:
For still, though all be dark elsewhere,   80
Some shining notice will be *there*,
Of open house and ready fare.

   The place to Benjamin right well
Is known, and by as strong a spell
As used to be that sign of love   85
And hope—the OLIVE-BOUGH and DOVE;
He knows it to his cost, good Man!
Who does not know the famous SWAN?
Object uncouth! and yet our boast,
For it was painted by the Host;   90
His own conceit the figure planned,
'Twas coloured all by his own hand;
And that frail Child of thirsty clay,
Of whom I sing this rustic lay,
Could tell with self-dissatisfaction   95
Quaint stories of the bird's attraction![1]

   Well! that is past—and in despite
Of open door and shining light.
And now the conqueror essays
The long ascent of Dunmail-raise;   100
And with his team is gentle here
As when he clomb from Rydal Mere;
His whip they do not dread—his voice
They only hear it to rejoice.
To stand or go is at *their* pleasure;   105
Their efforts and their time they measure
By generous pride within the breast;

  [1] This rude piece of self-taught art (such is the progress of refinement) has been supplanted by a professional production.

And while they strain, and while they rest,
He thus pursues his thoughts at leisure.

Now am I fairly safe to-night—   110
And with proud cause my heart is light:
I trespassed lately worse than ever—
But Heaven has blest a good endeavour;
And, to my soul's content, I find
The evil One is left behind.   115
Yes, let my master fume and fret,
Here am I—with my horses yet!
My jolly team, he finds that ye
Will work for nobody but me!
Full proof of this the Country gained;   120
It knows how ye were vexed and strained,
And forced unworthy stripes to bear,
When trusted to another's care.
Here was it—on this rugged slope,
Which now ye climb with heart and hope,   125
I saw you, between rage and fear,
Plunge, and fling back a spiteful ear,
And ever more and more confused,
As ye were more and more abused:
As chance would have it, passing by   130
I saw you in that jeopardy:
A word from me was like a charm;
Ye pulled together with one mind;
And your huge burthen, safe from harm,
Moved like a vessel in the wind!   135
—Yes, without me, up hills so high
'Tis vain to strive for mastery.
Then grieve not, jolly team! though tough
The road we travel, steep, and rough;
Though Rydal-heights and Dunmail-raise,   140
And all their fellow banks and braes,
Full often make you stretch and strain,
And halt for breath and halt again,

Yet to their sturdiness 'tis owing
That side by side we still are going! 145

    While Benjamin in earnest mood
His meditations thus pursued,
A storm, which had been smothered long,
Was growing inwardly more strong;
And, in its struggles to get free, 150
Was busily employed as he.
The thunder had begun to growl—
He heard not, too intent of soul;
The air was now without a breath—
He marked not that 'twas still as death. 155
But soon large rain-drops on his head
Fell with the weight of drops of lead;—
He starts—and takes, at the admonition,
A sage survey of his condition.
The road is black before his eyes, 160
Glimmering faintly where it lies;
Black is the sky—and every hill,
Up to the sky, is blacker still—
Sky, hill, and dale, one dismal room,
Hung round and overhung with gloom; 165
Save that above a single height
Is to be seen a lurid light,
Above Helm-crag [1]—a streak half dead,
A burning of portentous red;
And near that lurid light, full well 170
The ASTROLOGER, sage Sidrophel,
Where at his desk and book he sits,
Puzzling aloft his curious wits;
He whose domain is held in common
With no one but the ANCIENT WOMAN, 175

[1] A mountain of Grasmere, the broken summit of which presents two figures, full as distinctly shaped as that of the famous Cobbler near Arroquhar in Scotland.

Cowering beside her rifted cell,
As if intent on magic spell;—
Dread pair that, spite of wind and weather,
Still sit upon Helm-crag together!

   The ASTROLOGER was not unseen   180
By solitary Benjamin;
But total darkness came anon,
And he and every thing was gone:
And suddenly a ruffling breeze,
(That would have rocked the sounding trees, 185
Had aught of sylvan growth been there),
Swept through the Hollow long and bare:
The rain rushed down—the road was battered,
As with the force of billows shattered;
The horses are dismayed, nor know   190
Whether they should stand or go;
And Benjamin is groping near them,
Sees nothing, and can scarcely hear them.
He is astounded,—wonder not,—
With such a charge in such a spot;   195
Astounded in the mountain gap
With thunder-peals, clap after clap,
Close-treading on the silent flashes—
And somewhere, as he thinks, by crashes
Among the rocks; with weight of rain,   200
And sullen motions long and slow,
That to a dreary distance go—
Till, breaking in upon the dying strain,
A rending o'er his head begins the fray again.

   Meanwhile, uncertain what to do,   205
And oftentimes compelled to halt,
The horses cautiously pursue
Their way, without mishap or fault;
And now have reached that pile of stones,
Heaped over brave King Dunmail's bones, 210

He who had once supreme command,
Last king of rocky Cumberland ;
His bones, and those of all his Power,
Slain here in a disastrous hour !

When, passing through this narrow strait,
Stony, and dark, and desolate,   216
Benjamin can faintly hear
A voice that comes from some one near,
A female voice :—" Whoe'er you be,
Stop," it exclaimed, " and pity me !"   220
And less in pity than in wonder,
Amid the darkness and the thunder,
The Waggoner, with prompt command,
Summons his horses to a stand.

While, with increasing agitation,   225
The Woman urged her supplication,
In rueful words, with sobs between—
The voice of tears that fell unseen;
There came a flash—a startling glare,
And all Seat-Sandal was laid bare !   230
'Tis not a time for nice suggestion,
And Benjamin, without a question,
Taking her for some way-worn rover,
Said, " Mount, and get you under cover !"

Another voice, in tone as hoarse   235
As a swoln brook with rugged course,
Cried out, " Good brother, why so fast ?
I 've had a glimpse of you—*avast !*
Or, since it suits you to be civil,
Take her at once—for good and evil !'   240

" It is my Husband," softly said
The Woman, as if half afraid :
By this time she was snug within,

Through help of honest Benjamin;
She and her Babe, which to her breast   245
With thankfulness the Mother pressed;
And now the same strong voice more near
Said cordially, " My Friend, what cheer?
Rough doings these! as God's my judge,
The sky owes somebody a grudge!   250
We've had in half an hour or less
A twelvemonth's terror and distress!"

Then Benjamin entreats the Man
Would mount, too, quickly as he can:
The Sailor—Sailor now no more,   255
But such he had been heretofore—
To courteous Benjamin replied,
" Go you your way, and mind not me;
For I must have, whate'er betide,
My Ass and fifty things beside,—   260
Go, and I'll follow speedily!"

The Waggon moves—and with its load
Descends along the sloping road;
And the rough Sailor instantly
Turns to a little tent hard by: 265
For when, at closing-in of day,
The family had come that way,
Green pasture and the soft warm air
Tempted them to settle there.—
Green is the grass for beast to graze,   270
Around the stones of Dunmail-raise!

The Sailor gathers up his bed,
Takes down the canvas overhead;
And after farewell to the place,
A parting word—though not of grace,   275
Pursues, with Ass and all his store,
The way the Waggon went before.

CANTO SECOND.

If Wytheburne's modest House of prayer,
As lowly as the lowliest dwelling,
Had, with its belfry's humble stock,
A little pair that hang in air,
Been mistress also of a clock,
(And one, too, not in crazy plight),
Twelve strokes that clock would have been
    telling
Under the brow of old Helvellyn—
Its bead-roll of midnight,
Then, when the Hero of my tale   10
Was passing by, and, down the vale
(The vale now silent, hushed, I ween,
As if a storm had never been)
Proceeding with a mind at ease ;
While the old Familiar of the seas,   15
Intent to use his utmost haste,
Gained ground upon the Waggon fast,
And gives another lusty cheer ;
For, spite of rumbling of the wheels,
A welcome greeting he can hear ;—   20
It is a fiddle in its glee
Dinning from the CHERRY TREE !

    Thence the sound—the light is there—
As Benjamin is now aware,
Who, to his inward thoughts confined,   25
Had almost reached the festive door,
When, startled by the Sailor's roar,
He hears a sound and sees the light,
And in a moment calls to mind
That 'tis the village MERRY-NIGHT ! [1]   30

[1] A term well-known in the North of England, and applied to rural Festivals where young persons meet in the evening for the purpose of dancing.

Although before in no dejection,
At this insidious recollection
His heart with sudden joy is filled,—
His ears are by the music thrilled,
His eyes take pleasure in the road   35
Glittering before him bright and broad;
And Benjamin is wet and cold,
And there are reasons manifold
That make the good, tow'rds which he's yearn-
        ing,
Look fairly like a lawful earning.   40

Nor has thought time to come and go,
To vibrate between yes and no;
For cries the Sailor, " Glorious chance
That blew us hither!—let him dance,
Who can or will!—my honest soul,   45
Our treat shall be a friendly bowl!"
He draws him to the door—" Come in,
Come, come," cries he to Benjamin!
And Benjamin—ah, woe is me!
Gave the word—the horses heard   50
And halted, though reluctantly.

" Blithe souls and lightsome hearts have we,
Feasting at the Cherry Tree!"
This was the outside proclamation,
This was the inside salutation;   55
What bustling—jostling—high and low!
A universal overflow!
What tankards foaming from the tap!
What store of cakes in every lap!
What thumping—stumping—overhead!   60
The thunder had not been more busy:
With such a stir you would have said,
This little place may well be dizzy!
'Tis who can dance with greatest vigour—

'Tis what can be most prompt and eager; 65
As if it heard the fiddle's call,
The pewter clatters on the wall;
The very bacon shows its feeling,
Swinging from the smoky ceiling!

A steaming bowl, a blazing fire,   70
What greater good can heart desire?
'Twere worth a wise man's while to try
The utmost anger of the sky:
To *seek* for thoughts of a gloomy cast,
If such the bright amends at last.   75
Now should you say I judge amiss,
The CHERRY TREE shows proof of this;
For soon, of all the happy there,
Our Travellers are the happiest pair;
All care with Benjamin is gone—   80
A Cæsar past the Rubicon!
He thinks not of his long, long, strife;—
The Sailor, Man by nature gay,
Hath no resolves to throw away;
And he hath now forgot his Wife,   85
Hath quite forgotten her—or may be
Thinks her the luckiest soul on earth,
Within that warm and peaceful berth,
        Under cover,
        Terror over,   90
Sleeping by her sleeping Baby.

With bowl that sped from hand to hand,
The gladdest of the gladsome band,
Amid their own delight and fun,
They hear—when every dance is done,   95
When every whirling bout is o'er—
The fiddle's *squeak* [1]—that call to bliss,

[1] At the close of each strathspey, or jig, a particular
note from the fiddle summons the Rustic to the
agreeable duty of saluting his partner.

Ever followed by a kiss;
They envy not the happy lot,
But enjoy their own the more!   100

While thus our jocund Travellers fare,
Up springs the Sailor from his chair—
Limps (for I might have told before
That he was lame) across the floor—
Is gone—returns—and with a prize;   105
With what?—a Ship of lusty size;
A gallant stately Man-of-war,
Fixed on a smoothly-sliding car.
Surprise to all, but most surprise
To Benjamin, who rubs his eyes,   110
Not knowing that he had befriended
A Man so gloriously attended!

" This," cries the Sailor, " a Third-rate is—
Stand back, and you shall see her gratis!
This was the Flag-ship at the Nile,   115
The VANGUARD—you may smirk and smile,
But, pretty Maid, if you look near,
You'll find you've much in little here!
A nobler ship did never swim,
And you shall see her in full trim: 120
I'll set, my friends, to do you honour,
Set every inch of sail upon her."
So said, so done; and masts, sails, yards,
He names them all; and interlards
His speech with uncouth terms of art,   125
Accomplished in the showman's part;
And then, as from a sudden check,
Cries out—" 'Tis there, the quarter-deck
On which brave Admiral Nelson stood—
A sight that would have roused your blood!
One eye he had, which, bright as ten,   131
Burned like a fire among his men;

Let this be land, and that be sea,
Here lay the French—and *thus* came we!"

Hushed was by this the fiddle's sound, 135
The dancers all were gathered round,
And such the stillness of the house,
You might have heard a nibbling mouse;
While, borrowing helps where'er he may,
The Sailor through the story runs 140
Of ships to ships and guns to guns;
And does his utmost to display
The dismal conflict, and the might
And terror of that marvellous night!
" A bowl, a bowl of double measure," 145
Cries Benjamin, " a draught of length !
To Nelson, England's pride and treasure,
Her bulwark and her tower of strength !"
When Benjamin had seized the bowl,
The mastiff, from beneath the waggon, 150
Where he lay, watchful as a dragon,
Rattled his chain;—'twas all in vain,
For Benjamin, triumphant soul!
He heard the monitory growl;
Heard—and in opposition quaffed 155
A deep, determined, desperate draught!
Nor did the battered Tar forget,
Or flinch from what he deemed his debt:
Then, like a hero crowned with laurel,
Back to her place the ship he led; 160
Wheeled her back in full apparel;
And so, flag flying at mast head,
Re-yoked her to the Ass:—anon
Cries Benjamin, " We must be gone."
Thus, after two hours' hearty stay, 165
Again behold them on their way!

CANTO THIRD.

RIGHT gladly had the horses stirred,
When they the wished-for greeting heard,
The whip's loud notice from the door,
That they were free to move once more.
You think those doings must have bred
In them disheartening doubts and dread;
No, not a horse of all the eight,
Although it be a moonless night,
Fears either for himself or freight;
For this they know (and let it hide,   10
In part, the offences of their guide)
That Benjamin, with clouded brains,
Is worth the best with all their pains;
And, if they had a prayer to make,
The prayer would be that they may take 15
With him whatever comes in course,
The better fortune or the worse;
That no one else may have business near them,
And, drunk or sober, he may steer them.

So forth in dauntless mood they fare, 20
And with them goes the guardian pair.

Now, heroes, for the true commotion,
The triumph of your late devotion!
Can aught on earth impede delight,
Still mounting to a higher height;   25
And higher still—a greedy flight!
Can any low-born care pursue her,
Can any mortal clog come to her?
No notion have they—not a thought,
That is from joyless regions brought! 30
And, while they coast the silent lake,
Their inspiration I partake;

Share their empyreal spirits—yea,
With their enraptured vision see—
O fancy—what a jubilee! 35
What shifting pictures—clad in gleams
Of colour bright as feverish dreams!
Earth, spangled sky, and lake serene,
Involved and restless all—a scene
Pregnant with mutual exaltation, 40
Rich change, and multiplied creation!
This sight to me the Muse imparts ;—
And then, what kindness in their hearts!
What tears of rapture, what vow-making,
Profound entreaties, and hand-shaking! 45
What solemn, vacant, interlacing,
As if they 'd fall asleep embracing!
Then in the turbulence of glee,
And in the excess of amity,
Says Benjamin, " That Ass of thine, 50
He spoils thy sport, and hinders mine:
If he were tethered to the waggon,
He 'd drag as well what he is dragging ;
And we, as brother should with brother,
Might trudge it alongside each other! " 55

Forthwith, obedient to command,
The horses made a quiet stand ;
And to the waggon's skirts was tied
The Creature, by the Mastiff's side,
The Mastiff wondering, and perplext 60
With dread of what will happen next ;
And thinking it but sorry cheer
To have such company so near!

This new arrangement made, the Wain
Through the still night proceeds again ; 65
No moon hath risen her light to lend ;
But indistinctly may be kenned

The VANGUARD, following close behind,
Sails spread, as if to catch the wind!

"Thy wife and child are snug and warm,   70
Thy ship will travel without harm;
I like," said Benjamin, "her shape and stature:
And this of mine—this bulky creature
Of which I have the steering—this,
Seen fairly, is not much amiss!   75
We want your streamers, friend, you know;
But, altogether as we go,
We make a kind of handsome show!
Among these hills, from first to last,
We've weathered many a furious blast;   80
Hard passage forcing on, with head
Against the storm, and canvas spread.
I hate a boaster; but to thee
Will say 't, who know'st both land and sea,
The unluckiest hulk that stems the brine   85
Is hardly worse beset than mine,
When cross-winds on her quarter beat;
And, fairly lifted from my feet,
I stagger onward—heaven knows how;
But not so pleasantly as now: 90
Poor pilot I, by snows confounded,
And many a foundrous pit surrounded!
Yet here we are, by night and day
Grinding through rough and smooth our way;
Through foul and fair our task fulfilling;   95
And long shall be so yet—God willing!"

"Ay," said the Tar, "through fair and foul—
But save us from yon screeching owl!"
That instant was begun a fray
Which called their thoughts another way: 100
The Mastiff, ill-conditioned carl!
What must he do but growl and snarl,

Still more and more dissatisfied
With the meek comrade at his side!
Till, not incensed though put to proof,   105
The Ass, uplifting a hind hoof,
Salutes the Mastiff on the head;
And so were better manners bred,
And all was calmed and quieted.

"Yon screech-owl," says the Sailor, turning
Back to his former cause of mourning,   111
"Yon owl!—pray God that all be well!
'Tis worse than any funeral bell;
As sure as I've the gift of sight,
We shall be meeting ghosts to-night!"   115
—Said Benjamin, "This whip shall lay
A thousand, if they cross our way.
I know that Wanton's noisy station,
I know him and his occupation;
The jolly bird hath learned his cheer   120
Upon the banks of Windermere;
Where a tribe of them make merry,
Mocking the Man that keeps the ferry;
Hallooing from an open throat,
Like travellers shouting for a boat.   125
—The tricks he learned at Windermere
This vagrant owl is playing here—
That is the worst of his employment:
He's at the top of his enjoyment!"

This explanation stilled the alarm,   130
Cured the foreboder like a charm;
This, and the manner, and the voice,
Summoned the Sailor to rejoice;
His heart is up—he fears no evil
From life or death, from man or devil;   135
He wheels—and, making many stops,

Brandished his crutch against the mountain
      tops;
And, while he talked of blows and scars,
Benjamin, among the stars,
Beheld a dancing—and a glancing;   140
Such retreating and advancing
As, I ween, was never seen
In bloodiest battle since the days of Mars!

CANTO FOURTH.

Thus they, with freaks of proud delight,
Beguile the remnant of the night;
And many a snatch of jovial song
Regales them as they wind along;
While to the music, from on high,   5
The echoes make a glad reply.—
But the sage Muse the revel heeds
No farther than her story needs;
Nor will she servilely attend
The loitering journey to its end.   10
—Blithe spirits of her own impel
The Muse, who scents the morning air,
To take of this transported pair
A brief and unreproved farewell;
To quit the slow-paced waggon's side,   15
And wander down yon hawthorn dell,
With murmuring Greta for her guide.
—There doth she ken the awful form
Of Raven-crag—black as a storm—
Glimmering through the twilight pale   20
And Ghimmer-crag,[1] his tall twin brother,
Each peering forth to meet the other:—

    [1] The crag of the ewe lamb.

And, while she roves through St. John's Vale,
Along the smooth unpathwayed plain,
By sheep-track or through cottage lane,   25
Where no disturbance comes to intrude
Upon the pensive solitude,
Her unsuspecting eye, perchance,
With the rude shepherd's favoured glance,
Beholds the faeries in array,   30
Whose party-coloured garments gay
The silent company betray:
Red, green, and blue; a moment's sight!
For Skiddaw-top with rosy light
Is touched—and all the band take flight.   35
—Fly also, Muse! and from the dell
Mount to the ridge of Nathdale Fell;
Thence look thou forth o'er wood and lawn
Hoar with the frost-like dews of dawn;
Across yon meadowy bottom look,   40
Where close fogs hide their parent brook;
And see, beyond that hamlet small
The ruined towers of Threlkeld-hall,
Lurking in a double shade,
By trees and lingering twilight made!   45
There, at Blencathara's rugged feet,
Sir Lancelot gave a safe retreat
To noble Clifford; from annoy
Concealed the persecuted boy,
Well pleased in rustic garb to feed   50
His flock, and pipe on shepherd's reed
Among this multitude of hills,
Crags, woodlands, waterfalls, and rills;
Which soon the morning shall enfold,
From east to west, in ample vest   55
Of massy gloom and radiance bold.

The mists, that o'er the streamlet's bed
Hung low, begin to rise and spread;

Even while I speak, their skirts of grey
Are smitten by a silver ray;   60
And, lo!—up Castrigg's naked steep
(Where, smoothly urged, the vapours sweep
Along—and scatter and divide,
Like fleecy clouds self-multiplied)
The stately waggon is ascending,   65
With faithful Benjamin attending,
Apparent now beside his team—
Now lost amid a glittering steam:
And with him goes his Sailor-friend,
By this time near their journey's end;   70
And, after their high-minded riot,
Sickening into thoughtful quiet;
As if the morning's pleasant hour
Had for their joys a killing power.
And sooth for Benjamin a vein   75
Is opened of still deeper pain,
As if his heart by notes were stung
From out the lowly hedge-rows flung;
As if the warbler lost in light
Reproved his soarings of the night,   80
In strains of rapture pure and holy
Upbraided his distempered folly.

    Drooping is he, his step is dull;
But the horses stretch and pull;
With increasing vigour climb,   85
Eager to repair lost time;
Whether, by their own desert,
Knowing what cause there is for shame,
They are labouring to avert
As much as may be of the blame,   90
Which, they foresee, must soon alight
Upon *his* head, whom, in despite
Of all his failings, they love best;
Whether for him they are distrest;

Or, by length of fasting roused,   95
Are impatient to be housed:
Up against the hill they strain
Tugging at the iron chain,
Tugging all with might and main,
Last and foremost, every horse   100
To the utmost of his force!
And the smoke and respiration,
Rising like an exhalation,
Blend with the mist—a moving shroud
To form, an undissolving cloud;   105
Which, with slant ray, the merry sun
Takes delight to play upon.
Never golden-haired Apollo,
Pleased some favourite chief to follow
Through accidents of peace or war,   110
In a perilous moment threw
Around the object of his care
Veil of such celestial hue;
Interposed so bright a screen—
Him and his enemies between!   115

Alas! what boots it?—who can hide,
When the malicious Fates are bent
On working out an ill intent?
Can destiny be turned aside?
No—sad progress of my story!   120
Benjamin, this outward glory
Cannot shield thee from thy Master,
Who from Keswick has pricked forth,
Sour and surly as the north;
And, in fear of some disaster,   125
Comes to give what help he may,
And to hear what thou canst say;
If, as needs he must forbode,
Thou hast been loitering on the road!
His fears, his doubts, may now take flight— 130

The wished-for object is in sight;
Yet, trust the Muse, it rather hath
Stirred him up to livelier wrath;
Which he stifles, moody man!
With all the patience that he can;   135
To the end that, at your meeting,
He may give thee decent greeting.

There he is—resolved to stop,
Till the waggon gains the top;
But stop he cannot—must advance :   140
Him Benjamin, with lucky glance,
Espies—and instantly is ready,
Self-collected, poised, and steady :
And, to be the better seen,
Issues from his radiant shroud,   145
From his close-attending cloud,
With careless air and open mien.
Erect his port, and firm his going;
So struts yon cock that now is crowing;
And the morning light in grace   150
Strikes upon his lifted face,
Hurrying the pallid hue away
That might his trespasses betray.
But what can all avail to clear him,
Or what need of explanation,   155
Parley or interrogation?
For the Master sees, alas!
That unhappy Figure near him,
Limping o'er the dewy grass,
Where the road it fringes, sweet,   160
Soft and cool to way-worn feet;
And, O indignity! an Ass,
By his noble Mastiff's side,
Tethered to the waggon's tail:
And the ship, in all her pride,   165
Following after in full sail!

Not to speak of babe and mother;
Who, contented with each other,
And snug as birds in leafy arbour,
Find, within, a blessed harbour! [170]

With eager eyes the Master pries;
Looks in and out, and through and through;
Says nothing—till at last he spies
A wound upon the Mastiff's head,
A wound where plainly might be read   175
What feats an Ass's hoof can do!
But drop the rest:—this aggravation,
This complicated provocation,
A hoard of grievances unsealed;
All past forgiveness it repealed;   180
And thus, and through distempered blood
On both sides, Benjamin the good,
The patient, and the tender-hearted,
Was from his team and waggon parted;
When duty of that day was o'er,   185
Laid down his whip—and served no more.—
Nor could the waggon long survive,
Which Benjamin had ceased to drive:
It lingered on;—guide after guide
Ambitiously the office tried;   190
But each unmanageable hill
Called for *his* patience and *his* skill;—
And sure it is that through this night,
And what the morning brought to light,
Two losses had we to sustain,   195
We lost both WAGGONER and WAIN!
Accept, O Friend, for praise or blame,
The gift of this adventurous song;
A record which I dared to frame,
Though timid scruples checked me long;   200
They checked me—and I left the theme
Untouched;—in spite of many a gleam

Of fancy which thereon was shed,
Like pleasant sunbeams shifting still
Upon the side of a distant hill: 205
But Nature might not be gainsaid;
For what I have and what I miss
I sing of these;—it makes my bliss!
Nor is it I who play the part,
But a shy spirit in my heart,   210
That comes and goes—will sometimes leap
From hiding-places ten years deep;
Or haunts me with familiar face,
Returning, like a ghost unlaid,
Until the debt I owe be paid.   215
Forgive me then; for I had been
On friendly terms with this Machine :
In him, while he was wont to trace
Our roads, through many a long year's space,
A living almanack had we;   220
We had a speaking diary,
That in this uneventful place,
Gave to the days a mark and name
By which we knew them when they came.
—Yes, I, and all about me here,   225
Through all the changes of the year,
Had seen him through the mountains go,
In pomp of mist or pomp of snow,
Majestically huge and slow:
Or with a milder grace adorning   230
The landscape of a summer's morning;
While Grasmere smoothed her liquid plain
The moving image to detain;
And mighty Fairfield, with a chime
Of echoes, to his march kept time;   235
When little other business stirred,
And little other sound was heard;
In that delicious hour of balm,
Stillness, solitude, and calm,

While yet the valley is arrayed,   240
On this side with a sober shade;
On that is prodigally bright—
Crag, lawn, and wood—with rosy light.
—But most of all, thou lordly Wain!
I wish to have thee here again,   245
When windows flap and chimney roars,
And all is dismal out of doors;
And, sitting by my fire, I see
Eight sorry carts, no less a train!
Unworthy successors of thee,   250
Come straggling through the wind and rain:
And oft, as they pass slowly on,
Beneath my windows, one by one,
See, perched upon the naked height
The summit of a cumbrous freight,   255
·A single traveller—and there
Another; then perhaps a pair—
The lame, the sickly, and the old;
Men, women, heartless with the cold;
And babes in wet and starveling plight;   260
Which once, be weather as it might,
Had still a nest within a nest,
Thy shelter—and their mother's breast!
Then most of all, then far the most,
Do I regret what we have lost;   265
Am grieved for that unhappy sin
Which robbed us of good Benjamin;—
And of his stately Charge, which none
Could keep alive when He was gone!

1805.

POEMS OF THE IMAGINATION.

I.

THERE WAS A BOY.

THERE was a Boy; ye knew him well, ye cliffs
And islands of Winander!—many a time,
At evening, when the earliest stars began
To move along the edges of the hills,
Rising or setting, would he stand alone,   5
Beneath the trees, or by the glimmering lake;
And there, with fingers interwoven, both hands
Pressed closely palm to palm and to his mouth
Uplifted, he, as through an instrument,
Blew mimic hootings to the silent owls,   10
That they might answer him.—And they would
    shout
Across the watery vale, and shout again,
Responsive to his call,—with quivering peals,
And long halloos, and screams, and echoes loud
Redoubled and redoubled; concourse wild   15
Of jocund din! And, when there came a pause
Of silence such as baffled his best skill:
Then sometimes, in that silence, while he hung
Listening, a gentle shock of mild surprise
Has carried far into his heart the voice   20
Of mountain-torrents; or the visible scene
Would enter unawares into his mind
With all its solemn imagery, its rocks,
Its woods, and that uncertain heaven received
Into the bosom of the steady lake.   25

This boy was taken from his mates, and died

In childhood, ere he was full twelve years old.
Pre-eminent in beauty is the vale
Where he was born and bred: the church-yard
    hangs
Upon a slope above the village-school;   30
And through that church-yard when my way
    has led
On summer-evenings, I believe that there
A long half-hour together I have stood
Mute—looking at the grave in which he lies!

1798.

II.

TO THE CUCKOO.

O BLITHE New-comer! I have heard,
I hear thee and rejoice.
O Cuckoo! shall I call thee Bird,
Or but a wandering Voice?

While I am lying on the grass
Thy twofold shout I hear,
From hill to hill it seems to pass,
At once far off, and near.

Though babbling only to the Vale,
Of sunshine and of flowers,   10
Thou bringest unto me a tale
Of visionary hours.

Thrice welcome, darling of the Spring!
Even yet thou art to me
No bird, but an invisible thing,   15
A voice, a mystery;

The same whom in my school-boy days
I listened to ; that Cry
Which made me look a thousand ways
In bush, and tree, and sky.   20

To seek thee did I often rove
Through woods and on the green ;
And thou wert still a hope, a love ;
Still longed for, never seen.

And I can listen to thee yet ;   25
Can lie upon the plain
And listen, till I do beget
That golden time again.

O blessed Bird ! the earth we pace
Again appears to be   30
An unsubstantial, faery place ;
That is fit home for Thee !

March, 1802.

III.

A NIGHT-PIECE.

——— The sky is overcast
With a continuous cloud of texture close,
Heavy and wan, all whitened by the Moon,
Which through that veil is indistinctly seen,
A dull, contracted circle, yielding light   5
So feebly spread that not a shadow falls,
Chequering the ground—from rock, plant, tree,
        or tower.
At length a pleasant instantaneous gleam
Startles the pensive traveller while he treads
His lonesome path, with unobserving eye   10

Bent earthwards; he looks up—the clouds are
    split
Asunder,—and above his head he sees
The clear Moon, and the glory of the heavens.
There in a black-blue vault she sails along,
Followed by multitudes of stars, that, small 15
And sharp, and bright, along the dark abyss
Drive as she drives: how fast they wheel away,
Yet vanish not!—the wind is in the tree,
But they are silent;—still they roll along
Immeasurably distant; and the vault,   20
Built round by those white clouds, enormous
    clouds,
Still deepens its unfathomable depth.
At length the Vision closes; and the mind,
Not undisturbed by the delight it feels,
Which slowly settles into peaceful calm,   25
Is left to muse upon the solemn scene.

1798.

IV.

AIREY-FORCE VALLEY.

————Not a breath of air
Ruffles the bosom of this leafy glen.
From the brook's margin, wide around, the
    trees
Are steadfast as the rocks; the brook itself,
Old as the hills that feed it from afar,
Doth rather deepen than disturb the calm
Where all things else are still and motionless.
And yet, even now, a little breeze, perchance
Escaped from boisterous winds that rage with-
    out,

Has entered, by the sturdy oaks unfelt,   10
But to its gentle touch how sensitive
Is the light ash! that, pendent from the brow
Of yon dim cave, in seeming silence makes
A soft eye-music of slow-waving boughs,
Powerful almost as vocal harmony   15
To stay the wanderer's steps and soothe his
    thoughts.

                  1842. (?)

V.

YEW-TREES.

THERE is a Yew-tree, pride of Lorton Vale,
Which to this day stands single, in the midst
Of its own darkness, as it stood of yore:
Not loth to furnish weapons for the bands
Of Umfraville or Percy ere they marched   5
To Scotland's heaths; or those that crossed the
    sea
And drew their sounding bows at Azincour,
Perhaps at earlier Crecy, or Poictiers.
Of vast circumference and gloom profound
This solitary Tree! a living thing   10
Produced too slowly ever to decay;
Of form and aspect too magnificent
To be destroyed.   But worthier still of note
Are those fraternal Four of Borrowdale,
Joined in one solemn and capacious grove;   15
Huge trunks! and each particular trunk a
    growth
Of intertwisted fibres serpentine
Up-coiling, and inveterately convolved;
Nor uninformed with Phantasy, and looks
That threaten the profane;—a pillared shade,

Upon whose grassless floor of red-brown hue, 21
By sheddings from the pining umbrage tinged
Perennially—beneath whose sable roof
Of boughs, as if for festal purpose decked
With unrejoicing berries—ghostly Shapes   25
May meet at noontide; Fear and trembling
        Hope,
Silence and Foresight; Death the Skeleton
And Time the Shadow;—there to celebrate,
As in a natural temple scattered o'er
With altars undisturbed of mossy stone,   30
United worship; or in mute repose
To lie, and listen to the mountain flood
Murmuring from Glaramara's inmost caves.

1803.

VI.

NUTTING.

——————— It seems a day
(I speak of one from many singled out)
One of those heavenly days that cannot die;
When, in the eagerness of boyish hope,
I left our cottage-threshold, sallying forth   5
With a huge wallet o'er my shoulders slung,
A nutting-crook in hand; and turned my steps
Tow'rd some far distant wood, a Figure quaint,
Tricked out in proud disguise of cast-off weeds
Which for that service had been husbanded, 10
By exhortation of my frugal Dame—
Motley accoutrement, of power to smile
At thorns, and brakes, and brambles,—and in
        truth

More raggèd than need was! O'er pathless
    rocks,
Through beds of matted fern, and tangled
    thickets,   15
Forcing my way, I came to one dear nook
Unvisited, where not a broken bough
Drooped with its withered leaves, ungracious
    sign
Of devastation; but the hazels rose
Tall and erect, with tempting clusters hung, 20
A virgin scene!—A little while I stood,
Breathing with such suppression of the heart
As joy delights in; and with wise restraint
Voluptuous, fearless of a rival, eyed
The banquet;—or beneath the trees I sate 25
Among the flowers, and with the flowers I
    played;
A temper known to those who, after long
And weary expectation, have been blest
With sudden happiness beyond all hope.
Perhaps it was a bower beneath whose leaves
The violets of five seasons re-appear   31
And fade, unseen by any human eye;
Where fairy water-breaks do murmur on
For ever; and I saw the sparkling foam,
And—with my cheek on one of those green
    stones   35
That, fleeced with moss, under the shady trees,
Lay round me, scattered like a flock of sheep—
I heard the murmur and the murmuring sound,
In that sweet mood when pleasure loves to pay
Tribute to ease; and, of its joy secure,   40
The heart luxuriates with indifferent things,
Wasting its kindliness on stocks and stones,
And on the vacant air. Then up I rose,
And dragged to earth both branch and bough,
    with crash

And merciless ravage: and the shady nook 45
Of hazels, and the green and mossy bower,
Deformed and sullied, patiently gave up
Their quiet being: and unless I now
Confound my present feelings with the past,
Ere from the mutilated bower I turned 50
Exulting, rich beyond the wealth of kings,
I felt a sense of pain when I beheld
The silent trees, and saw the intruding sky.—
Then, dearest Maiden, move along these shades
In gentleness of heart; with gentle hand 55
Touch—for there is a spirit in the woods.

1799.

VII.

THE SIMPLON PASS.

————Brook and road
Were fellow-travellers in this gloomy Pass,
And with them did we journey several hours
At a slow step. The immeasurable height
Of woods decaying, never to be decayed, 5
The stationary blasts of waterfalls,
And in the narrow rent, at every turn,
Winds thwarting winds bewildered and forlorn,
The torrents shooting from the clear blue sky,
The rocks that muttered close upon our ears, 10
Black drizzling crags that spake by the wayside
As if a voice were in them, the sick sight
And giddy prospect of the raving stream,
The unfettered clouds and region of the
            heavens, 14
Tumult and peace, the darkness and the light—
Were all like workings of one mind, the features

Of the same face, blossoms upon one tree,
Characters of the great Apocalypse,
The types and symbols of Eternity,
Of first, and last, and midst, and without end. 20

1804.

VIII.

SHE was a Phantom of delight
When first she gleamed upon my sight;
A lovely Apparition, sent
To be a moment's ornament;
Her eyes as stars of Twilight fair;
Like Twilight's, too, her dusky hair;
But all things else about her drawn
From May-time and the cheerful Dawn;
A dancing Shape, an Image gay,
To haunt, to startle, and way-lay. 10

I saw her upon nearer view,
A Spirit, yet a Woman too!
Her household motions light and free,
And steps of virgin-liberty;
A countenance in which did meet 15
Sweet records, promises as sweet;
A Creature not too bright or good
For human nature's daily food;
For transient sorrows, simple wiles,
Praise, blame, love, kisses, tears, and smiles.

And now I see with eye serene 21
The very pulse of the machine;
A Being breathing thoughtful breath,
A Traveller between life and death;
The reason firm, the temperate will, 25

Endurance, foresight, strength, and skill;
A perfect Woman, nobly planned,
To warn, to comfort, and command;
And yet a Spirit still, and bright
With something of angelic light.   30

1804.

IX.

O NIGHTINGALE! thou surely art
A creature of a " fiery heart":—
These notes of thine—they pierce and pierce;
Tumultuous harmony and fierce!
Thou sing'st as if the God of wine
Had helped thee to a Valentine;
A song in mockery and despite
Of shades, and dews, and silent night;
And steady bliss, and all the loves
Now sleeping in these peaceful groves.   10

I heard a Stock-dove sing or say
His homely tale, this very day;
His voice was buried among trees,
Yet to be come-at by the breeze:
He did not cease; but cooed—and cooed;   15
And somewhat pensively he wooed:
He sang of love, with quiet blending,
Slow to begin, and never ending;
Of serious faith, and inward glee;
That was the song—the song for me   20

1806.

X.

THREE years she grew in sun and shower,
Then Nature said, " A lovelier flower
On earth was never sown ;
This Child I to myself will take ;
She shall be mine, and I will make   5
A Lady of my own.

Myself will to my darling be
Both law and impulse : and with me
The Girl, in rock and plain,
In earth and heaven, in glade and bower, 10
Shall feel an overseeing power
To kindle or restrain.

She shall be sportive as the fawn
That wild with glee across the lawn
Or up the mountain springs ;   15
And hers shall be the breathing balm,
And hers the silence and the calm
Of mute insensate things.

The floating clouds their state shall lend
To her ; for her the willow bend ;   20
Nor shall she fail to see
Even in the motions of the Storm
Grace that shall mould the Maiden's form
By silent sympathy.

The stars of midnight shall be dear   25
To her ; and she shall lean her ear
In many a secret place
Where rivulets dance their wayward round,
And beauty born of murmuring sound
Shall pass into her face.   30

And vital feelings of delight
Shall rear her form to stately height,
Her virgin bosom swell;
Such thoughts to Lucy I will give
While she and I together live   35
Here in this happy dell."

Thus Nature spake—The work was done—
How soon my Lucy's race was run!
She died, and left to me
This heath, this calm, and quiet scene;   40
The memory of what has been,
And never more will be.

                                        1799.

XI.

A SLUMBER did my spirit seal;
   I had no human fears ::
She seemed a thing that could not feel
   The touch of earthly years.

No motion has she now, no force;
   She neither hears nor sees;
Rolled round in earth's diurnal course,
   With rocks, and stones, and trees.

                                        1799.

XII.

I WANDERED lonely as a cloud
That floats on high o'er vales and hills,
When all at once I saw a crowd,
A host, of golden daffodils;

II.   H

Beside the lake, beneath the trees,
Fluttering and dancing in the breeze.

Continuous as the stars that shine
And twinkle on the milky way,
They stretched in never-ending line
Along the margin of a bay :   10
Ten thousand saw I at a glance,
Tossing their heads in sprightly dance.

The waves beside them danced ; but they
Out-did the sparkling waves in glee :
A poet could not but be gay,   15
In such a jocund company :
I gazed—and gazed—but little thought
What wealth the show to me had brought :

For oft, when on my couch I lie
In vacant or in pensive mood,   20
They flash upon that inward eye
Which is the bliss of solitude ;
And then my heart with pleasure fills,
And dances with the daffodils.

                              1804.

XIII.

THE REVERIE OF POOR SUSAN.

AT the corner of Wood Street, when daylight
          appears,
Hangs a Thrush that sings loud, it has sung
          for three years :
Poor Susan has passed by the spot, and has heard
In the silence of morning the song of the Bird.

'Tis a note of enchantment; what ails her?
    She sees   5
A mountain ascending, a vision of trees;
Bright volumes of vapour through Lothbury
    glide,
And a river flows on through the vale of Cheap-
    side.

Green pastures she views in the midst of the
    dale,
Down which she so often has tripped with her
    pail;   10
And a single small cottage, a nest like a dove's,
The one only dwelling on earth that she loves.

She looks, and her heart is in heaven : but they
    fade,
The mist and the river, the hill and the shade :
The stream will not flow, and the hill will not
    rise,   15
And the colours have all passed away from her
    eyes!

                           1797.

XIV.

POWER OF MUSIC.

An Orpheus! an Orpheus! yes, Faith may
    grow bold,
And take to herself all the wonders of old;—
Near the stately Pantheon you 'll meet with
    the same
In the street that from Oxford hath borrowed
    its name.   4

His station is there ; and he works on the crowd,
He sways them with harmony merry and loud ;
He fills with his power all their hearts to the
        brim—
Was aught ever heard like his fiddle and him ?

What an eager assembly ! what an empire is
        this !   9
The weary have life, and the hungry have bliss ;
The mourner is cheered, and the anxious have
        rest ;
And the guilt-burthened soul is no longer
        opprest.

As the Moon brightens round her the clouds of
        the night,
So He, where he stands, is a centre of light ;
It gleams on the face, there, of dusky-browed
        Jack,   15
And the pale-visaged Baker's, with basket on
        back.

That errand-bound 'Prentice was passing in
        haste—
What matter ! he 's caught—and his time runs
        to waste ;
The Newsman is stopped, though he stops on
        the fret ;
And the half-breathless Lamplighter—he 's in
        the net !   20

The Porter sits down on the weight which he
        bore ;
The Lass with her barrow wheels hither her
        store ;—
If a thief could be here he might pilfer at ease ;
She sees the Musician, 'tis all that she sees !

He stands, backed by the wall ;—he abates not
    his din ;   25
His hat gives him vigour, with boons dropping in,
From the old and the young, from the poorest ;
    and there !
The one-pennied Boy has his penny to spare.

O blest are the hearers, and proud be the hand
Of the pleasure it spreads through so thankful
    a band ;   30
I am glad for him, blind as he is !—all the while
If they speak 'tis to praise, and they praise
    with a smile.

That tall Man, a giant in bulk and in height,
Not an inch of his body is free from delight ;
Can he keep himself still, if he would ? oh,
    not he !   35
The music stirs in him like wind through a tree.

Mark that Cripple who leans on his crutch ;
    like a tower
That long has leaned forward, leans hour after
    hour !—
That Mother, whose spirit in fetters is bound,
While she dandles the Babe in her arms to the
    sound.   40

Now, coaches and chariots ! roar on like a
    stream ;
Here are twenty souls happy as souls in a dream :
They are deaf to your murmurs—they care not
    for you,
Nor what ye are flying, nor what ye pursue !

                        1806.

XV.

STAR-GAZERS.

WHAT crowd is this? what have we here! we
  must not pass it by;
A Telescope upon its frame, and pointed to the
  sky:
Long is it as a barber's pole, or mast of little
  boat,
Some little pleasure skiff, that doth on Thames's
  waters float.

The Show-man chooses well his place, 'tis
  Leicester's busy Square; 5
And is as happy in his night, for the heavens
  are blue and fair;
Calm, though impatient, is the crowd; each
  stands ready with the fee,
And envies him that's looking;—what an
  insight must it be!

Yet, Show-man, where can lie the cause? Shall
  thy Implement have blame,
A boaster that, when he is tried, fails, and is
  put to shame?
Or is it good as others are, and be their eyes
  in fault?
Their eyes, or minds? or, finally, is yon resplen-
  dent vault?

Is nothing of that radiant pomp so good as we
  have here?
Or gives a thing but small delight that never
  can be dear?

The silver moon with all her vales, and hills of
    mightiest fame, 15
Doth she betray us when they're seen? or are
    they but a name?

Or is it rather that Conceit rapacious is and
    strong,
And bounty never yields so much but it seems
    to do her wrong?
Or is it that, when human Souls a journey long
    have had
And are returned into themselves, they cannot
    but be sad? 20

Or must we be constrained to think that these
    Spectators rude,
Poor in estate, of manners base, men of the
    multitude,
Have souls which never yet have risen, and
    therefore prostrate lie?
No, no, this cannot be;—men thirst for power
    and majesty!

Does, then, a deep and earnest thought the
    blissful mind employ 25
Of him who gazes, or has gazed? a grave and
    steady joy,
That doth reject all show of pride, admits no
    outward sign,
Because not of this noisy world, but silent and
    divine!

Whatever be the cause, 'tis sure that they who
    pry and pore
Seem to meet with little gain, seem less happy
    than before: 30

One after One they take their turn, nor have I
    one espied
That doth not slackly go away, as if dissatisfied.

1806.

XVI.

WRITTEN IN MARCH,

WHILE RESTING ON THE BRIDGE AT THE FOOT OF BROTHER'S WATER.

THE Cock is crowing,
   The stream is flowing,
   The small birds twitter,
   The lake doth glitter,
The green field sleeps in the sun;
   The oldest and youngest
   Are at work with the strongest;
   The cattle are grazing,
   Their heads never raising;
There are forty feeding like one!   10

   Like an army defeated
   The snow hath retreated,
   And now doth fare ill
   On the top of the bare hill;
The Ploughboy is whooping—anon—anon: 15
   There's joy in the mountains;
   There's life in the fountains;
   Small clouds are sailing,
   Blue sky prevailing;
The rain is over and gone!   20

April 16, 1802.

XVII.

LYRE! though such power do in thy magic live
  As might from India's farthest plain
  Recall the not unwilling Maid,
      Assist me to detain
      The lovely Fugitive: 5
Check with thy notes the impulse which,
  betrayed
By her sweet farewell looks, I longed to aid.
Here let me gaze enrapt upon that eye,
The impregnable and awe-inspiring fort
Of contemplation, the calm port   10
By reason fenced from winds that sigh
Among the restless sails of vanity.
But if no wish be hers that we should part,
A humbler bliss would satisfy my heart.
      Where all things are so fair,   15
Enough by her dear side to breathe the air
      Of this Elysian weather;
And on or in, or near, the brook, espy
  Shade upon the sunshine lying
      Faint and somewhat pensively;   20
And downward Image gaily vying
      With its upright living tree
'Mid silver clouds, and openings of blue sky
As soft almost and deep as her cerulean eye.

Nor less the joy with many a glance   25
Cast up the Stream or down at her beseeching,
To mark its eddying foam-balls prettily distrest
By ever-changing shape and want of rest;
      Or watch, with mutual teaching,
      The current as it plays   30

    In flashing leaps and stealthy creeps
    Adown a rocky maze;
Or note (translucent summer's happiest chance!)
In the slope-channel floored with pebbles bright,
Stones of all hues, gem emulous of gem,   35
So vivid that they take from keenest sight
The liquid veil that seeks not to hide them.

                            1842. (?)

XVIII.

BEGGARS.

SHE had a tall man's height or more;
Her face from summer's noontide heat
No bonnet shaded, but she wore
A mantle, to her very feet
Descending with a graceful flow,   5
And on her head a cap as white as new-fallen
    snow.

Her skin was of Egyptian brown:
Haughty, as if her eye had seen
Its own light to a distance thrown,
She towered, fit person for a Queen   10
To lead those ancient Amazonian files;
Or ruling Bandit's wife among the Grecian isles.

Advancing, forth she stretched her hand
And begged an alms with doleful plea
That ceased not; on our English land   15
Such woes, I knew, could never be;
And yet a boon I gave her, for the creature
Was beautiful to see—a weed of glorious
    feature.

I left her, and pursued my way;
And soon before me did espy   20
A pair of little Boys at play,
Chasing a crimson butterfly;
The taller followed with his hat in hand,
Wreathed round with yellow flowers the gayest
    of the land.

The other wore a rimless crown   25
With leaves of laurel stuck about;
And while both followed up and down,
Each whooping with a merry shout,
In their fraternal features I could trace
Unquestionable lines of that wild Suppliant's
    face.   30

Yet *they*, so blithe of heart, seemed fit
For finest tasks of earth or air:
Wings let them have, and they might flit
Precursors to Aurora's car,
Scattering fresh flowers; though happier far, I
    ween,   35
To hunt their fluttering game o'er rock and
    level green.

They dart across my path—but lo,
Each ready with a plaintive whine!
Said I, "not half an hour ago
Your Mother has had alms of mine."   40
"That cannot be," one answered—"she is
    dead:"—
I looked reproof—they saw—but neither hung
    his head.

"She has been dead, Sir, many a day."—
"Hush, boys! you're telling me a lie;

It was your Mother, as I say!"   45
And, in the twinkling of an eye,
"Come! come!" cried one, and without more
        ado
Off to some other play the joyous Vagrants flew!

                    March 13, 14, 1802.

XIX.

SEQUEL TO THE FOREGOING,

COMPOSED MANY YEARS AFTER.

WHERE are they now, those wanton Boys?
For whose free range the dædal earth
Was filled with animated toys,
And implements of frolic mirth;
With tools for ready wit to guide;
And ornaments of seemlier pride,
More fresh, more bright, than princes wear;
For what one moment flung aside,
Another could repair;
What good or evil have they seen   10
Since I their pastime witnessed here,
Their daring wiles, their sportive cheer?
I ask—but all is dark between!

  They met me in a genial hour,
When universal nature breathed   15
As with the breath of one sweet flower,—
A time to overrule the power
Of discontent, and check the birth
Of thoughts with better thoughts at strife,
The most familiar bane of life   20
Since parting Innocence bequeathed

Mortality to Earth!
Soft clouds, the whitest of the year,
Sailed through the sky—the brooks ran clear;
The lambs from rock to rock were bounding;
With songs the budded groves resounding; 26
And to my heart are still endeared
The thoughts with which it then was cheered;
The faith which saw that gladsome pair
Walk through the fire with unsinged hair. 30
Or, if such faith must needs deceive—
Then, Spirits of beauty and of grace,
Associates in that eager chase;
Ye, who within the blameless mind
Your favourite seat of empire find— 35
Kind Spirits! may we not believe
That they, so happy and so fair
Through your sweet influence, and the care
Of pitying Heaven, at least were free
From touch of *deadly* injury? 40
Destined, whate'er their earthly doom,
For mercy and immortal bloom?

1817.

XX.

GIPSIES.

YET are they here the same unbroken knot
Of human Beings, in the self-same spot!
    Men, women, children, yea the frame
    Of the whole spectacle the same!
Only their fire seems bolder, yielding light, 5
Now deep and red, the colouring of night;
    That on their Gipsy-faces falls,
    Their bed of straw and blanket-walls.

—Twelve hours, twelve bounteous hours are
    gone, while I
Have been a traveller under open sky,   10
    Much witnessing of change and cheer,
    Yet as I left I find them here!
The weary Sun betook himself to rest;—
Then issued Vesper from the fulgent west,
    Outshining like a visible God   15
    The glorious path in which he trod.
And now, ascending, after one dark hour
And one night's diminution of her power,
    Behold the mighty Moon! this way
    She looks as if at them—but they   20
Regard not her:—oh better wrong and strife
(By nature transient) than this torpid life;
    Life which the very stars reprove
    As on their silent tasks they move!
Yet, witness all that stirs in heaven or earth!
In scorn I speak not;—they are what their
    birth   26
    And breeding suffer them to be;
    Wild outcasts of society!

1807.

XXI.

RUTH.

WHEN Ruth was left half desolate,
Her Father took another Mate;
And Ruth, not seven years old,
A slighted child, at her own will
Went wandering over dale and hill,
In thoughtless freedom, bold.

And she had made a pipe of straw,
And music from that pipe could draw
Like sounds of winds and floods;
Had built a bower upon the green,   10
As if she from her birth had been
An infant of the woods.

Beneath her father's roof, alone
She seemed to live; her thoughts her own;
Herself her own delight;   15
Pleased with herself, nor sad, nor gay;
And, passing thus the live-long day,
She grew to woman's height.

There came a Youth from Georgia's shore—
A military casque he wore,   20
With splendid feathers drest;
He brought them from the Cherokees;
The feathers nodded in the breeze,
And made a gallant crest.

From Indian blood you deem he sprung: 25
But no! he spake the English tongue,
And bore a soldier's name;
And, when America was free
From battle and from jeopardy,
He 'cross the ocean came.   30

With hues of genius on his cheek
In finest tones the Youth could speak:
—While he was yet a boy,
The moon, the glory of the sun,
And streams that murmur as they run,   35
Had been his dearest joy.

He was a lovely Youth !   I guess
The panther in the wilderness
Was not so fair as he ;
And, when he chose to sport and play,   40
No dolphin ever was so gay
Upon the tropic sea.

Among the Indians he had fought,
And with him many tales he brought
Of pleasure and of fear ;   45
Such tales as told to any maid
By such a Youth, in the green shade,
Were perilous to hear.

He told of girls—a happy rout !
Who quit their fold with dance and shout, 50
Their pleasant Indian town,
To gather strawberries all day long ;
Returning with a choral song
When daylight is gone down.

He spake of plants that hourly change   55
Their blossoms, through a boundless range
Of intermingling hues ;
With budding, fading, faded flowers
They stand the wonder of the bowers
From morn to evening dews.   60

He told of the magnolia, spread
High as a cloud, high over head !
The cypress and her spire ;
—Of flowers that with one scarlet gleam
Cover a hundred leagues, and seem   65
To set the hills on fire.

The Youth of green savannahs spake,
And many an endless, endless lake,
With all its fairy crowds
Of islands, that together lie   70
As quietly as spots of sky
Among the evening clouds.

"How pleasant," then he said, "it were
A fisher or a hunter there,
In sunshine or in shade   75
To wander with an easy mind;
And build a household fire, and find
A home in every glade!

What days and what bright years! Ah me!
Our life were life indeed, with thee   80
So passed in quiet bliss,
And all the while," said he, "to know
That we were in a world of woe,
On such an earth as this!"

And then he sometimes interwove   85
Fond thoughts about a father's love:
"For there," said he, "are spun
Around the heart such tender ties,
That our own children to our eyes
Are dearer than the sun.   90

Sweet Ruth! and could you go with me
My helpmate in the woods to be,
Our shed at night to rear;
Or run, my own adopted bride,
A sylvan huntress at my side,   95
And drive the flying deer!

II.   I

Beloved Ruth!"—No more he said.
The wakeful Ruth at midnight shed
A solitary tear:
She thought again—and did agree   100
With him to sail across the sea,
And drive the flying deer.

" And now, as fitting is and right,
We in the church our faith will plight,
A husband and a wife."   105
Even so they did; and I may say
That to sweet Ruth that happy day
Was more than human life.

Through dream and vision did she sink,
Delighted all the while to think   110
That on those lonesome floods,
And green savannahs, she should share
His board with lawful joy, and bear
His name in the wild woods.

But, as you have before been told,   115
This Stripling, sportive, gay, and bold,
And, with his dancing crest,
So beautiful, through savage lands
Had roamed about, with vagrant bands
Of Indians in the West.   120

The wind, the tempest roaring high,
The tumult of a tropic sky,
Might well be dangerous food
For him, a Youth to whom was given
So much of earth—so much of heaven,   125
And such impetuous blood.

Whatever in those climes he found
Irregular in sight or sound
Did to his mind impart
A kindred impulse, seemed allied   130
To his own powers, and justified
The workings of his heart.

Nor less, to feed voluptuous thought,
The beauteous forms of nature wrought,
Fair trees and gorgeous flowers ;   135
The breezes their own languor lent ;
The stars had feelings, which they sent
Into those favoured bowers.

Yet, in his worst pursuits I ween
That sometimes there did intervene   140
Pure hopes of high intent :
For passions linked to forms so fair
And stately needs must have their share
Of noble sentiment.

But ill he lived, much evil saw,   145
With men to whom no better law
Nor better life was known ;
Deliberately, and undeceived,
Those wild men's vices he received,
And gave them back his own.   150

His genius and his moral frame
Were thus impaired, and he became
The slave of low desires :
A Man who without self-control
Would seek what the degraded soul   155
Unworthily admires.

And yet he with no feigned delight
Had wooed the Maiden, day and night
Had loved her, night and morn :
What could he less than love a Maid   160
Whose heart with so much nature played ?
So kind and so forlorn !

Sometimes, most earnestly, he said,
"O Ruth ! I have been worse than dead ;
False thoughts, thoughts bold and vain,   165
Encompassed me on every side
When I, in confidence and pride,
Had crossed the Atlantic main.

Before me shone a glorious world—
Fresh as a banner bright, unfurled   170
To music suddenly :
I looked upon those hills and plains,
And seemed as if let loose from chains,
To live at liberty.

No more of this ; for now, by thee   175
Dear Ruth ! more happily set free
With nobler zeal I burn ;
My soul from darkness is released,
Like the whole sky when to the east
The morning doth return."   180

Full soon that better mind was gone ;
No hope, no wish remained, not one,—
They stirred him now no more ;
New objects did new pleasure give,
And once again he wished to live   185
As lawless as before.

Meanwhile, as thus with him it fared,
They for the voyage were prepared,
And went to the sea-shore,
But, when they thither came, the Youth 190
Deserted his poor Bride, and Ruth
Could never find him more.

God help thee, Ruth!—Such pains she had,
That she in half a year was mad,
And in a prison housed; 195
And there, with many a doleful song
Made of wild words, her cup of wrong
She fearfully caroused.

Yet sometimes milder hours she knew,
Nor wanted sun, nor rain, nor dew, 200
Nor pastimes of the May;
—They all were with her in her cell;
And a clear brook with cheerful knell
Did o'er the pebbles play.

When Ruth three seasons thus had lain, 205
There came a respite to her pain;
She from her prison fled;
But of the Vagrant none took thought;
And where it liked her best she sought
Her shelter and her bread. 210

Among the fields she breathed again:
The master-current of her brain
Ran permanent and free;
And, coming to the Banks of Tone,
There did she rest; and dwell alone 215
Under the greenwood tree.

The engines of her pain, the tools
That shaped her sorrow, rocks and pools,
And airs that gently stir
The vernal leaves—she loved them still; 220
Nor ever taxed them with the ill
Which had been done to her.

A Barn her *winter* bed supplies;
But, till the warmth of summer skies
And summer days is gone,   225
(And all do in this tale agree)
She sleeps beneath the greenwood tree,
And other home hath none.

An innocent life, yet far astray!
And Ruth will, long before her day,   230
Be broken down and old:
Sore aches she needs must have! but less
Of mind than body's wretchedness,
From damp, and rain, and cold.

If she is prest by want of food,   235
She from her dwelling in the wood
Repairs to a roadside;
And there she begs at one steep place
Where up and down with easy pace
The horsemen-travellers ride.   240

That oaten pipe of hers is mute,
Or thrown away; but with a flute
Her loneliness she cheers:
This flute, made of a hemlock stalk,
At evening in his homeward walk   245
The Quantock woodman hears.

I, too, have passed her on the hills
Setting her little water-mills
By spouts and fountains wild—
Such small machinery as she turned   250
Ere she had wept, ere she had mourned,
A young and happy Child!

Farewell! and when thy days are told,
Ill-fated Ruth, in hallowed mould
Thy corpse shall buried be,   255
For thee a funeral bell shall ring,
And all the congregation sing
A Christian psalm for thee.

1799.

XXII.

RESOLUTION AND INDEPENDENCE.

I.

THERE was a roaring in the wind all night;
The rain came heavily and fell in floods;
But now the sun is rising calm and bright;
The birds are singing in the distant woods;   4
Over his own sweet voice the Stock-dove broods;
The Jay makes answer as the Magpie chatters;
And all the air is filled with pleasant noise of
    waters.

II.

All things that love the sun are out of doors;
The sky rejoices in the morning's birth;
The grass is bright with rain-drops;—on the
    moors   10
The hare is running races in her mirth;

And with her feet she from the plashy earth
Raises a mist; that, glittering in the sun,
Runs with her all the way, wherever she doth
    run.

III.

I was a Traveller then upon the moor;   15
I saw the hare that raced about with joy;
I heard the woods and distant waters roar;
Or heard them not, as happy as a boy:
The pleasant season did my heart employ:
My old remembrances went from me wholly; 20
And all the ways of men, so vain and melan-
    choly.

IV.

But, as it sometimes chanceth, from the might
Of joy in minds that can no further go,
As high as we have mounted in delight
In our dejection do we sink as low;   25
To me that morning did it happen so;
And fears and fancies thick upon me came;
Dim sadness—and blind thoughts, I knew not,
    nor could name.

V.

I heard the sky-lark warbling in the sky;
And I bethought me of the playful hare: 30
Even such a happy Child of earth am I;
Even as these blissful creatures do I fare;
Far from the world I walk, and from all care;
But there may come another day to me—
Solitude, pain of heart, distress, and poverty. 35

VI.

My whole life I have lived in pleasant thought
As if life's business were a summer mood;
As if all needful things would come unsought

To genial faith, still rich in genial good;
But how can He expect that others should   40
Build for him, sow for him, and at his call
Love him, who for himself will take no heed at
    all?

VII.

I thought of Chatterton, the marvellous Boy,
The sleepless Soul that perished in his pride;
Of Him who walked in glory and in joy   45
Following his plough, along the mountain-side:
By our own spirits are we deified:
We Poets in our youth begin in gladness;
But thereof come in the end despondency and
    madness.

VIII.

Now, whether it were by peculiar grace,   50
A leading from above, a something given,
Yet it befell that, in this lonely place,
When I with these untoward thoughts had
    striven,
Beside a pool bare to the eye of heaven
I saw a Man before me unawares: 55
The oldest man he seemed that ever wore grey
    hairs.

IX.

As a huge stone is sometimes seen to lie
Couched on the bald top of an eminence;
Wonder to all who do the same espy,
By what means it could thither come, and
    whence;   60
So that it seems a thing endued with sense:
Like a sea-beast crawled forth, that on a shelf
Of rock or sand reposeth, there to sun itself;

X.

Such seemed this Man, not all alive nor dead,
Nor all asleep—in his extreme old age: 65
His body was bent double, feet and head
Coming together in life's pilgrimage;
As if some dire constraint of pain, or rage
Of sickness felt by him in times long past,
A more than human weight upon his frame had
    cast.   70

XI.

Himself he propped, limbs, body, and pale face,
Upon a long grey staff of shaven wood:
And, still as I drew near with gentle pace,
Upon the margin of that moorish flood
Motionless as a cloud the old Man stood,   75
That heareth not the loud winds when they
    call;
And moveth all together, if it move at all.

XII.

At length, himself unsettling, he the pond
Stirred with his staff, and fixedly did look
Upon the muddy water, which he conned,   80
As if he had been reading in a book:
And now a stranger's privilege I took;
And, drawing to his side, to him did say,
"This morning gives us promise of a glorious
    day."

XIII.

A gentle answer did the old Man make,   85
In courteous speech which forth he slowly drew:
And him with further words I thus bespake,
"What occupation do you there pursue?
This is a lonesome place for one like you."
Ere he replied, a flash of mild surprise   90
Broke from the sable orbs of his yet-vivid eyes.

XIV.

His words came feebly, from a feeble chest,
But each in solemn order followed each,
With something of a lofty utterance drest—
Choice word and measured phrase, above the
     reach   95
Of ordinary men ; a stately speech ;
Such as grave Livers do in Scotland use,
Religious men, who give to God and man their
     dues.

XV.

He told that to these waters he had come
To gather leeches, being old and poor :   100
Employment hazardous and wearisome !
And he had many hardships to endure :
From pond to pond he roamed, from moor to
     moor ;
Housing, with God's good help, by choice or
     chance ;
And in this way he gained an honest mainte-
     nance.   105

XVI.

The old Man still stood talking by my side ;
But now his voice to me was like a stream
Scarce heard ; nor word from word could I
     divide ;
And the whole body of the Man did seem
Like one whom I had met with in a dream ; 110
Or like a man from some far region sent,
To give me human strength, by apt admonish-
     ment.

XVII.

My former thoughts returned : the fear that
     kills ;
And hope that is unwilling to be fed ;

Cold, pain, and labour, and all fleshly ills ; 115
And mighty Poets in their misery dead.
—Perplexed, and longing to be comforted,
My question eagerly did I renew,
"How is it that you live, and what is it you
    do ?"

XVIII.

He with a smile did then his words repeat ; 120
And said that, gathering leeches, far and wide
He travelled ; stirring thus about his feet
The waters of the pools where they abide.
" Once I could meet with them on every side ;
But they have dwindled long by slow decay ; 125
Yet still I persevere, and find them where I
    may."

XIX.

While he was talking thus, the lonely place,
The old Man's shape, and speech—all troubled
    me :
In my mind's eye I seemed to see him pace
About the weary moors continually,   130
Wandering about alone and silently.
While I these thoughts within myself pursued,
He, having made a pause, the same discourse
    renewed.

XX.

And soon with this he other matter blended,
Cheerfully uttered, with demeanour kind,   135
But stately in the main, and, when he ended,
I could have laughed myself to scorn to find
In that decrepit Man so firm a mind.
" God," said I, " be my help and stay secure ;
I'll think of the Leech-gatherer on the lonely
    moor ! "   140

May-July, 1802.

XXIII.

THE THORN.

I.

"There is a Thorn—it looks so old,
In truth, you'd find it hard to say
How it could ever have been young,
It looks so old and grey.
Not higher than a two years' child
It stands erect, this aged Thorn ;
No leaves it has, no prickly points ;
It is a mass of knotted joints,
A wretched thing forlorn.
It stands erect, and like a stone   10
With lichens is it overgrown.

II.

Like rock or stone, it is o'ergrown,
With lichens to the very top,
And hung with heavy tufts of moss,
A melancholy crop :   15
Up from the earth these mosses creep,
And this poor Thorn they clasp it round
So close, you'd say that they are bent
With plain and manifest intent
To drag it to the ground ;   20
And all have joined in one endeavour
To bury this poor Thorn for ever.

III.

High on a mountain's highest ridge,
Where oft the stormy winter gale
Cuts like a scythe, while through the clouds 25
It sweeps from vale to vale;

Not five yards from the mountain path,
This Thorn you on your left espy ;
And to the left, three yards beyond,
You see a little muddy pond   30
Of water—never dry,
Though but of compass small, and bare
To thirsty suns and parching air.

IV.

And, close beside this aged Thorn,
There is a fresh and lovely sight,   35
A beauteous heap, a hill of moss,
Just half a foot in height.
All lovely colours there you see,
All colours that were ever seen ;
And mossy network too is there,   40
As if by hand of lady fair
The work had woven been ;
And cups, the darlings of the eye,
So deep is their vermilion dye.

V.

Ah me ! what lovely tints are there   45
Of olive green and scarlet bright,
In spikes, in branches, and in stars,
Green, red, and pearly white !
This heap of earth o'ergrown with moss,
Which close beside the Thorn you see,   50
So fresh in all its beauteous dyes,
Is like an infant's grave in size,
As like as like can be :
But never, never any where,
An infant's grave was half so fair.   55

VI.

Now would you see this aged Thorn,
This pond, and beauteous hill of moss,

You must take care and choose your time
The mountain when to cross.
For oft there sits between the heap, 60
So like an infant's grave in size,
And that same pond of which I spoke,
A Woman in a scarlet cloak,
And to herself she cries,
' Oh misery ! oh misery ! 65
Oh woe is me ! oh misery !'

VII.

At all times of the day and night
This wretched Woman thither goes ;
And she is known to every star,
And every wind that blows ; 70
And there, beside the Thorn, she sits
When the blue daylight's in the skies,
And when the whirlwind's on the hill,
Or frosty air is keen and still,
And to herself she cries, 75
' Oh misery ! oh misery !
Oh woe is me ! oh misery !'"

VIII.

" Now wherefore, thus, by day and night,
In rain, in tempest, and in snow,
Thus to the dreary mountain-top 80
Does this poor Woman go ?
And why sits she beside the Thorn
When the blue daylight's in the sky
Or when the whirlwind's on the hill,
Or frosty air is keen and still, 85
And wherefore does she cry ?—
O wherefore ? wherefore ? tell me why
Does she repeat that doleful cry ?"

IX.

"I cannot tell; I wish I could;
For the true reason no one knows: 90
But would you gladly view the spot,
The spot to which she goes;
The hillock like an infant's grave,
The pond—and Thorn, so old and grey;
Pass by her door—'tis seldom shut—   95
And if you see her in her hut—
Then to the spot away!
I never heard of such as dare
Approach the spot when she is there."

X.

"But wherefore to the mountain-top   100
Can this unhappy Woman go,
Whatever star is in the skies,
Whatever wind may blow?"
"Full twenty years are past and gone
Since she (her name is Martha Ray)   105
Gave with a maiden's true good-will
Her company to Stephen Hill;
And she was blithe and gay,
While friends and kindred all approved
Of him whom tenderly she loved.   110

XI.

And they had fixed the wedding day,
The morning that must wed them both;
But Stephen to another Maid
Had sworn another oath;
And, with this other Maid, to church   115
Unthinking Stephen went—
Poor Martha! on that woeful day
A pang of pitiless dismay
Into her soul was sent;

A fire was kindled in her breast,   120
Which might not burn itself to rest.

XII.

They say full six months after this,
While yet the summer leaves were green,
She to the mountain-top would go,
And there was often seen.   125
What could she seek?—or wish to hide?
Her state to any eye was plain;
She was with child, and she was mad;
Yet often was she sober sad
From her exceeding pain.   130
O guilty Father—would that death
Had saved him from that breach of faith!

XIII.

Sad case for such a brain to hold
Communion with a stirring child!
Sad case, as you may think, for one   135
Who had a brain so wild!
Last Christmas-eve we talked of this,
And grey-haired Wilfred of the glen
Held that the unborn infant wrought
About its mother's heart, and brought   140
Her senses back again:
And, when at last her time drew near,
Her looks were calm, her senses clear.

XIV.

More know I not, I wish I did,
And it should all be told to you;   145
For what became of this poor child
No mortal ever knew;
Nay—if a child to her was born
No earthly tongue could ever tell;
And if 'twas born alive or dead,   150

II.   K

Far less could this with proof be said;
For some remember well
That Martha Ray about this time
Would up the mountain often climb.

xv.

And all that winter, when at night   155
The wind blew from the mountain-peak,
'Twas worth your while, though in the dark,
The churchyard path to seek:
For many a time and oft were heard
Cries coming from the mountain head: 160
Some plainly living voices were;
And others, I've heard many swear,
Were voices of the dead:
I cannot think, whate'er they say,
They had to do with Martha Ray.   165

xvi.

But that she goes to this old Thorn,
The Thorn which I described to you,
And there sits in a scarlet cloak,
I will be sworn is true.
For one day with my telescope,   170
To view the ocean wide and bright,
When to this country first I came,
Ere I had heard of Martha's name,
I climbed the mountain's height:—
A storm came on, and I could see   175
No object higher than my knee.

xvii.

'Twas mist and rain, and storm and rain:
No screen, no fence could I discover;
And then the wind! in sooth, it was
A wind full ten times over.   180

I looked around, I thought I saw
A jutting crag,—and off I ran,
Head-foremost, through the driving rain,
The shelter of the crag to gain;
And, as I am a man,   185
Instead of jutting crag I found
A Woman seated on the ground.

XVIII.

I did not speak—I saw her face;
Her face!—it was enough for me;
I turned about and heard her cry,   190
'Oh misery! oh misery!'
And there she sits, until the moon
Through half the clear blue sky will go;
And when the little breezes make
The waters of the pond to shake,   195
As all the country know,
She shudders, and you hear her cry,
'Oh misery! oh misery!'"

XIX.

"But what's the Thorn? and what the pond?
And what the hill of moss to her?   200
And what the creeping breeze that comes
The little pond to stir?"
"I cannot tell; but some will say
She hanged her baby on the tree;
Some say she drowned it in the pond,   205
Which is a little step beyond :
But all and each agree,
The little Babe was buried there,
Beneath that hill of moss so fair.

XX.

I've heard, the moss is spotted red   210
With drops of that poor infant's blood;

But kill a new-born infant thus,
I do not think she could!
Some say if to the pond you go,
And fix on it a steady view,   215
The shadow of a babe you trace,
A baby and a baby's face,
And that it looks at you;
Whene'er you look on it, 'tis plain
The baby looks at you again.   220

XXI.

And some had sworn an oath that she
Should be to public justice brought;
And for the little infant's bones
With spades they would have sought.
But instantly the hill of moss   225
Before their eyes began to stir!
And, for full fifty yards around,
The grass—it shook upon the ground!
Yet all do still aver
The little Babe lies buried there,   230
Beneath that hill of moss so fair.

XXII.

I cannot tell how this may be,
But plain it is the Thorn is bound
With heavy tufts of moss that strive
To drag it to the ground;   235
And this I know, full many a time,
When she was on the mountain high,
By day, and in the silent night,
When all the stars shone clear and bright,
That I have heard her cry,   240
'Oh misery! oh misery!
Oh woe is me! oh misery!'"

1798.

XXIV.

HART-LEAP WELL.

Hart-Leap Well is a small spring of water, about five miles from Richmond in Yorkshire, and near the side of the road that leads from Richmond to Askrigg. Its name is derived from a remarkable Chase, the memory of which is preserved by the monuments spoken of in the second Part of the following Poem, which monuments do now exist as I have there described them.

THE Knight had ridden down from Wensley
    Moor
With the slow motion of a summer's cloud,
And now, as he approached a vassal's door,
" Bring forth another horse! " he cried aloud.

"Another horse!"—That shout the vassal heard
And saddled his best Steed, a comely grey;   6
Sir Walter mounted him; he was the third
Which he had mounted on that glorious day.

Joy sparkled in the prancing courser's eyes;
The horse and horseman are a happy pair;   10
But, though Sir Walter like a falcon flies,
There is a doleful silence in the air.

A rout this morning left Sir Walter's Hall,
That as they galloped made the echoes roar;
But horse and man are vanished, one and all;
Such race, I think, was never seen before.   16

Sir Walter, restless as a veering wind,
Calls to the few tired dogs that yet remain :
Blanch, Swift, and Music, noblest of their kind,
Follow, and up the weary mountain strain.   20

The Knight hallooed, he cheered and chid them
    on
With suppliant gestures and upbraidings stern;
But breath and eyesight fail; and, one by one,
The dogs are stretched among the mountain
    fern.

Where is the throng, the tumult of the race? 25
The bugles that so joyfully were blown?
—This chase it looks not like an earthly chase;
Sir Walter and the Hart are left alone.

The poor Hart toils along the mountain-side;
I will not stop to tell how far he fled,   30
Nor will I mention by what death he died;
But now the Knight beholds him lying dead.

Dismounting then he leaned against a thorn;
He had no follower, dog, nor man, nor boy:
He neither cracked his whip, nor blew his horn,
But gazed upon the spoil with silent joy.   36

Close to the thorn on which Sir Walter leaned
Stood his dumb partner in this glorious feat;
Weak as a lamb the hour that it is yeaned;
And white with foam as if with cleaving sleet.

Upon his side the Hart was lying stretched: 41
His nostril touched a spring beneath a hill,
And with the last deep groan his breath had
    fetched
The waters of the spring were trembling still.

And now, too happy for repose or rest,   45
(Never had living man such joyful lot!)
Sir Walter walked all round, north, south, and
    west,
And gazed and gazed upon that darling spot.

And climbing up the hill—(it was at least
Four roods of sheer ascent) Sir Walter found
Three several hoof-marks which the hunted
      Beast   51
Had left imprinted on the grassy ground.

Sir Walter wiped his face, and cried, " Till now
Such sight was never seen by human eyes:
Three leaps have borne him from this lofty
      brow   55
Down to the very fountain where he lies.

I'll build a pleasure-house upon this spot,
And a small arbour, made for rural joy ;
'Twill be the traveller's shed, the pilgrim's cot,
A place of love for damsels that are coy.   60

A cunning artist will I have to frame
A basin for that fountain in the dell !
And they who do make mention of the same,
From this day forth, shall call it HART-LEAP
      WELL.

And, gallant Stag ! to make thy praises known,
Another monument shall here be raised ;   66
Three several pillars, each a rough-hewn stone,
And planted where thy hoofs the turf have
      grazed.

And in the summer-time, when days are long,
I will come hither with my Paramour;   70
And with the dancers and the minstrel's song
We will make merry in that pleasant bower.

Till the foundations of the mountains fail
My mansion with its arbour shall endure ;—
The joy of them who till the fields of Swale, 75
And them who dwell among the woods of Ure ! "

Then home he went, and left the Hart stone-
     dead,
With breathless nostrils stretched above the
     spring.
—Soon did the Knight perform what he had
     said;
And far and wide the fame thereof did ring. 80

Ere thrice the Moon into her port had steered,
A cup of stone received the living well;
Three pillars of rude stone Sir Walter reared,
And built a house of pleasure in the dell.

And, near the fountain, flowers of stature tall 85
With trailing plants and trees were inter-
     twined,—
Which soon composed a little sylvan hall,
A leafy shelter from the sun and wind.

And thither, when the summer days were long,
Sir Walter led his wondering Paramour;   90
And with the dancers and the minstrel's song
Made merriment within that pleasant bower.

The Knight, Sir Walter, died in course of time,
And his bones lie in his paternal vale.—
But there is matter for a second rhyme,   95
And I to this would add another tale.

PART SECOND.

The moving accident is not my trade;
To freeze the blood I have no ready arts:
'Tis my delight, alone in summer shade,
To pipe a simple song for thinking hearts. 100

As I from Hawes to Richmond did repair,
It chanced that I saw standing in a dell
Three aspens at three corners of a square;
And one, not four yards distant, near a well.

What this imported I could ill divine: 105
And, pulling now the rein my horse to stop,
I saw three pillars standing in a line,—
The last stone-pillar on a dark hill-top.

The trees were grey, with neither arms nor
        head;   109
Half wasted the square mound of tawny green;
So that you just might say, as then I said,
" Here in old time the hand of man hath been."

I looked upon the hill both far and near,
More doleful place did never eye survey;   114
It seemed as if the spring-time came not here,
And Nature here were willing to decay.

I stood in various thoughts and fancies lost,
When one, who was in shepherd's garb attired,
Came up the hollow:—him did I accost,   119
And what this place might be I then inquired.

The Shepherd stopped, and that same story
        told
Which in my former rhyme I have rehearsed.
" A jolly place," said he, " in times of old!
But something ails it now: the spot is curst. 124

You see these lifeless stumps of aspen wood—
Some say that they are beeches, others elms—
These were the bower; and here a mansion
        stood,
The finest palace of a hundred realms!

The arbour does its own condition tell;
You see the stones, the fountain, and the
    stream;   130
But as to the great Lodge! you might as well
Hunt half a day for a forgotten dream.

There's neither dog nor heifer, horse nor sheep,
Will wet his lips within that cup of stone;
And oftentimes, when all are fast asleep,   135
This water doth send forth a dolorous groan.

Some say that here a murder has been done,
And blood cries out for blood: but, for my part,
I've guessed, when I've been sitting in the sun,
That it was all for that unhappy Hart.   140

What thoughts must through the creature's
    brain have past!
Even from the topmost stone, upon the steep,
Are but three bounds—and look, Sir, at this
    last—
O Master! it has been a cruel leap.

For thirteen hours he ran a desperate race; 145
And in my simple mind we cannot tell
What cause the Hart might have to love this
    place,
And come and make his death-bed near the well.

Here on the grass perhaps asleep he sank,
Lulled by the fountain in the summer-tide; 150
This water was perhaps the first he drank
When he had wandered from his mother's side.

In April here beneath the flowering thorn
He heard the birds their morning carols sing;
And he perhaps, for aught we know, was born
Not half a furlong from that self-same spring. 156

Now, here is neither grass nor pleasant shade;
The sun on drearier hollow never shone;
So will it be, as I have often said,
Till trees, and stones, and fountain, all are
    gone." 160

"Grey-headed Shepherd, thou hast spoken
    well;
Small difference lies between thy creed and
    mine:
This Beast not unobserved by Nature fell;
His death was mourned by sympathy divine.

The Being that is in the clouds and air, 165
That is in the green leaves among the groves,
Maintains a deep and reverential care
For the unoffending creatures whom he loves.

The pleasure-house is dust:—behind, before,
This is no common waste, no common gloom;
But Nature, in due course of time, once more
Shall here put on her beauty and her bloom. 172

She leaves these objects to a slow decay,
That what we are, and have been, may be
    known;
But at the coming of the milder day 175
These monuments shall all be overgrown.

One lesson, Shepherd, let us two divide,
Taught both by what she shows, and what
    conceals;
Never to blend our pleasure or our pride 179
With sorrow of the meanest thing that feels."

                      1800.

XXV.

SONG AT THE FEAST OF BROUGHAM CASTLE,

UPON THE RESTORATION OF LORD CLIFFORD,
THE SHEPHERD, TO THE ESTATES AND
HONOURS OF HIS ANCESTORS.

HIGH in the breathless Hall the Minstrel sate,
And Emont's murmur mingled with the Song.—
The words of ancient time I thus translate,
A festal strain that hath been silent long :—

  " From town to town, from tower to tower, 5
The red rose is a gladsome flower.
Her thirty years of winter past,
The red rose is revived at last ;
She lifts her head for endless spring,
For everlasting blossoming :   10
Both roses flourish, red and white :
In love and sisterly delight
The two that were at strife are blended,
And all old troubles now are ended.—
Joy ! joy to both ! but most to her   15
Who is the flower of Lancaster !
Behold her how She smiles to-day
On this great throng, this bright array !
Fair greeting doth she send to all
From every corner of the hall ;   20
But chiefly from above the board
Where sits in state our rightful Lord,
A Clifford to his own restored !

    They came with banner, spear, and shield ;
And it was proved in Bosworth-field.   25

Not long the Avenger was withstood—
Earth helped him with the cry of blood:
St. George was for us, and the might
Of blessed Angels crowned the right.
Loud voice the Land has uttered forth, 30
We loudest in the faithful north:
Our fields rejoice, our mountains ring,
Our streams proclaim a welcoming;
Our strong-abodes and castles see
The glory of their loyalty. 35

How glad is Skipton at this hour—
Though lonely, a deserted Tower;
Knight, squire, and yeoman, page and groom:
We have them at the feast of Brough'm.
How glad Pendragon—though the sleep 40
Of years be on her!—She shall reap
A taste of this great pleasure, viewing
As in a dream her own renewing.
Rejoiced is Brough, right glad, I deem,
Beside her little humble stream; 45
And she that keepeth watch and ward
Her statelier Eden's course to guard;
They both are happy at this hour,
Though each is but a lonely Tower:—
But here is perfect joy and pride 50
For one fair House by Emont's side.
This day, distinguished without peer,
To see her Master and to cheer—
Him, and his Lady-mother dear!

Oh! it was a time forlorn 55
When the fatherless was born—
Give her wings that she may fly,
Or she sees her infant die!
Swords that are with slaughter wild
Hunt the Mother and the Child. 60

Who will take them from the light?
—Yonder is a man in sight—
Yonder is a house—but where?
No, they must not enter there.
To the caves, and to the brooks,   65
To the clouds of heaven she looks;
She is speechless, but her eyes
Pray in ghostly agonies.
Blissful Mary, Mother mild,
Maid and Mother undefiled,   70
Save a Mother and her Child!

   Now Who is he that bounds with joy
On Carrock's side, a Shepherd-boy?
No thoughts hath he but thoughts that pass
Light as the wind along the grass.   75
Can this be He who hither came
In secret, like a smothered flame?
O'er whom such thankful tears were shed
For shelter, and a poor man's bread!
God loves the Child; and God hath willed   80
That those dear words should be fulfilled,
The Lady's words, when forced away
The last she to her Babe did say:
'My own, my own, thy Fellow-guest
I may not be; but rest thee, rest,   85
For lowly shepherd's life is best!'

   Alas! when evil men are strong
No life is good, no pleasure long.
The Boy must part from Mosedale's groves,
And leave Blencathara's rugged coves,   90
And quit the flowers that summer brings
To Glenderamakin's lofty springs;
Must vanish, and his careless cheer
Be turned to heaviness and fear.
—Give Sir Lancelot Threlkeld praise!   95

Hear it, good man, old in days!
Thou tree of covert and of rest
For this young Bird that is distrest;
Among thy branches safe he lay,
And he was free to sport and play, 100
When falcons were abroad for prey.

A recreant harp, that sings of fear
And heaviness in Clifford's ear!
I said, when evil men are strong,
No life is good, no pleasure long, 105
A weak and cowardly untruth!
Our Clifford was a happy Youth,
And thankful through a weary time,
That brought him up to manhood's prime.
—Again he wanders forth at will, 110
And tends a flock from hill to hill:
His garb is humble; ne'er was seen
Such garb with such a noble mien;
Among the shepherd-grooms no mate
Hath he, a Child of strength and state! 115
Yet lacks not friends for simple glee,
Nor yet for higher sympathy.
To his side the fallow-deer
Came, and rested without fear;
The eagle, lord of land and sea, 120
Stooped down to pay him fealty;
And both the undying fish that swim
Through Bowscale-tarn did wait on him;
The pair were servants of his eye
In their immortality; 125
And glancing, gleaming, dark or bright,
Moved to and fro, for his delight.
He knew the rocks which Angels haunt
Upon the mountains visitant;
He hath kenned them taking wing: 130
And into caves where Faeries sing

He hath entered; and been told
By Voices how men lived of old.
Among the heavens his eye can see
The face of thing that is to be;   135
And, if that men report him right,
His tongue could whisper words of might.
—Now another day is come,
Fitter hope, and nobler doom;
He hath thrown aside his crook,   140
And hath buried deep his book;
Armour rusting in his halls
On the blood of Clifford calls;—
' Quell the Scot,' exclaims the Lance—
Bear me to the heart of France,   145
Is the longing of the Shield—
Tell thy name, thou trembling Field;
Field of death, where'er thou be,
Groan thou with our victory!
Happy day, and mighty hour,   150
When our Shepherd in his power,
Mailed and horsed, with lance and sword,
To his ancestors restored
Like a re-appearing Star,
Like a glory from afar,   155
First shall head the flock of war!"

Alas! the impassioned minstrel did not know
How, by Heaven's grace, this Clifford's heart
            was framed:
How he, long forced in humble walks to go, 159
Was softened into feeling, soothed, and tamed.

Love had he found in huts where poor men lie;
His daily teachers had been woods and rills,
The silence that is in the starry sky,
The sleep that is among the lonely hills.

In him the savage virtue of the Race,   165
Revenge, and all ferocious thoughts were dead:
Nor did he change; but kept in lofty place
The wisdom which adversity had bred.

Glad were the vales, and every cottage-hearth;
The Shepherd-lord was honoured more and
          more;   170
And, ages after he was laid in earth,
"The good Lord Clifford" was the name he
          bore.

                              1807.

XXVI.

LINES

COMPOSED A FEW MILES ABOVE TINTERN ABBEY,
ON REVISITING THE BANKS OF THE WYE
DURING A TOUR. JULY 13, 1798.

FIVE years have past; five summers, with the
          length
Of five long winters! and again I hear
These waters, rolling from their mountain-
          springs
With a soft inland murmur.[1]—Once again
Do I behold these steep and lofty cliffs,
That on a wild secluded scene impress
Thoughts of more deep seclusion; and connect
The landscape with the quiet of the sky.
The day is come when I again repose
Here, under this dark sycamore, and view   10
These plots of cottage-ground, these orchard-
          tufts,

---

[1] The river is not affected by the tides a few miles
above Tintern.

Which at this season, with their unripe fruits,
Are clad in one green hue, and lose themselves
'Mid groves and copses.   Once again I see
These hedge-rows, hardly hedge-rows, little
    lines   15
Of sportive wood run wild: these pastoral
    farms,
Green to the very door; and wreaths of smoke
Sent up, in silence, from among the trees!
With some uncertain notice, as might seem
Of vagrant dwellers in the houseless woods, 20
Or of some Hermit's cave, where by his fire
The Hermit sits alone.

            These beauteous forms,
Through a long absence, have not been to me
As is a landscape to a blind man's eye:
But oft, in lonely rooms, and 'mid the din   25
Of towns and cities, I have owed to them,
In hours of weariness, sensations sweet,
Felt in the blood, and felt along the heart;
And passing even into my purer mind,
With tranquil restoration:—feelings too   30
Of unremembered pleasure: such, perhaps,
As have no slight or trivial influence
On that best portion of a good man's life,
His little, nameless, unremembered, acts
Of kindness and of love.   Nor less, I trust, 35
To them I may have owed another gift,
Of aspect more sublime; that blessed mood,
In which the burthen of the mystery,
In which the heavy and the weary weight
Of all this unintelligible world,   40
Is lightened:—that serene and blessed mood,
In which the affections gently lead us on,—
Until, the breath of this corporeal flame
And even the motion of our human blood

Almost suspended, we are laid asleep   45
In body, and become a living soul:
While with an eye made quiet by the power
Of harmony, and the deep power of joy,
We see into the life of things.
                                        If this
Be but a vain belief, yet, oh! how oft—   50
In darkness and amid the many shapes
Of joyless daylight; when the fretful stir
Unprofitable, and the fever of the world,
Have hung upon the beatings of my heart—
How oft, in spirit, have I turned to thee,   55
O sylvan Wye! thou wanderer thro' the woods,
How often has my spirit turned to thee!

    And now, with gleams of half-extinguished
        thought,
With many recognitions dim and faint,
And somewhat of a sad perplexity,   60
The picture of the mind revives again:
While here I stand, not only with the sense
Of present pleasure, but with pleasing thoughts
That in this moment there is life and food
For future years.   And so I dare to hope,   65
Though changed, no doubt, from what I was
        when first
I came among these hills; when like a roe
I bounded o'er the mountains, by the sides
Of the deep rivers, and the lonely streams,
Wherever nature led: more like a man   70
Flying from something that he dreads than
        one
Who sought the thing he loved.   For nature
        then
(The coarser pleasures of my boyish days,
And their glad animal movements all gone by)
To me was all in all.—I cannot paint   75

What then I was.   The sounding cataract
Haunted me like a passion: the tall rock,
The mountain, and the deep and gloomy wood,
Their colours and their forms, were then to me
An appetite; a feeling and a love,   80
That had no need of a remoter charm,
By thought supplied, nor any interest
Unborrowed from the eye.—That time is past,
And all its aching joys are now no more,
And all its dizzy raptures.   Not for this   85
Faint I, nor mourn nor murmur; other gifts
Have followed; for such loss, I would believe,
Abundant recompense.   For I have learned
To look on nature, not as in the hour
Of thoughtless youth; but hearing oftentimes
The still, sad music of humanity,   91
Nor harsh nor grating, though of ample power
To chasten and subdue.   And I have felt
A presence that disturbs me with the joy
Of elevated thoughts; a sense sublime   95
Of something far more deeply interfused,
Whose dwelling is the light of setting suns,
And the round ocean and the living air,
And the blue sky, and in the mind of man:
A motion and a spirit, that impels   100
All thinking things, all objects of all thought,
And rolls through all things.   Therefore am I
         still
A lover of the meadows and the woods,
And mountains; and of all that we behold 104
From this green earth; of all the mighty world
Of eye, and ear,—both what they half create,[1]
And what perceive; well pleased to recognize

This line has a close resemblance to an admirable
line of Young's, the exact expression of which I do
not recollect.

In nature and the language of the sense
The anchor of my purest thoughts, the nurse,
The guide, the guardian of my heart, and soul
Of all my moral being.

              Nor perchance,   111
If I were not thus taught, should I the more
Suffer my genial spirits to decay :
For thou art with me here upon the banks
Of this fair river ; thou my dearest Friend, 115
My dear, dear Friend ; and in thy voice I catch
The language of my former heart, and read
My former pleasures in the shooting lights
Of thy wild eyes. Oh! yet a little while
May I behold in thee what I was once,   120
My dear, dear Sister! and this prayer I make,
Knowing that Nature never did betray
The heart that loved her ; 'tis her privilege,
Through all the years of this our life, to lead
From joy to joy : for she can so inform   125
The mind that is within us, so impress
With quietness and beauty, and so feed
With lofty thoughts, that neither evil tongues,
Rash judgments, nor the sneers of selfish men,
Nor greetings where no kindness is, nor all 130
The dreary intercourse of daily life,
Shall e'er prevail against us, or disturb
Our cheerful faith, that all which we behold
Is full of blessings. Therefore let the moon
Shine on thee in thy solitary walk ;   135
And let the misty mountain-winds be free
To blow against thee : and, in after years,
When these wild ecstasies shall be matured
Into a sober pleasure ; when thy mind
Shall be a mansion for all lovely forms,   140
Thy memory be as a dwelling-place
For all sweet sounds and harmonies ; oh! then,
If solitude, or fear, or pain, or grief,

Should be thy portion, with what healing
      thoughts
Of tender joy wilt thou remember me,   145
And these my exhortations ! Nor, perchance—
If I should be where I no more can hear
Thy voice, nor catch from thy wild eyes these
      gleams
Of past existence—wilt thou then forget
That on the banks of this delightful stream 150
We stood together ; and that I, so long
A worshipper of Nature, hither came
Unwearied in that service : rather say
With warmer love—oh ! with far deeper zeal
Of holier love.   Nor wilt thou then forget   155
That after many wanderings, many years
Of absence, these steep woods and lofty cliffs,
And this green pastoral landscape, were to me
More dear, both for themselves and for thy sake

1798.

XXVII.

It is no Spirit who from heaven hath flown,
And is descending on his embassy ;
Nor Traveller gone from earth the heavens to
      espy !
'Tis Hesperus—there he stands with glittering
      crown,
First admonition that the sun is down !   5
For yet it is broad day-light : clouds pass by ;
A few are near him still—and now the sky,
He hath it to himself—'tis all his own.
O most ambitious Star ! an inquest wrought
Within me when I recognized thy light ;   10
A moment I was startled at the sight :
And, while I gazed, there came to me a thought

That I might step beyond my natural race
As thou seem'st now to do; might one day
    trace
Some ground not mine; and, strong her
    strength above,   15
My Soul, an Apparition in the place,
Tread there with steps that no one shall reprove!

                  1803.

XXVIII.

FRENCH REVOLUTION,

AS IT APPEARED TO ENTHUSIASTS AT ITS COM-
MENCEMENT.[1] REPRINTED FROM
"THE FRIEND."

OH! pleasant exercise of hope and joy!
For mighty were the auxiliars which then stood
Upon our side, we who were strong in love!
Bliss was it in that dawn to be alive,
But to be young was very heaven!—Oh! times,
In which the meagre, stale, forbidding ways 6
Of custom, law, and statute, took at once
The attraction of a country in romance!
When Reason seemed the most to assert her
    rights,
When most intent on making of herself   10
A prime Enchantress—to assist the work
Which then was going forward in her name!
Not favoured spots alone, but the whole earth,

---

[1] This and the Extract, Vol. i. pages 197-199, and the
first Piece of this Class, are from the unpublished
Poem of which some account is given in the Preface
to THE EXCURSION.

The beauty wore of promise, that which sets
(As at some moment might not be unfelt   15
Among the bowers of paradise itself)
The budding rose above the rose full blown.
What temper at the prospect did not wake
To happiness unthought of?   The inert
Were roused, and lively natures rapt away! 20
They who had fed their childhood upon dreams,
The playfellows of fancy, who had made
All powers of swiftness, subtilty, and strength
Their ministers,—who in lordly wise had stirred
Among the grandest objects of the sense,   25
And dealt with whatsoever they found there
As if they had within some lurking right
To wield it;—they, too, who, of gentle mood,
Had watched all gentle motions, and to these
Had fitted their own thoughts, schemers more
          mild,   30
And in the region of their peaceful selves;—
Now was it that both found, the meek and lofty
Did both find, helpers to their heart's desire,
And stuff at hand, plastic as they could wish;
Were called upon to exercise their skill,   35
Not in Utopia, subterranean fields,
Or some secreted island, Heaven knows where!
But in the very world, which is the world
Of all of us,—the place where in the end
We find our happiness, or not at all!   40
                                    1805.

XXIX.

Yes, it was the mountain Echo,
Solitary, clear, profound,
Answering to the shouting Cuckoo,
Giving to her sound for sound!

Unsolicited reply   5
To a babbling wanderer sent;
Like her ordinary cry,
Like—but oh, how different!

Hears not also mortal Life?
Hear not we, unthinking Creatures!   10
Slaves of folly, love, or strife—
Voices of two different natures?

Have not *we* too?—yes, we have
Answers, and we know not whence;
Echoes from beyond the.grave,   15
Recognised intelligence!

Such rebounds our inward ear
Catches sometimes from afar—
Listen, ponder, hold them dear;
For of God,—of God they are.   20

                                    1806.

XXX.

TO A SKY-LARK.

ETHEREAL minstrel! pilgrim of the sky!
Dost thou despise the earth where cares abound?
Or, while the wings aspire, are heart and eye
Both with thy nest upon the dewy ground?
Thy nest which thou canst drop into at will, 5
Those quivering wings composed, that music
        still!

Leave to the nightingale her shady wood;
A privacy of glorious light is thine;

Whence thou dost pour upon the world a flood
Of harmony, with instinct more divine;　　10
Type of the wise who soar, but never roam;
True to the kindred points of Heaven and Home!

　　　　　　　　　　　　　　　　1825.

XXXI.

LAODAMIA.

" WITH sacrifice before the rising morn
Vows have I made by fruitless hope inspired;
And from the infernal Gods, 'mid shades forlorn
Of night, my slaughtered Lord have I required:
Celestial pity I again implore;—　　　　5
Restore him to my sight—great Jove, restore!"

So speaking, and by fervent love endowed
With faith, the Suppliant heavenward lifts her
　　　　hands;
While, like the sun emerging from a cloud,
Her countenance brightens—and her eye
　　　　expands;　　　　　　　　　　　10
Her bosom heaves and spreads, her stature
　　　　grows;
And she expects the issue in repose.

O terror! what hath she perceived?—O joy!
What doth she look on?—whom doth she
　　　　behold?
Her Hero slain upon the beach of Troy?　　15
His vital presence? his corporeal mould?
It is—if sense deceive her not—'tis He!
And a God leads him, winged Mercury!

Mild Hermes spake—and touched her with his
    wand
That calms all fear ; " Such grace hath crowned
    thy prayer,   20
Laodamía! that at Jove's command
Thy Husband walks the paths of upper air :
He comes to tarry with thee three hours' space ;
Accept the gift, behold him face to face ! "

Forth sprang the impassioned Queen her Lord
    to clasp ;   25
Again that consummation she essayed ;
But unsubstantial Form eludes her grasp
As often as that eager grasp was made.
The Phantom parts—but parts to re-unite,
And re-assume his place before her sight.   30

" Protesiláus, lo ! thy guide is gone !
Confirm, I pray, the vision with thy voice :
This is our palace,—yonder is thy throne ;
Speak, and the floor thou tread'st on will re-
    joice.
Not to appal me have the gods bestowed   35
This precious boon ; and blest a sad abode."

" Great Jove, Laodamía ! doth not leave
His gifts imperfect :—Spectre though I be,
I am not sent to scare thee or deceive ;
But in reward of thy fidelity.   40
And something also did my worth obtain ;
For fearless virtue bringeth boundless gain.

Thou knowest the Delphic oracle foretold
That the first Greek who touched the Trojan
    strand

Should die; but me the threat could not with-
     hold :   45
A generous cause a victim did demand ;
And forth I leapt upon the sandy plain ;
A self-devoted chief—by Hector slain."

" Supreme of Heroes—bravest, noblest, best !
Thy matchless courage I bewail no more,   50
Which then, when tens of thousands were
     deprest
By doubt, propelled thee to the fatal shore ;
Thou found'st—and I forgive thee—here thou
     art—
A nobler counsellor than my poor heart.

But thou, though capable of sternest deed,   55
Wert kind as resolute, and good as brave ;
And he, whose power restores thee, hath de-
     creed
Thou should'st elude the malice of the grave :
Redundant are thy locks, thy lips as fair   59
As when their breath enriched Thessalian air.

No Spectre greets me,—no vain Shadow this ;
Come, blooming Hero, place thee by my side !
Give, on this well-known couch, one nuptial
     kiss
To me, this day, a second time thy bride ! "
Jove frowned in heaven : the conscious Parcæ
     threw   65
Upon those roseate lips a Stygian hue.

" This visage tells thee that my doom is past :
Nor should the change be mourned, even if the
     joys

Of sense were able to return as fast
And surely as they vanish. Earth destroys 70
Those raptures duly—Erebus disdains:
Calm pleasures there abide—majestic pains.

Be taught, O faithful Consort, to control
Rebellious passion: for the Gods approve
The depth, and not the tumult, of the soul; 75
A fervent, not ungovernable, love.
Thy transports moderate; and meekly mourn
When I depart, for brief is my sojourn—"

" Ah, wherefore?—Did not Hercules by force
Wrest from the guardian Monster of the tomb
Alcestis, a reanimated corse,   81
Given back to dwell on earth in vernal bloom?
Medea's spells dispersed the weight of years,
And Æson stood a youth 'mid youthful peers.

The Gods to us are merciful—and they   85
Yet further may relent: for mightier far
Than strength of nerve and sinew, or the sway
Of magic potent over sun and star,
Is love, though oft to agony distrest,
And   though   his   favourite   seat   be   feeble
    woman's breast.   90

But if thou goest, I follow—" " Peace!" he
    said,—
She looked upon him and was calmed and
    cheered ;
The ghastly colour from his lips had fled ;
In his deportment, shape, and mien, appeared
Elysian beauty, melancholy grace,   95
Brought from a pensive though a happy place.

He spake of love, such love as Spirits feel
In worlds whose course is equable and pure;
No fears to beat away—no strife to heal—
The past unsighed for, and the future sure; 100
Spake of heroic arts in graver mood
Revived, with finer harmony pursued;

Of all that is most beauteous—imaged there
In happier beauty; more pellucid streams,
An ampler ether, a diviner air,   105
And fields invested with purpureal gleams;
Climes which the sun, who sheds the brightest
        day
Earth knows, is all unworthy to survey.

Yet there the Soul shall enter which hath
        earned
That privilege by virtue.—"Ill," said he,   110
"The end of man's existence I discerned,
Who from ignoble games and revelry
Could draw, when we had parted, vain delight,
While tears were thy best pastime, day and
        night;

And while my youthful peers before my eyes
(Each hero following his peculiar bent)   116
Prepared themselves for glorious enterprise
By martial sports,—or, seated in the tent,
Chieftains and kings in council were detained;
What time the fleet at Aulis lay enchained. 120

The wished-for wind was given:—I then re-
        volved
The oracle, upon the silent sea;
And, if no worthier led the way, resolved

That, of a thousand vessels, mine should be
The foremost prow in pressing to the strand,— 125
Mine the first blood that tinged the Trojan
    sand.

Yet bitter, oft-times bitter, was the pang
When of thy loss I thought, belovèd Wife!
On thee too fondly did my memory hang,
And on the joys we shared in mortal life,— 130
The paths which we had trod—these fountains,
    flowers;
My new-planned cities, and unfinished towers.

But should suspense permit the Foe to cry,
' Behold they tremble!—haughty their array,
Yet of their number no one dares to die?' 135
In soul I swept the indignity away:
Old frailties then recurred:—but lofty thought,
In act embodied, my deliverance wrought.

And Thou, though strong in love, art all too
    weak
In reason, in self-government too slow;   140
I counsel thee by fortitude to seek
Our blest re-union in the shades below.
The invisible world with thee hath sympathised;
Be thy affections raised and solemnised.

Learn, by a mortal yearning, to ascend— 145
Seeking a higher object.   Love was given,
Encouraged, sanctioned, chiefly for that end;
For this the passion to excess was driven—
That self might be annulled: her bondage
    prove
The fetters of a dream opposed to love."— 150

Aloud she shrieked! for Hermes re-appears!
Round the dear Shade she would have clung—
   'tis vain:
The hours are past—too brief had they been
   years;
And him no mortal effort can detain:
Swift, toward the realms that know not earthly
   day,   155
He through the portal takes his silent way,
And on the palace-floor a lifeless corse She lay.

Thus, all in vain exhorted and reproved,
She perished; and, as for a wilful crime,
By the just Gods whom no weak pity moved, 160
Was doomed to wear out her appointed time,
Apart from happy Ghosts, that gather flowers
Of blissful quiet 'mid unfading bowers.

—Yet tears to human suffering are due;
And mortal hopes defeated and o'erthrown 165
Are mourned by man, and not by man alone,
As fondly he believes.—Upon the side
Of Hellespont (such faith was entertained)
A knot of spiry trees for ages grew   169
From out the tomb of him for whom she died;
And ever, when such stature they had gained
That Ilium's walls were subject to their view,
The trees' tall summits withered at the sight;
A constant interchange of growth and blight![1]
          1814.

[1] For the account of these long-lived trees, see
Pliny's "Natural History," lib. xvi. cap. 44; and for
the features in the character of Protesilaus see the
"Iphigenia in Aulis" of Euripides. Virgil places the
Shade of Laodamia in a mournful region, among un-
happy Lovers,
     —— His Laodamia
  It Comes.——

XXXII.

DION.

(SEE PLUTARCH.)

I.

SERENE, and fitted to embrace,
Where'er he turned, a swan-like grace
Of haughtiness without pretence,
And to unfold a still magnificence,
Was princely Dion, in the power
And beauty of his happier hour.
And what pure homage *then* did wait
On Dion's virtues, while the lunar beam
Of Plato's genius, from its lofty sphere,
Fell round him in the grove of Academe,   10
Softening their inbred dignity austere—
   That he, not too elate
   With self-sufficing solitude,
But with majestic lowliness endued,
Might in the universal bosom reign,   15
And from affectionate observance gain
Help, under every change of adverse fate.

II.

Five thousand warriors—O the rapturous day!
Each crowned with flowers, and armed with
     spear and shield,
Or ruder weapon which their course might
     yield,   20
To Syracuse advance in bright array.
Who leads them on ?—The anxious people see
Long-exiled Dion marching at their head,
He also crowned with flowers of Sicily,

II.   M

And in a white, far-beaming, corslet clad!   25
Pure transport undisturbed by doubt or fear
The gazers feel; and, rushing to the plain,
Salute those strangers as a holy train
Or blest procession (to the Immortals dear)
That brought their precious liberty again.   30
Lo! when the gates are entered, on each hand,
Down the long street, rich goblets filled with
       wine
          In seemly order stand,
On tables set, as if for rites divine;—
And, as the great Deliverer marches by,   35
He looks on festal ground with fruits bestrown;
And flowers are on his person thrown
   In boundless prodigality;
Nor doth the general voice abstain from prayer, ·
Invoking Dion's tutelary care,   40
As if a very Deity he were!

III.

Mourn, hills and groves of Attica! and mourn
Ilissus, bending o'er thy classic urn!
Mourn, and lament for him whose spirit dreads
Your once sweet memory, studious walks and
       shades!   45
For him who to divinity aspired,
Not on the breath of popular applause,
But through dependence on the sacred laws
Framed in the schools where Wisdom dwelt
       retired,
Intent to trace the ideal path of right   50
(More fair than heaven's broad causeway paved
       with stars)
Which Dion learned to measure with sublime
       delight;—
But He hath overleaped the eternal bars;

And, following guides whose craft holds no
  consent   54
With aught that breathes the ethereal element,
Hath stained the robes of civil power with
  blood,
Unjustly shed, though for the public good.
Whence doubts that came too late, and wishes
  vain,
Hollow excuses, and triumphant pain;
And oft his cogitations sink as low   60
As, through the abysses of a joyless heart,
The heaviest plummet of despair can go—
But whence that sudden check? that fearful
  start!
   He hears an uncouth sound—
   Anon his lifted eyes   65
Saw, at a long-drawn gallery's dusky bound,
A Shape of more than mortal size
And hideous aspect, stalking round and round!
   A woman's garb the Phantom wore,
   And fiercely swept the marble floor,— 70
   Like Auster whirling to and fro,
   His force on Caspian foam to try;
Or Boreas when he scours the snow
That skins the plains of Thessaly,
Or when aloft on Mænalus he stops 75
His flight, 'mid eddying pine-tree tops!

      IV.
So, but from toil less sign of profit reaping,
The sullen Spectre to her purpose bowed,
   Sweeping—vehemently sweeping—
No pause admitted, no design avowed! 80
"Avaunt, inexplicable Guest!—avaunt,"
Exclaimed the Chieftain—"let me rather see
The coronal that coiling vipers make;
The torch that flames with many a lurid flake,

And the long train of doleful pageantry   85
Which they behold, whom vengeful Furies
    haunt;
Who, while they struggle from the scourge to
    flee,
Move where the blasted soil is not unworn,
And, in their anguish, bear what other minds
    have borne!"

V.

But Shapes, that come not at an earthly call, 90
Will not depart when mortal voices bid;
Lords of the visionary eye whose lid,
Once raised, remains aghast, and will not fall!
Ye Gods, thought He, that servile Implement
    Obeys a mystical intent!   95
Your Minister would brush away
The spots that to my soul adhere;
But should she labour night and day,
They will not, cannot disappear;
Whence angry perturbations,—and that look
Which no philosophy can brook!   101

VI.

Ill-fated Chief! there are whose hopes are
    built
Upon the ruins of thy glorious name;
Who, through the portal of one moment's guilt,
Pursue thee with their deadly aim!   105
O matchless perfidy! portentous lust
Of monstrous crime!—that horror-striking
    blade,
Drawn in defiance of the Gods, hath laid
The noble Syracusan low in dust!
Shuddered the walls—the marble city wept—
And sylvan places heaved a pensive sigh;   111
But in calm peace the appointed Victim slept,

As he had fallen in magnanimity;
Of spirit too capacious to require
That Destiny her course should change; too
     just   115
To his own native greatness to desire
That wretched boon, days lengthened by mis-
     trust.
So were the hopeless troubles, that involved
The soul of Dion, instantly dissolved.
Released from life and cares of princely state,
He left this moral grafted on his Fate;   121
" Him only pleasure leads, and peace attends,
Him, only him, the shield of Jove defends,
Whose means are fair and spotless as his ends."

                                 1816.

XXXIII.

THE PASS OF KIRKSTONE.

I.

WITHIN the mind strong fancies work,
A deep delight the bosom thrills,
Oft as I pass along the fork
Of these fraternal hills:
Where, save the rugged road, we find   5
No appanage of human kind,
Nor hint of man; if stone or rock
Seem not his handy-work to mock
By something cognizably shaped;
Mockery—or model roughly hewn,   10
And left as if by earthquake strewn,
Or from the Flood escaped:
Altars for Druid service fit;
(But where no fire was ever lit,

Unless the glow-worm to the skies   15
Thence offer nightly sacrifice)
Wrinkled Egyptian monument;
Green moss-grown tower; or hoary tent;
Tents of a camp that never shall be raised—
On which four thousand years have gazed!   20

II.

Ye plough-shares sparkling on the slopes!
Ye snow-white lambs that trip
Imprisoned 'mid the formal props
Of restless ownership!
Ye trees, that may to-morrow fall   25
To feed the insatiate Prodigal!
Lawns, houses, chattels, groves, and fields,
All that the fertile valley shields;
Wages of folly—baits of crime,
Of life's uneasy game the stake,   30
Playthings that keep the eyes awake
Of drowsy, dotard Time;—
O care! O guilt!—O vales and plains,
Here, 'mid his own unvexed domains,
A Genius dwells, that can subdue   35
At once all memory of You,—
Most potent when mists veil the sky,
Mists that distort and magnify,
While the coarse rushes, to the sweeping
    breeze,
Sigh forth their ancient melodies!   40

III.

List to those shriller notes!—*that* march
Perchance was on the blast,
When, through this Height's inverted arch,
Rome's earliest legion passed!
—They saw, adventurously impelled,   45
And older eyes than theirs beheld,

This block—and yon, whose church-like frame
Gives to this savage Pass its name.
Aspiring Road! that lov'st to hide
Thy daring in a vapoury bourn,   50
Not seldom may the hour return
When thou shalt be my guide:
And I (as all men may find cause,
When life is at a weary pause,
And they have panted up the hill   55
Of duty with reluctant will)
Be thankful, even though tired and faint,
For the rich bounties of constraint;
Whence oft invigorating transports flow
That choice lacked courage to bestow!   60

IV.

My Soul was grateful for delight
That wore a threatening brow;
A veil is lifted—can she slight
The scene that opens now?
Though habitation none appear,   65
The greenness tells, man must be there;
The shelter—that the pérspective
Is of the clime in which we live;
Where Toil pursues his daily round;
Where Pity sheds sweet tears—and Love,   70
In woodbine bower or birchen grove,
Inflicts his tender wound.
—Who comes not hither ne'er shall know
How beautiful the world below;
Nor can he guess how lightly leaps   75
The brook adown the rocky steeps.
Farewell, thou desolate Domain!
Hope, pointing to the cultured plain,
Carols like a shepherd-boy;
And who is she?—Can that be Joy!   80
Who, with a sunbeam for her guide,

Smoothly skims the meadows wide ;
While Faith, from yonder opening cloud,
To hill and vale proclaims aloud,
"Whate'er the weak may dread, the wicked
    dare,   85
Thy lot, O Man, is good, thy portion fair !"
                        1817.

XXXIV.

TO ENTERPRISE.

KEEP for the Young the impassioned smile
Shed from thy countenance, as I see thee stand
High on that chalky cliff of Britain's Isle,
A slender volume grasping in thy hand—
(Perchance the pages that relate
The various turns of Crusoe's fate)—
Ah, spare the exulting smile,
And drop thy pointing finger bright
As the first flash of beacon light ;
But neither veil thy head in shadows dim,   10
Nor turn thy face away
From One who, in the evening of his day,
To thee would offer no presumptuous hymn !

I.

Bold Spirit ! who art free to rove
Among the starry courts of Jove,   15
And oft in splendour dost appear
Embodied to poetic eyes,
While traversing this nether sphere,
Where Mortals call thee ENTERPRISE.
Daughter of Hope ! her favourite Child,   20
Whom she to young Ambition bore,
When hunter's arrow first defiled

The grove, and stained the turf with gore;
Thee wingèd Fancy took, and nursed
On broad Euphrates' palmy shore,   25
And where the mightier Waters burst
From caves of Indian mountains hoar!
She wrapped thee in a panther's skin;
And Thou, thy favourite food to win,
The flame-eyed eagle oft wouldst scare   30
From her rock-fortress in mid air,
With infant shout; and often sweep,
Paired with the ostrich, o'er the plain;
Or, tired with sport, wouldst sink asleep
Upon the couchant lion's mane!   35
With rolling years thy strength increased;
And, far beyond thy native East,
To thee, by varying titles known
As variously thy power was shown,
Did incense-bearing altars rise,   40
Which caught the blaze of sacrifice,
From suppliants panting for the skies!

II.

What though this ancient Earth be trod
No more by step of Demi-god
Mounting from glorious deed to deed   45
As thou from clime to clime didst lead;
Yet still the bosom beating high,
And the hushed farewell of an eye
Where no procrastinating gaze
A last infirmity betrays,   50
Prove that thy heaven-descended sway
Shall ne'er submit to cold decay.
By thy divinity impelled,
The Stripling seeks the tented field;
The aspiring Virgin kneels; and, pale   55
With awe, receives the hallowed veil,
A soft and tender Heroine

Vowed to severer discipline;
Inflamed by thee, the blooming Boy
Makes of the whistling shrouds a toy,   60
And of the ocean's dismal breast
A play-ground,—or a couch of rest;
'Mid the blank world of snow and ice,
Thou to his dangers dost enchain
The Chamois-chaser awed in vain   65
By chasm or dizzy precipice;
And hast Thou not with triumph seen
How soaring Mortals glide between
Or through the clouds, and brave the light
With bolder than Icarian flight?   70
How they, in bells of crystal, dive—
Where winds and waters cease to strive—
For no unholy visitings,
Among the monsters of the Deep;
And all the sad and precious things   75
Which there in ghastly silence sleep?
Or adverse tides and currents headed,
And breathless calms no longer dreaded,
In never-slackening voyage go
Straight as an arrow from the bow;   80
And, slighting sails and scorning oars,
Keep faith with Time on distant shores?
—Within our fearless reach are placed
The secrets of the burning Waste;
Egyptian tombs unlock their dead,   85
Nile trembles at his fountain head;
Thou speak'st—and lo! the polar Seas
Unbosom their last mysteries.
—But oh! what transports, what sublime
        reward,
Won from the world of mind, dost thou prepare
For philosophic Sage; or high-souled Bard   91
Who, for thy service trained in lonely woods,
Hath fed on pageants floating through the air,

Or calentured in depth of limpid floods;
Nor grieves—tho' doomed thro' silent night to
     bear   95
The domination of his glorious themes,
Or struggle in the net-work of thy dreams!

III.

If there be movements in the Patriot's soul,
From source still deeper, and of higher worth,
'Tis thine the quickening impulse to control,
And in due season send the mandate forth; 101
Thy call a prostrate Nation can restore,
When but a single Mind resolves to crouch no
     more.

IV.

Dread Minister of wrath!   104
Who to their destined punishment dost urge
The Pharaohs of the earth, the men of hardened
     heart!
Not unassisted by the flattering stars,
Thou strew'st temptation o'er the path
When they in pomp depart
With trampling horses and refulgent cars— 110
Soon to be swallowed by the briny surge;
Or cast, for lingering death, on unknown strands;
Or caught amid a whirl of desert sands—
An Army now, and now a living hill
That a brief while heaves with convulsive
     throes—   115
Then all is still;
Or, to forget their madness and their woes,
Wrapt in a winding-sheet of spotless snows!

V.

Back flows the willing current of my Song:
If to provoke such doom the Impious dare, 120

Why should it daunt a blameless prayer?
—Bold Goddess! range our Youth among;
Nor let thy genuine impulse fail to beat
In hearts no longer young;
Still may a veteran Few have pride   125
In thoughts whose sternness makes them sweet;
In fixed resolves by Reason justified;
That to their object cleave like sleet
Whitening a pine tree's northern side,
When fields are naked far and wide,   130
And withered leaves, from earth's cold breast
Up-caught in whirlwinds, nowhere can find rest.

VI.

But if such homage thou disdain
As doth with mellowing years agree,
One rarely absent from thy train   135
More humble favours may obtain
For thy contented Votary.
She who incites the frolic lambs
In presence of their heedless dams,
And to the solitary fawn   140
Vouchsafes her lessons, bounteous Nymph
That wakes the breeze, the sparkling lymph
Doth hurry to the lawn;
She who inspires that strain of joyance holy
Which the sweet Bird, misnamed the melancholy,
Pours forth in shady groves, shall plead for me;
And vernal mornings opening bright   147
With views of undefined delight,
And cheerful songs, and suns that shine
On busy days, with thankful nights, be mine.

VII.

But thou, O Goddess! in thy favourite Isle 151
(Freedom's impregnable redoubt,
The wide earth's store-house fenced about

With breakers roaring to the gales
That stretch a thousand thousand sails) 155
Quicken the slothful, and exalt the vile!—
Thy impulse is the life of Fame;
Glad Hope would almost cease to be
If torn from thy society;
And Love, when worthiest of his name, 160
Is proud to walk the earth with Thee!

1820. (?)

XXXV.

TO ———,

ON HER FIRST ASCENT TO THE SUMMIT OF
HELVELLYN.

INMATE of a mountain-dwelling,
Thou hast clomb aloft, and gazed
From the watch-towers of Helvellyn;
Awed, delighted, and amazed!

Potent was the spell that bound thee
Not unwilling to obey;
For blue Ether's arms, flung round thee,
Stilled the pantings of dismay.

Lo! the dwindled woods and meadows;
What a vast abyss is there!   10
Lo! the clouds, the solemn shadows,
And the glistenings—heavenly fair!

And a record of commotion
Which a thousand ridges yield;
Ridge, and gulf, and distant ocean   15
Gleaming like a silver shield!

Maiden! now take flight;—inherit
Alps or Andes—they are thine!
With the morning's roseate Spirit
Sweep their length of snowy line;   20

Or survey their bright dominions
In the gorgeous colours drest
Flung from off the purple pinions,
Evening spreads throughout the west!

Thine are all the choral[1] fountains   25
Warbling in each sparry vault
Of the untrodden lunar mountains;
Listen to their songs!—or halt,

To Niphates' top invited,
Whither spiteful Satan steered;   30
Or descend where the ark alighted,
When the green earth re-appeared;

For the power of hills is on thee,
As was witnessed through thine eye
Then, when old Helvellyn won thee   35
To confess their majesty!

                                    1816.

XXXVI.

TO A YOUNG LADY,

WHO HAD BEEN REPROACHED FOR TAKING
LONG WALKS IN THE COUNTRY.

DEAR Child of Nature, let them rail!
—There is a nest in a green dale,
A harbour and a hold;

[1] " Choral " edd. 1820, 1827 ; " coral " 1832-1849.

Where thou, a Wife and Friend, shalt see
Thy own heart-stirring days, and be
A light to young and old.

There, healthy as a shepherd boy,
And treading among flowers of joy
Which at no season fade,
Thou, while thy babes around thee cling,   10
Shalt show us how divine a thing
A Woman may be made.

Thy thoughts and feelings shall not die,
Nor leave thee, when grey hairs are nigh,
A melancholy slave;   15
But an old age serene and bright,
And lovely as a Lapland night,
Shall lead thee to thy grave.

1805.

XXXVII.

WATER-FOWL.

" Let me be allowed the aid of verse to describe the
    evolutions which these visitants sometimes perform,
    on a fine day towards the close of winter."—*Extract*
    from the Author's Book on the Lakes.

MARK how the feathered tenants of the flood,
With grace of motion that might scarcely seem
Inferior to angelical, prolong
Their curious pastime! shaping in mid air
(And sometimes with ambitious wing that soars
High as the level of the mountain-tops)   6
A circuit ampler than the lake beneath—
Their own domain; but ever, while intent

On tracing and retracing that large round,
Their jubilant activity evolves   10
Hundreds of curves and circlets, to and fro,
Upward and downward, progress intricate
Yet unperplexed, as if one spirit swayed
Their indefatigable flight.   'Tis done—
Ten times, or more, I fancied it had ceased; 15
But lo! the vanished company again
Ascending; they approach—I hear their wings,
Faint, faint at first; and then an eager sound,
Past in a moment—and as faint again!
They tempt the sun to sport amid their plumes;
They tempt the water, or the gleaming ice,   21
To show them a fair image; 'tis themselves,
Their own fair forms, upon the glimmering
      plain,
Painted more soft and fair as they descend
Almost to touch;—then up again aloft,   25
Up with a sally and a flash of speed,
As if they scorned both resting-place and rest;

                                        1804.

XXXVIII.

VIEW FROM THE TOP OF

BLACK COMB.

THIS Height a ministering Angel might select:
For from the summit of BLACK COMB (dread
      name
Derived from clouds and storms!) the amplest
      range
Of unobstructed prospect may be seen
That British ground commands:—low dusky
      tracts,   5

Where Trent is nursed, far southward!   Cam-
    brian hills
To the south-west, a multitudinous show;
And, in a line of eye-sight linked with these,
The hoary peaks of Scotland that give birth
To Tiviot's stream, to Annan, Tweed, and
    Clyde:—   10
Crowding the quarter whence the sun comes forth
Gigantic mountains rough with crags; beneath,
Right at the imperial station's western base,
Main ocean, breaking audibly, and stretched
Far into silent regions blue and pale;—   15
And visibly engirding Mona's Isle
That, as we left the plain, before our sight
Stood like a lofty mount, uplifting slowly
(Above the convex of the watery globe)
Into clear view the cultured fields that streak
Her habitable shores, but now appears   21
A dwindled object, and submits to lie
At the spectator's feet.—Yon azure ridge,
Is it a perishable cloud?   Or there
Do we behold the line of Erin's coast?   25
Land sometimes by the roving shepherd-swain
(Like the bright confines of another world)
Not doubtfully perceived.—Look homeward
    now!
In depth, in height, in circuit, how serene
The spectacle, how pure!—Of Nature's works,
In earth, and air, and earth-embracing sea, 31
A revelation infinite it seems;
Display august of man's inheritance,
Of Britain's calm felicity and power!

1813.

    Black Comb stands at the southern extremity of
Cumberland: its base covers a much greater extent
of ground than any other mountain in those parts;
and, from its situation, the summit commands a more
extensive view than any other point in Britain.

XXXIX.

THE HAUNTED TREE.

TO ———.

THOSE silver clouds collected round the sun
His mid-day warmth abate not, seeming less
To overshade than multiply his beams
By soft reflection—grateful to the sky,
To rocks, fields, woods.   Nor doth our human
     sense   5
Ask, for its pleasure, screen or canopy
More ample than the time-dismantled Oak
Spreads o'er this tuft of heath, which now,
     attired
In the whole fulness of its bloom, affords
Couch beautiful as e'er for earthly use   10
Was fashioned; whether by the hand of Art,
That eastern Sultan, amid flowers enwrought
On silken tissue, might diffuse his limbs
In languor; or by Nature, for repose
Of panting Wood-nymph, wearied with the
     chase.   15
O Lady! fairer in thy Poet's sight
Than fairest spiritual creature of the groves,
Approach;—and, thus invited, crown with rest
The noon-tide hour: though truly some there
     are
Whose footsteps superstitiously avoid   20
This venerable Tree; for, when the wind
Blows keenly, it sends forth a creaking sound
(Above the general roar of woods and crags)
Distinctly heard from far—a doleful note!
As if (so Grecian shepherds would have
     deemed)   25

The Hamadryad, pent within, bewailed
Some bitter wrong.   Nor is it unbelieved,
By ruder fancy, that a troubled ghost
Haunts the old trunk; lamenting deeds of which
The flowery ground is conscious. But no wind 30
Sweeps now along this elevated ridge;
Not even a zephyr stirs;—the obnoxious Tree
Is mute; and, in his silence, would look down,
O lovely Wanderer of the trackless hills,
On thy reclining form with more delight   35
Than his coevals in the sheltered vale
Seem to participate, the while they view
Their own far-stretching arms and leafy heads
Vividly pictured in some glassy pool,
That, for a brief space, checks the hurrying
    stream !   40

                                    1819.

XL.

THE TRIAD.

Show me the noblest Youth of present time,
Whose trembling fancy would to love give
    birth;
Some God or Hero, from the Olympian clime
Returned, to seek a Consort upon earth;
Or, in no doubtful prospect, let me see
The brightest star of ages yet to be,
And I will mate and match him blissfully.

I will not fetch a Naiad from a flood
Pure as herself—(song lacks not mightier
    power)
Nor leaf-crowned Dryad from a pathless wood,
Nor Sea-nymph glistening from her coral
    bower;   11

Mere Mortals, bodied forth in vision still,
Shall with Mount Ida's triple lustre fill
The chaster coverts of a British hill.

  " Appear!—obey my lyre's command!   15
Come, like the Graces, hand in hand!
For ye, though not by birth allied,
Are Sisters in the bond of love;
Nor shall the tongue of envious pride
Presume those interweavings to reprove   20
In you, which that fair progeny of Jove
Learned from the tuneful spheres that glide
In endless union, earth and sea above."
—I sing in vain;—the pines have hushed their
       waving:
A peerless Youth expectant at my side,   25
Breathless as they, with unabated craving
Looks to the earth, and to the vacant air;
And, with a wandering eye that seems to chide,
Asks of the clouds what occupants they hide:—
But why solicit more than sight could bear, 30
By casting on a moment all we dare?
Invoke we those bright Beings one by one;
And what was boldly promised, truly shall be
      done.

  " Fear not a constraining measure!
—Yielding to this gentle spell,   35
Lucida! from domes of pleasure,
Or from cottage-sprinkled dell,
Come to regions solitary,
Where the eagle builds her aery,
Above the hermit's long-forsaken cell!"   40
—She comes!—behold
That Figure, like a ship with snow-white sail!
Nearer she draws; a breeze uplifts her veil;
Upon her coming wait
As pure a sunshine and as soft a gale   45

As e'er, on herbage covering earthly mould,
Tempted the bird of Juno to unfold
His richest splendour—when his veering gait
And every motion of his starry train
Seem governed by a strain   50
Of music, audible to him alone.

"O Lady, worthy of earth's proudest throne!
Nor less, by excellence of nature, fit
Beside an unambitious hearth to sit
Domestic queen, where grandeur is unknown;
What living man could fear   56
The worst of Fortune's malice, wert Thou near,
Humbling that lily-stem, thy sceptre meek,
That its fair flowers may from his cheek
Brush the too happy tear?   60
——Queen, and handmaid lowly!
Whose skill can speed the day with lively cares,
And banish melancholy
By all that mind invents or hand prepares;
O Thou, against whose lip, without its smile 65
And in its silence even, no heart is proof;
Whose goodness, sinking deep, would reconcile
The softest Nursling of a gorgeous palace
To the bare life beneath the hawthorn-roof   69
Of Sherwood's Archer, or in caves of Wallace—
Who that hath seen thy beauty could content
His soul with but a *glimpse* of heavenly day?
Who that hath loved thee, but would lay
His strong hand on the wind, if it were bent
To take thee in thy majesty away?   75
—Pass onward (even the glancing deer
Till we depart intrude not here;)
That mossy slope, o'er which the woodbine
        throws
A canopy, is smoothed for thy repose!"
Glad moment is it when the throng   80

Of warblers in full concert strong
Strive, and not vainly strive, to rout
The lagging shower, and force coy Phœbus out,
Met by the rainbow's form divine,
Issuing from her cloudy shrine;—   85
So may the thrillings of the lyre
Prevail to further our desire,
While to these shades a sister Nymph I call.

   " Come, if the notes thine ear may pierce,
Come, youngest of the lovely Three,   90
Submissive to the might of verse
And the dear voice of harmony,
By none more deeply felt than Thee!"
—I sang; and lo! from pastimes virginal
She hastens to the tents   95
Of nature, and the lonely elements.
Air sparkles round her with a dazzling sheen;
But mark her glowing cheek, her vesture green!
And, as if wishful to disarm
Or to repay the potent Charm,   100
She bears the strìngèd lute of old romance,
That cheered the trellised arbour's privacy,
And soothed war-wearied knights in raftered
    hall.
How vivid, yet how delicate, her glee!
So tripped the Muse, inventress of the dance;
So, truant in waste woods, the blithe Euphro-
    syne!   106

But the ringlets of that head
Why are they ungarlanded?
Why bedeck her temples less
Than the simplest shepherdess?   110
Is it not a brow inviting
Choicest flowers that ever breathed,
Which the myrtle would delight in

With Idalian rose enwreathed?
But her humility is well content   115
With *one* wild floweret (call it not forlorn)
FLOWER OF THE WINDS, beneath her bosom
     worn—
Yet more for love than ornament.

Open, ye thickets! let her fly,
Swift as a Thracian Nymph o'er field and
     height!   120
For She, to all but those who love her, shy,
Would gladly vanish from a Stranger's sight;
Though, where she is beloved and loves,
Light as the wheeling butterfly she moves;
Her happy spirit as a bird is free,   125
That rifles blossoms on a tree,
Turning them inside out with arch audacity.
Alas! how little can a moment show
Of an eye where feeling plays
In ten thousand dewy rays;   130
A face o'er which a thousand shadows go!
—She stops—is fastened to that rivulet's side;
And there (while, with sedater mien,
O'er timid waters that have scarcely left
Their birth-place in the rocky cleft   135
She bends) at leisure may be seen
Features to old ideal grace allied,
Amid their smiles and dimples dignified—
Fit countenance for the soul of primal truth;
The bland composure of eternal youth!   140

What more changeful than the sea?
But over his great tides
Fidelity presides;
And this light-hearted Maiden constant is as he.
High is her aim as heaven above,   145
And wide as ether her good-will;

And, like the lowly reed, her love
Can drink its nurture from the scantiest rill:
Insight as keen as frosty star
Is to *her* charity no bar,   150
Nor interrupts her frolic graces
When she is, far from these wild places,
Encircled by familiar faces.

O the charm that manners draw,
Nature, from thy genuine law!   155
If from what her hand would do,
Her voice would utter, aught ensue
Untoward or unfit;
She, in benign affections pure,
In self-forgetfulness secure,   160
Sheds round the transient harm or vague mis-
          chance
A light unknown to tutored elegance:
Hers is not a cheek shame-stricken,
But her blushes are joy-flushes;
And the fault (if fault it be)   165
Only ministers to quicken
Laughter-loving gaiety,
And kindle sportive wit—
Leaving this Daughter of the mountains free,
As if she knew that Oberon king of Faery 170
Had crossed her purpose with some quaint
          vagary,
And heard his viewless bands
Over their mirthful triumph clapping hands.

" Last of the Three, though eldest born,
Reveal thyself, like pensive Morn   175
Touched by the skylark's earliest note,
Ere humbler gladness be afloat.
But whether in the semblance drest
Of Dawn—or Eve, fair vision of the west,

Come with each anxious hope subdued   180
By woman's gentle fortitude,
Each grief, through meekness, settling into rest.
—Or I would hail thee when some high-wrought
    page
Of a closed volume lingering in thy hand
Has raised thy spirit to a peaceful stand   185
Among the glories of a happier age."

Her brow hath opened on me—see it there,
Brightening the umbrage of her hair;
So gleams the crescent moon, that loves
To be descried through shady groves.   190
Tenderest bloom is on her cheek;
Wish not for a richer streak;
Nor dread the depth of meditative eye;
But let thy love, upon that azure field
Of thoughtfulness and beauty, yield   195
Its homage offered up in purity.
What would'st thou more? In sunny glade,
Or under leaves of thickest shade,
Was such a stillness e'er diffused
Since earth grew calm while angels mused? 200
Softly she treads, as if her foot were loth
To crush the mountain dew-drops—soon to melt
On the flower's breast; as if she felt
That flowers themselves, whate'er their hue,
With all their fragrance, all their glistening,
Call to the heart for inward listening—   206
And though for bridal wreaths and tokens true
Welcomed wisely; though a growth
Which the careless shepherd sleeps on,
As fitly spring from turf the mourner weeps
    on—   210
And without wrong are cropped the marble
    tomb to strew.
The Charm is over; the mute Phantoms gone,

Nor will return—but droop not, favoured
    Youth;
The apparition that before thee shone
Obeyed a summons covetous of truth.   215
From these wild rocks thy footsteps I will guide
To bowers in which thy fortune may be tried,
And one of the bright Three become thy happy
    Bride.

                            1828.

XLI.

THE WISHING-GATE.

In the vale of Grasmere, by the side of the old high-
   way leading to Ambleside, is a gate, which, time
   out of mind, has been called the Wishing-gate,
   from a belief that wishes formed or indulged there
   have a favourable issue.

HOPE rules a land for ever green:
All powers that serve the bright-eyed Queen
    Are confident and gay;
Clouds at her bidding disappear;
Points she to aught?—the bliss draws near, 5
    And Fancy smooths the way.

Not such the land of Wishes—there
Dwell fruitless day-dreams, lawless prayer,
    And thoughts with things at strife;
Yet how forlorn, should *ye* depart,   10
Ye superstitions of the *heart*,
    How poor, were human life!

When magic lore abjured its might,
Ye did not forfeit one dear right,

One tender claim abate; 15
Witness this symbol of your sway,
Surviving near the public way,
    The rustic Wishing-gate!

Inquire not if the faery race
Shed kindly influence on the place, 20
    Ere northward they retired;
If here a warrior left a spell,
Panting for glory as he fell;
    Or here a saint expired.

Enough that all around is fair, 25
Composed with Nature's finest care,
    And in her fondest love—
Peace to embosom and content—
To overawe the turbulent,
    The selfish to reprove. 30

Yea! even the Stranger from afar,
Reclining on this moss-grown bar,
    Unknowing, and unknown,
The infection of the ground partakes,
Longing for his Beloved—who makes 35
    All happiness her own.

Then why should conscious Spirits fear
The mystic stirrings that are here,
    The ancient faith disclaim?
The local Genius ne'er befriends 40
Desires whose course in folly ends,
    Whose just reward is shame.

Smile if thou wilt, but not in scorn,
If some, by ceaseless pains outworn,
    Here crave an easier lot; 45
If some have thirsted to renew

A broken vow, or bind a true,
    With firmer, holier knot.

And not in vain, when thoughts are cast
Upon the irrevocable past,   50
    Some Penitent sincere
May for a worthier future sigh,
While trickles from his downcast eye
    No unavailing tear.

The Worldling, pining to be freed   55
From turmoil, who would turn or speed
    The current of his fate,
Might stop before this favoured scene,
At Nature's call, nor blush to lean
    Upon the Wishing-gate.   60

The Sage, who feels how blind, how weak
Is man, though loth such help to *seek*,
    Yet, passing, here might pause,
And thirst for insight to allay
Misgiving, while the crimson day   65
    In quietness withdraws;

Or when the church-clock's knell profound
To Time's first step across the bound
    Of midnight makes reply;
Time pressing on with starry crest   70
To filial sleep upon the breast
    Of dread eternity.

                         1828.

XLII.

THE WISHING-GATE DESTROYED.

'Tis gone—with old belief and dream
That round it clung, and tempting scheme
    Released from fear and doubt;
And the bright landscape too must lie,
By this blank wall, from every eye,   5
    Relentlessly shut out.

Bear witness ye who seldom passed
That opening—but a look ye cast
    Upon the lake below,
What spirit-stirring power it gained   10
From faith which here was entertained,
    Though reason might say no.

Blest is that ground, where, o'er the springs
Of history, Glory claps her wings,
    Fame sheds the exulting tear;   15
Yet earth is wide, and many a nook
Unheard of is, like this, a book
    For modest meanings dear.

It was in sooth a happy thought
That grafted, on so fair a spot,   20
    So confident a token
Of coming good;—the charm is fled;
Indulgent centuries spun a thread,
    Which one harsh day has broken.

Alas! for him who gave the word;   25
Could he no sympathy afford,

    Derived from earth or heaven,
To hearts so oft by hope betrayed;
Their very wishes wanted aid
    Which here was freely given?   30

Where, for the love-lorn maiden's wound,
Will now so readily be found
    A balm of expectation?
Anxious for far-off children, where
Shall mothers breathe a like still air   35
    Of home-felt consolation?

And not unfelt will prove the loss
'Mid trivial care and petty cross
    And each day's shallow grief;
Though the most easily beguiled   40
Were oft among the first that smiled
    At their own fond belief.

If still the reckless change we mourn,
A reconciling thought may turn
    To harm that might lurk here,   45
Ere judgment prompted from within
Fit aims, with courage to begin,
    And strength to persevere.

Not Fortune's slave is Man: our state
Enjoins, while firm resolves await   50
    On wishes just and wise,
That strenuous action follow both,
And life be one perpetual growth
    Of heaven-ward enterprise.

So taught, so trained, we boldly face   55
All accidents of time and place;
    Whatever props may fail,
Trust in that sovereign law can spread

New glory o'er the mountain's head,
  Fresh beauty through the vale.   60

That truth informing mind and heart,
The simplest cottager may part,
    Ungrieved, with charm and spell;
And yet, lost Wishing-gate, to thee
The voice of grateful memory   65
    Shall bid a kind farewell![1]

                  1842. (?)

XLIII.

THE PRIMROSE OF THE ROCK.

A ROCK there is whose homely front
  The passing traveller slights;
Yet there the glow-worms hang their lamps,
  Like stars, at various heights;
And one coy Primrose to that Rock
  The vernal breeze invites.

What hideous warfare hath been waged,
  What kingdoms overthrown,
Since first I spied that Primrose-tuft
  And marked it for my own;   10
A lasting link in Nature's chain
  From highest heaven let down!

The flowers, still faithful to the stems,
  Their fellowship renew;
The stems are faithful to the root,   15
  That worketh out of view;
And to the rock the root adheres
  In every fibre true.

[1] See Note at end of this volume.

Close clings to earth the living rock,
   Though threatening still to fall;   20
The earth is constant to her sphere;
   And God upholds them all:
So blooms this lonely Plant, nor dreads
   Her annual funeral.

      *   *   *   *   *

Here closed the meditative strain;   25
   But air breathed soft that day,
The hoary mountain-heights were cheered,
   The sunny vale looked gay;
And to the Primrose of the Rock
   I gave this after-lay.   30

I sang—Let myriads of bright flowers,
   Like Thee, in field and grove
Revive unenvied;—mightier far,
   Than tremblings that reprove
Our vernal tendencies to hope,   35
   Is God's redeeming love;

That love which changed—for wan disease,
   For sorrow that had bent
O'er hopeless dust, for withered age—
   Their moral element,   40
And turned the thistles of a curse
   To types beneficent.

Sin-blighted though we are, we too,
   The reasoning Sons of Men,
From one oblivious winter called   45
   Shall rise, and breathe again;
And in eternal summer lose
   Our threescore years and ten.

To humbleness of heart descends,
  This prescience from on high,   50
The faith that elevates the just,
  Before and when they die;
And makes each soul a separate heaven,
  A court for Deity.

                          1831.

XLIV.

PRESENTIMENTS.

PRESENTIMENTS! they judge not right
Who deem that ye from open light
  Retire in fear of shame;
All *heaven-born* Instincts shun the touch
Of vulgar sense,—and, being such,   5
  Such privilege ye claim.

The tear whose source I could not guess,
The deep sigh that seemed fatherless,
  Were mine in early days;
And now, unforced by time to part   10
With fancy, I obey my heart,
  And venture on your praise.

What though some busy foes to good,
Too potent over nerve and blood,
  Lurk near you—and combine   15
To taint the health which ye infuse;
This hides not from the moral Muse
  Your origin divine.

How oft from you, derided Powers!
Comes Faith that in auspicious hours   20

Builds castles, not of air:
Bodings unsanctioned by the will
Flow from your visionary skill,
   And teach us to beware.

The bosom-weight, your stubborn gift,   25
That no philosophy can lift,
   Shall vanish, if ye please,
Like morning mist: and, where it lay,
The spirits at your bidding play
   In gaiety and ease.   30

Star-guided contemplations move
Through space, though calm, not raised above
   Prognostics that ye rule;
The naked Indian of the wild,
And haply too the cradled Child,   35
   Are pupils of your school.

But who can fathom your intents,
Number their signs or instruments?
   A rainbow, a sunbeam,
A subtle smell that Spring unbinds,   40
Dead pause abrupt of midnight winds,
   An echo, or a dream.

The laughter of the Christmas hearth
With sighs of self-exhausted mirth
   Ye feelingly reprove;   45
And daily, in the conscious breast,
Your visitations are a test
   And exercise of love.

When some great change gives boundless scope
To an exulting Nation's hope,   50
   Oft, startled and made wise
By your low-breathed interpretings,

The simply-meek foretaste the springs
  Of bitter contraries.

Ye daunt the proud array of war,   55
Pervade the lonely ocean far
  As sail hath been unfurled;
For dancers in the festive hall
What ghastly partners hath your call
  Fetched from the shadowy world.   60

'Tis said that warnings ye dispense,
Emboldened by a keener sense;
  That men have lived for whom,
With dread precision, ye made clear
The hour that in a distant year   65
  Should knell them to the tomb.

Unwelcome insight! Yet there are
Blest times when mystery is laid bare,
  Truth shows a glorious face,
While on that isthmus which commands 70
The councils of both worlds she stands,
  Sage Spirits! by your grace.

God, who instructs the brutes to scent
All changes of the element,
  Whose wisdom fixed the scale   75
Of natures, for our wants provides
By higher, sometimes humbler, guides,
  When lights of reason fail.

                           1830.

XLV.

·VERNAL ODE.

" Rerum Natura tota est nusquam magis quam in
    minimis." PLIN. *Nat. Hist.*

I.

BENEATH the concave of an April sky,
When all the fields with freshest green were
    dight,
Appeared, in presence of the spiritual eye
That aids or supersedes our grosser sight,
The form and rich habiliments of One   5
Whose countenance bore resemblance to the
    sun,
When it reveals, in evening majesty,
Features half lost amid their own pure light.
Poised like a weary cloud, in middle air
He hung,—then floated with angelic ease   10
(Softening that bright effulgence by degrees)
Till he had reached a summit sharp and bare,
Where oft the venturous heifer drinks the noon-
    tide breeze.
Upon the apex of that lofty cone
Alighted, there the Stranger stood alone;   15
Fair as a gorgeous Fabric of the east
Suddenly raised by some enchanter's power,
Where nothing was; and firm as some old
    Tower
Of Britain's realm, whose leafy crest   19
Waves high, embellished by a gleaming shower!

II.

Beneath the shadow of his purple wings
Rested a golden harp;—he touched the strings;
And, after prelude of unearthly sound

Poured through the echoing hills around,
He sang—

   "No wintry desolations,   25
Scorching blight or noxious dew,
Affect my native habitations ;
Buried in glory, far beyond the scope
Of man's inquiring gaze, but to his hope
Imaged, though faintly, in the hue   30
Profound of night's ethereal blue ;
And in the aspect of each radiant orb ;—
Some fixed, some wandering with no timid
   curb ;
But wandering star and fixed, to mortal eye,
Blended in absolute serenity,   35
And free from semblance of decline ;—
Fresh as if Evening brought their natal hour,
Her darkness splendour gave, her silence power,
To testify of Love and Grace divine.

III.

What if those bright fires   40
Shine subject to decay,
Sons haply of extinguished sires,
Themselves to lose their light, or pass away
Like clouds before the wind,
Be thanks poured out to Him whose hand
   bestows,   45
Nightly, on human kind
That vision of endurance and repose.
—And though to every draught of vital breath,
Renewed throughout the bounds of earth or
   ocean,
The melancholy gates of Death   50
Respond with sympathetic motion ;
Though all that feeds on nether air,
Howe'er magnificent or fair,
Grows but to perish, and entrust

Its ruins to their kindred dust;   55
Yet, by the Almighty's ever-during care,
Her procreant vigils Nature keeps
Amid the unfathomable deeps;
And saves the peopled fields of earth
From dread of emptiness or dearth.   60
Thus, in their stations, lifting tow'rd the sky
The foliaged head in cloud-like majesty,
The shadow-casting race of trees survive:
Thus, in the train of Spring, arrive
Sweet flowers;—what living eye hath viewed
Their myriads?—endlessly renewed,   66
Wherever strikes the sun's glad ray;
Where'er the subtle waters stray;
Wherever sportive breezes bend
Their course, or genial showers descend!   70
Mortals, rejoice! the very Angels quit
Their mansions unsusceptible of change,
Amid your pleasant bowers to sit,
And through your sweet vicissitudes to range!"

                          IV.

O, nursed at happy distance from the cares   75
Of a too-anxious world, mild pastoral Muse!
That to the sparkling crown Urania wears,
And to her sister Clio's laurel wreath,
Preferr'st a garland culled from purple heath,
Or blooming thicket moist with morning dews;
Was such bright Spectacle vouchsafed to me?
And was it granted to the simple ear   82
Of thy contented Votary
Such melody to hear!
Him rather suits it, side by side with thee,   85
Wrapped in a fit of pleasing indolence,
While thy tired lute hangs on the hawthorn-
        tree,
To lie and listen—till o'er-drowsèd sense

Sinks, hardly conscious of the influence—
To the soft murmur of the vagrant Bee.   90
—A slender sound! yet hoary Time
Doth to the *Soul* exalt it with the chime
Of all his years;—a company
Of ages coming, ages gone;
(Nations from before them sweeping,   95
Regions in destruction steeping,)
But every awful note in unison
With that faint utterance, which tells
Of treasure sucked from buds and bells,
For the pure keeping of those waxen cells; 100
Where She—a statist prudent to confer
Upon the common weal; a warrior bold,
Radiant all over with unburnished gold,
And armed with living spear for mortal fight;
    A cunning forager   105
That spreads no waste; a social builder; one
In whom all busy offices unite
With all fine functions that afford delight—
Safe through the winter storm in quiet dwells!

v.

And is She brought within the power   110
Of vision?—o'er this tempting flower
Hovering until the petals stay
Her flight, and take its voice away!—
Observe each wing!—a tiny van!
The structure of her laden thigh,   115
How fragile! yet of ancestry
Mysteriously remote and high;
High as the imperial front of man;
The roseate bloom on woman's cheek;
The soaring eagle's curvèd beak;   120
The white plumes of the floating swan;
Old as the tiger's paw, the lion's mane
Ere shaken by that mood of stern disdain

At which the desert trembles.—Humming Bee!
Thy sting was needless then, perchance un-
        known,   125
The seeds of malice were not sown;
All creatures met in peace, from fierceness free,
And no pride blended with their dignity.
—Tears had not broken from their source;
Nor Anguish strayed from her Tartarean den;
The golden years maintained a course   131
Not undiversified though smooth and even;
We were not mocked with glimpse and shadow
        then,
Bright Seraphs mixed familiarly with men;
And earth and stars composed a universal
        heaven!   135

                                        1817.

XLVI.

DEVOTIONAL INCITEMENTS.

> "Not to the earth confined,
>   Ascend to heaven."

WHERE will they stop, those breathing Powers,
The Spirits of the new-born flowers?
They wander with the breeze, they wind
Where'er the streams a passage find;
Up from their native ground they rise
In mute aërial harmonies;
From humble violet—modest thyme—
Exhaled, the essential odours climb,
As if no space below the sky
Their subtle flight could satisfy: 10
Heaven will not tax our thoughts with pride
If like ambition be *their* guide.

Roused by this kindliest of May-showers,
The spirit-quickener of the flowers,
That with moist virtue softly cleaves   15
The buds, and freshens the young leaves,
The birds pour forth their souls in notes
Of rapture from a thousand throats—
Here checked by too impetuous haste,
While there the music runs to waste,   20
With bounty more and more enlarged,
Till the whole air is overcharged;
Give ear, O Man! to their appeal,
And thirst for no inferior zeal,
Thou, who canst *think*, as well as feel.   25

Mount from the earth; aspire! aspire!
So pleads the town's cathedral quire,
In strains that from their solemn height
Sink, to attain a loftier flight;
While incense from the altar breathes   30
Rich fragrance in embodied wreaths;
Or, flung from swinging censer, shrouds
The taper-lights, and curls in clouds
Around angelic Forms, the still
Creation of the painter's skill,   35
That on the service wait concealed
One moment, and the next revealed.
—Cast off your bonds, awake, arise,
And for no transient ecstasies!
What else can mean the visual plea   40
Of still or moving imagery—
The iterated summons loud,
Not wasted on the attendant crowd,
Nor wholly lost upon the throng
Hurrying the busy streets along?   45

Alas! the sanctities combined
By art to unsensualise the mind

Decay and languish; or, as creeds
And humours change, are spurned like weeds:
The priests are from their altars thrust;   50
Temples are levelled with the dust;
And solemn rites and awful forms
Founder amid fanatic storms.
Yet evermore, through years renewed
In undisturbed vicissitude   55
Of seasons balancing their flight
On the swift wings of day and night,
Kind Nature keeps a heavenly door
Wide open for the scattered Poor.
Where flower-breathed incense to the skies   60
Is wafted in mute harmonies;
And ground fresh-cloven by the plough
Is fragrant with a humbler vow;
Where birds and brooks from leafy dells
Chime forth unwearied canticles,   65
And vapours magnify and spread
The glory of the sun's bright head—
Still constant in her worship, still
Conforming to the eternal Will,
Whether men sow or reap the fields,   70
Divine monition Nature yields,
That not by bread alone we live,
Or what a hand of flesh can give;
That every day should leave some part
Free for a sabbath of the heart: 75
So shall the seventh be truly blest,
From morn to eve, with hallowed rest.

                              1832.

XLVII.

THE CUCKOO-CLOCK.

WOULDST thou be taught, when sleep has taken
    flight,
By a sure voice that can most sweetly tell,
How far-off yet a glimpse of morning light,
And if to lure the truant back be well,
Forbear to covet a Repeater's stroke,   5
That, answering to thy touch, will sound the
    hour;
Better provide thee with a Cuckoo-clock,
For service hung behind thy chamber-door;
And in due time the soft spontaneous shock,
The double note, as if with living power,   10
Will to composure lead—or make thee blithe
    as bird in bower.

List, Cuckoo—Cuckoo!—oft tho' tempests howl,
Or nipping frost remind thee trees are bare,
How cattle pine, and droop the shivering fowl,
Thy spirits will seem to feed on balmy air: 15
I speak with knowledge,—by that Voice
    beguiled,
Thou wilt salute old memories as they throng
Into thy heart; and fancies, running wild
Through fresh green fields, and budding groves
    among,
Will make thee happy, happy as a child;   20
Of sunshine wilt thou think, and flowers, and
    song,
And breathe as in a world where nothing can
    go wrong.

And know—that, even for him who shuns the
    day
And nightly tosses on a bed of pain;   24
Whose joys, from all but memory swept away,
Must come unhoped for, if they come again;
Know—that, for him whose waking thoughts,
    severe
As his distress is sharp, would scorn my theme,
The mimic notes, striking upon his ear
In sleep, and intermingling with his dream, 30
Could from sad regions send him to a dear
Delightful land of verdure, shower and gleam,
To mock the *wandering* Voice beside some
    haunted stream.

O bounty without measure! while the grace
Of Heaven doth in such wise, from humblest
    springs,   35
Pour pleasure forth, and solaces that trace
A mazy course along familiar things,
Well may our hearts have faith that blessings
    come,
Streaming from founts above the starry sky,
With angels when their own untroubled home
They leave, and speed on nightly embassy 41
To visit earthly chambers,—and for whom?
Yea, both for souls who God's forbearance try,
And those that seek his help, and for his mercy
    sigh.

                    1842. (?)

XLVIII.

TO THE CLOUDS.

ARMY of Clouds! ye wingèd Host in troops
Ascending from behind the motionless brow
Of that tall rock, as from a hidden world,
O whither with such eagerness of speed?
What seek ye, or what shun ye? of the gale 5
Companions, fear ye to be left behind,
Or racing o'er your blue ethereal field
Contend ye with each other? of the sea
Children, thus post ye over vale and height
To sink upon your mother's lap—and rest? 10
Or were ye rightlier hailed, when first mine eyes
Beheld in your impetuous march the likeness
Of a wide army pressing on to meet
Or overtake some unknown enemy?—
But your smooth motions suit a peaceful aim;
And Fancy, not less aptly pleased, compares 16
Your squadrons to an endless flight of birds
Aerial, upon due migration bound
To milder climes; or rather do ye urge
In caravan your hasty pilgrimage 20
To pause at last on more aspiring heights
Than these, and utter your devotion there
With thunderous voice? Or are ye jubilant,
And would ye, tracking your proud lord the
        Sun,
Be present at his setting; or the pomp 25
Of Persian mornings would ye fill, and stand
Poising your splendours high above the heads
Of worshippers kneeling to their up-risen God?
Whence, whence, ye Clouds! this eagerness of
        speed?

Speak, silent creatures.—They are gone, are fled,
Buried together in yon gloomy mass   31
That loads the middle heaven; and clear and
     bright
And vacant doth the region which they
     thronged
Appear; a calm descent of sky conducting
Down to the unapproachable abyss,   35
Down to that hidden gulf from which they rose
To vanish—fleet as days and months and years,
Fleet as the generations of mankind,
Power, glory, empire, as the world itself,
The lingering world, when time hath ceased to
     be.   40
But the winds roar, shaking the rooted trees,
And see! a bright precursor to a train
Perchance as numerous, overpeers the rock
That sullenly refuses to partake
Of the wild impulse. From a fount of life   45
Invisible, the long procession moves
Luminous or gloomy, welcome to the vale
Which they are entering, welcome to mine eye
That sees them, to my soul that owns in them,
And in the bosom of the firmament   50
O'er which they move, wherein they are con-
     tained,
A type of her capacious self and all
Her restless progeny.   A humble walk
Here is my body doomed to tread, this path,
A little hoary line and faintly traced,   55
Work, shall we call it, of the shepherd's foot
Or of his flock?—joint vestige of them both.
I pace it unrepining, for my thoughts
Admit no bondage and my words have wings.
Where is the Orphean lyre, or Druid harp,   60
To accompany the verse? The mountain blast

Shall be our *hand* of music ; he shall sweep
The rocks, and quivering trees, and billowy lake,
And search the fibres of the caves, and they
Shall answer, for our song is of the Clouds, 65
And the wind loves them; and the gentle
     gales—
Which by their aid re-clothe the naked lawn
With annual verdure, and revive the woods,
And moisten the parched lips of thirsty flowers—
Love them ; and every idle breeze of air   70
Bends to the favourite burthen. Moon and stars
Keep their most solemn vigils when the Clouds
Watch also, shifting peaceably their place
Like bands of ministering Spirits, or when
    they lie,
As if some Protean art the change had wrought,
In listless quiet o'er the ethereal deep   76
Scattered, a Cyclades of various shapes
And all degrees of beauty. O ye Lightnings!
Ye are their perilous offspring ; and the Sun—
Source inexhaustible of life and joy,   80
And type of man's far-darting reason, therefore
In old time worshipped as the god of verse,
A blazing intellectual deity—
Loves his own glory in their looks, and showers
Upon that unsubstantial brotherhood   85
Visions with all but beatific light
Enriched—too transient, were they not renewed
From age to age, and did not, while we gaze
In silent rapture, credulous desire   89
Nourish the hope that memory lacks not power
To keep the treasure unimpaired. Vain thought!
Yet why repine, created as we are
For joy and rest, albeit to find them only
Lodged in the bosom of eternal things?

                      1842. (?)

XLIX.

SUGGESTED BY A PICTURE OF THE
BIRD OF PARADISE.

The gentlest Poet, with free thoughts endowed,
And a true master of the glowing strain,
Might scan the narrow province with disdain
That to the Painter's skill is here allowed.
This, this the Bird of Paradise! disclaim   5
The daring thought, forget the name;
This the Sun's Bird, whom Glendoveers might
      own
As no unworthy Partner in their flight
Through seas of ether, where the ruffling sway
Of r.ether air's rude billows is unknown;   10
Whom Sylphs, if e'er for casual pastime they
Through India's spicy regions wing their way,
Might bow to as their Lord.   What character,
O sovereign Nature! I appeal to thee,
Of all thy feathered progeny   15
Is so unearthly, and what shape so fair?
So richly decked in variegated down,
Green, sable, shining yellow, shadowy brown,
Tints softly with each other blended,
Hues doubtfully begun and ended;   20
Or intershooting, and to sight
Lost and recovered, as the rays of light
Glance on the conscious plumes touched here
      and there?
Full surely, when with such proud gifts of life
Began the pencil's strife,   25
O'erweening Art was caught as in a snare.

A sense of seemingly presumptuous wrong

Gave the first impulse to the Poet's song;
But, of his scorn repenting soon, he drew
A juster judgment from a calmer view;   30
And, with a spirit freed from discontent,
Thankfully took an effort that was meant
Not with God's bounty, Nature's love, to vie,
Or made with hope to please that inward eye
Which ever strives in vain itself to satisfy, 35
But to recall the truth by some faint trace
Of power ethereal and celestial grace,
That in the living Creature find on earth a place.

1842. (?)

L.

A JEWISH FAMILY.

(IN A SMALL VALLEY OPPOSITE ST. GOAR,
UPON THE RHINE.)

GENIUS of Raphael! if thy wings
  Might bear thee to this glen,
With faithful memory left of things
  To pencil dear and pen,
Thou wouldst forego the neighbouring Rhine, 5
  And all his majesty—
A studious forehead to incline
  O'er this poor family.

The Mother—her thou must have seen,
  In spirit, ere she came 10
To dwell these rifted rocks between,
  Or found on earth a name;
An image, too, of that sweet Boy,
  Thy inspirations give—
Of playfulness, and love, and joy, 15
  Predestined here to live.

II.   P

Downcast, or shooting glances far,
  How beautiful his eyes,
That blend the nature of the star
  With that of summer skies!   20
I speak as if of sense beguiled;
  Uncounted months are gone,
Yet am I with the Jewish Child,
  That exquisite Saint John.

I see the dark-brown curls, the brow,   25
  The smooth transparent skin,
Refined, as with intent to show
  The holiness within;
The grace of parting Infancy
  By blushes yet untamed;   30
Age faithful to the mother's knee,
  Nor of her arms ashamed.

Two lovely Sisters, still and sweet
  As flowers, stand side by side;
Their soul-subduing looks might cheat   35
  The Christian of his pride:
Such beauty hath the Eternal poured
  Upon them not forlorn,
Though of a lineage once abhorred,
  Nor yet redeemed from scorn.   40

Mysterious safeguard, that, in spite
  Of poverty and wrong,
Doth here preserve a living light,
  From Hebrew fountains sprung;
That gives this ragged group to cast   45
  Around the dell a gleam
Of Palestine, of glory past,
  And proud Jerusalem!

                          1828.

LI.

ON THE POWER OF SOUND.

ARGUMENT.

The Ear addressed, as occupied by a spiritual func-
tionary, in communion with sounds, individual, or
combined in studied harmony.—Sources and effects
of those sounds (to the close of 6th Stanza).—The
power of music, whence proceeding, exemplified in
the idiot.—Origin of music, and its effect in early
ages—how produced (to the middle of 10th Stanza).
—The mind recalled to sounds acting casually and
severally.—Wish uttered (11th Stanza) that these
could be united into a scheme or system for moral
interests and intellectual contemplation.—(Stanza
12th).—The Pythagorean theory of numbers and
music, with their supposed power over the motions
of the universe—imaginations consonant with such
a theory.—Wish expressed (in 11th Stanza) realized,
in some degree, by the representation of all sounds
under the form of thanksgiving to the Creator.—
(Last Stanza) the destruction of earth and the
planetary system—the survival of audible harmony,
and its support in the Divine Nature, as revealed
in Holy Writ.

I.

THY functions are ethereal,
As if within thee dwelt a glancing mind,
Organ of vision! And a Spirit aërial
Informs the cell of Hearing, dark and blind;
Intricate labyrinth, more dread for thought   5
To enter than oracular cave;
Strict passage, through which sighs are brought,
And whispers for the heart, their slave;
And shrieks, that revel in abuse
Of shivering flesh; and warbled air,   10

Whose piercing sweetness can unloose
The chains of frenzy, or entice a smile
Into the ambush of despair;
Hosannas pealing down the long-drawn aisle,
And requiems answered by the pulse that beats
Devoutly, in life's last retreats!   16

II.

The headlong streams and fountains
Serve Thee, invisible Spirit, with untired
        powers;
Cheering the wakeful tent on Syrian moun-
        tains,
They lull perchance ten thousand thousand
        flowers.   20
That roar, the prowling lion's *Here I am*,
How fearful to the desert wide!
That bleat, how tender! of the dam
Calling a straggler to her side.
Shout, cuckoo!—let the vernal soul   25
Go with thee to the frozen zone;
Toll from thy loftiest perch, lone bell-bird, toll!
At the still hour to Mercy dear,
Mercy from her twilight throne
Listening to nun's faint throb of holy fear,   30
To sailor's prayer breathed from a darkening
        sea,
Or widow's cottage-lullaby.

III.

Ye Voices, and ye Shadows
And Images of voice—to hound and horn   34
From rocky steep and rock-bestudded meadows
Flung back, and, in the sky's blue caves, re-
        born—
On with your pastime! till the church-tower
        bells

A greeting give of measured glee;
And milder echoes from their cells
Repeat the bridal symphony.   40
Then, or far earlier, let us rove
Where mists are breaking up or gone,
And from aloft look down into a cove
Besprinkled with a careless quire,
Happy milk-maids, one by one   45
Scattering a ditty each to her desire,
A liquid concert matchless by nice Art,
A stream as if from one full heart.

IV.

Blest be the song that brightens
The blind man's gloom, exalts the veteran's
    mirth;   50
Unscorned the peasant's whistling breath, that
    lightens
His duteous toil of furrowing the green earth.
For the tired slave, Song lifts the languid oar,
And bids it aptly fall, with chime
That beautifies the fairest shore,   55
And mitigates the harshest clime.
Yon pilgrims see—in lagging file
They move; but soon the appointed way
A choral *Ave Marie* shall beguile,
And to their hope the distant shrine   60
Glisten with a livelier ray;
Nor friendless he, the prisoner of the mine,
Who from the well-spring of his own clear
    breast
Can draw, and sing his griefs to rest.

V.

When civic renovation   65
Dawns on a kingdom, and for needful haste
Best eloquence avails not, Inspiration

Mounts with a tune, that travels like a blast
Piping through cave and battlemented tower;
Then starts the sluggard, pleased to meet   70
That voice of Freedom, in its power
Of promises, shrill, wild, and sweet!
Who, from a martial *pageant*, spreads
Incitements of a battle-day,
Thrilling the unweaponed crowd with plumeless
   heads?—   75
Even She whose Lydian airs inspire
Peaceful striving, gentle play
Of timid hope and innocent desire
Shot from the dancing Graces, as they move
Fanned by the plausive wings of Love.   80

VI.

How oft along thy mazes,
Regent of sound, have dangerous Passions trod!
O Thou, through whom the temple rings with
   praises,
And blackening clouds in thunder speak of God,
Betray not by the cozenage of sense   85
Thy votaries, wooingly resigned
To a voluptuous influence
That taints the purer, better, mind;
But lead sick Fancy to a harp
That hath in noble tasks been tried;   90
And, if the virtuous feel a pang too sharp,
Soothe it into patience,—stay
The uplifted arm of Suicide;
And let some mood of thine in firm array
Knit every thought the impending issue needs,
Ere martyr burns, or patriot bleeds!   96

VII.

As Conscience, to the centre
Of being, smites with irresistible pain,

So shall a solemn cadence, if it enter
The mouldy vaults of the dull idiot's brain, 100
Transmute him to a wretch from quiet hurled—
Convulsed as by a jarring din;
And then aghast, as at the world
Of reason partially let in
By concords winding with a sway 105
Terrible for sense and soul!
Or awed he weeps, struggling to quell dismay.
Point not these mysteries to an Art
Lodged above the starry pole;
Pure modulations flowing from the heart 110
Of divine Love, where Wisdom, Beauty, Truth
With Order dwell, in endless youth?

VIII.

Oblivion may not cover
All treasures hoarded by the miser, Time.
Orphean Insight! truth's undaunted lover, 115
To the first leagues of tutored passion climb,
When Music deigned within this grosser sphere
Her subtle essence to enfold,
And voice and shell drew forth a tear
Softer than Nature's self could mould. 120
Yet *strenuous* was the infant Age:
Art, daring because souls could feel,
Stirred nowhere but an urgent equipage
Of rapt imagination sped her march
Through the realms of woe and weal: 125
Hell to the lyre bowed low; the upper arch
Rejoiced that clamorous spell and magic verse
Her wan disasters could disperse.

IX.

The GIFT to king Amphion
That walled a city with its melody 130
Was for belief no dream:—thy skill, Arion!

Could humanize the creatures of the sea,
Where men were monsters. A last grace he
    craves,
Leave for one chant;—the dulcet sound
Steals from the deck o'er willing waves,   135
And listening dolphins gather round.
Self-cast, as with a desperate course,
'Mid that strange audience, he bestrides
A proud One docile as a managed horse;
And singing, while the accordant hand   140
Sweeps his harp, the Master rides;
So shall he touch at length a friendly strand,
And he, with his preserver, shine star-bright
In memory, through silent night.

X.

The pipe of Pan, to shepherds   145
Couched in the shadow of Mænalian pines,
Was passing sweet; the eyeballs of the leopards,
That in high triumph drew the Lord of vines,
How did they sparkle to the cymbal's clang!
While Fauns and Satyrs beat the ground   150
In cadence,—and Silenus swang
This way and that, with wild-flowers crowned.
To life, to *life* give back thine ear:
Ye who are longing to be rid
Of fable, though to truth subservient, hear   155
The little sprinkling of cold earth that fell
Echoed from the coffin-lid;
The convict's summons in the steeple's knell;
" The vain distress-gun," from a leeward shore,
Repeated—heard, and heard no more!   160

XI.

For terror, joy, or pity,
Vast is the compass and the swell of notes :
From the babe's first cry to voice of regal city,

Rolling a solemn sea-like bass, that floats
Far as the woodlands—with the trill to blend
Of that shy songstress, whose love-tale   166
Might tempt an angel to descend,
While hovering o'er the moonlight vale.
Ye wandering Utterances, has earth no scheme,
No scale of moral music—to unite   170
Powers that survive but in the faintest dream
Of memory?—O that ye might stoop to bear
Chains, such precious chains of sight
As laboured minstrelsies through ages wear!
O for a balance fit the truth to tell   175
Of the Unsubstantial, pondered well!

XII.

By one pervading spirit
Of tones and numbers all things are controlled,
As sages taught, where faith was found to merit
Initiation in that mystery old.   180
The heavens, whose aspect makes our minds as
     still
As they themselves appear to be,
Innumerable voices fill
With everlasting harmony;
The towering headlands, crowned with mist, 185
Their feet among the billows, know
That Ocean is a mighty harmonist;
Thy pinions, universal Air,
Ever waving to and fro,
Are delegates of harmony, and bear   190
Strains that support the Seasons in their round;
Stern Winter loves a dirge-like sound.

XIII.

Break forth into thanksgiving,
Ye banded instruments of wind and chords;
Unite, to magnify the Ever-living,   195

Your inarticulate notes with the voice of words!
Nor hushed be service from the lowing mead,
Nor mute the forest hum of noon;
Thou too be heard, lone eagle! freed
From snowy peak and cloud, attune   200
Thy hungry barkings to the hymn
Of joy, that from her utmost walls
The six-days' Work by flaming Seraphim
Transmits to Heaven! As Deep to Deep
Shouting through one valley calls,   205
All worlds, all natures, mood and measure keep
For praise and ceaseless gratulation, poured
Into the ear of God, their Lord!

XIV.

A Voice to Light gave Being;
To Time, and Man his earth-born chronicler; 210
A Voice shall finish doubt and dim foreseeing,
And sweep away life's visionary stir;
The trumpet (we, intoxicate with pride,
Arm at its blast for deadly wars)
To archangelic lips applied,   215
The grave shall open, quench the stars.
O Silence! are Man's noisy years
No more than moments of thy life?
Is Harmony, blest queen of smiles and tears,
With her smooth tones and discords just,   220
Tempered into rapturous strife,
Thy destined bond-slave? No! though earth
            be dust
And vanish, though the heavens dissolve, her
            stay
Is in the WORD, that shall not pass away.
                                    1828.

PETER BELL.

A TALE.

" What's in a *Name?*

*　　*　　*　　*　　*

Brutus will start a Spirit as soon as Cæsar ! "

TO ROBERT SOUTHEY, ESQ., P.L., ETC., ETC.

My Dear Friend,
The Tale of Peter Bell, which I now
introduce to your notice, and to that of the Public,
has, in its Manuscript state, nearly survived its
minority:—for it first saw the light in the summer
of 1798. During this long interval, pains have been
taken at different times to make the production less
unworthy of a favourable reception; or rather to
fit it for filling *permanently* a station, however
humble, in the Literature of our Country. This
has, indeed, been the aim of all my endeavours in
Poetry, which, you know, have been sufficiently
laborious to prove that I deem the Art not lightly
to be approached; and that the attainment of excel-
lence in it may laudably be made the principal
object of intellectual pursuit by any man, who, with
reasonable consideration of circumstances, has faith
in his own impulses.

The Poem of Peter Bell, as the Prologue will show,
was composed under a belief that the Imagination
not only does not require for its exercise the inter-
vention of supernatural agency, but that, though
such agency be excluded, the faculty may be called
forth as imperiously, and for kindred results of plea-
sure, by incidents within the compass of poetic
probability, in the humblest departments of daily
life. Since that Prologue was written, *you* have
exhibited most splendid effects of judicious daring
in the opposite and usual course. Let this acknow-
ledgement make my peace with the lovers of the
supernatural; and I am persuaded it will be ad-

mitted that to you, as a Master in that province of
the art, the following Tale, whether from contrast or
congruity, is not an unappropriate offering. Accept
it, then, as a public testimony of affectionate admira-
tion from one with whose name yours has been often
coupled (to use your own words) for evil and for
good ; and believe me to be, with earnest wishes that
life and health may be granted you to complete the
many important works in which you are engaged,
and with high respect,
Most faithfully yours,
WILLIAM WORDSWORTH.

RYDAL MOUNT,
April 7, 1819.

PROLOGUE.

THERE'S something in a flying horse,
There's something in a huge balloon;
But through the clouds I'll never float
Until I have a little Boat,
Shaped like the crescent-moon.

And now I *have* a little Boat,
In shape a very crescent-moon :
Fast through the clouds my Boat can sail;
But if perchance your faith should fail,
Look up—and you shall see me soon !   10

The woods, my Friends, are round you roaring,
Rocking and roaring like a sea ;
The noise of danger's in your ears,
And ye have all a thousand fears
Both for my little Boat and me !   15

Meanwhile untroubled I admire
The pointed horns of my canoe ;
And, did not pity touch my breast
To see how ye are all distrest,
Till my ribs ached I'd laugh at you !   20

Away we go, my Boat and I—
Frail man ne'er sate in such another;
Whether among the winds we strive,
Or deep into the clouds we dive,
Each is contented with the other.   25

Away we go—and what care we
For treasons, tumults, and for wars?
We are as calm in our delight
As is the crescent-moon so bright
Among the scattered stars.   30

Up goes my Boat among the stars
Through many a breathless field of light,
Through many a long blue field of ether,
Leaving ten thousand stars beneath her:
Up goes my little Boat so bright!   35

The Crab, the Scorpion, and the Bull—
We pry among them all; have shot
High o'er the red-haired race of Mars,
Covered from top to toe with scars;
Such company I like it not!   40

The towns in Saturn are decayed,
And melancholy Spectres throng them;—
The Pleiads, that appear to kiss
Each other in the vast abyss,
With joy I sail among them.   45

Swift Mercury resounds with mirth,
Great Jove is full of stately bowers;
But these, and all that they contain,
What are they to that tiny grain,
That little Earth of ours?   50

Then back to Earth, the dear green Earth :—
Whole ages if I here should roam,
The world for my remarks and me
Would not a whit the better be ;
I've left my heart at home.   55

See ! there she is, the matchless Earth !
There spreads the famed Pacific Ocean !
Old Andes thrusts yon craggy spear
Through the grey clouds ; the Alps are here,
Like waters in commotion !   60

Yon tawny slip is Libya's sands ;
That silver thread the river Dnieper ;
And look, where clothed in brightest green
Is a sweet Isle, of isles the Queen ;
Ye fairies, from all evil keep her !   65

And see the town where I was born !
Around those happy fields we span
In boyish gambols ;—I was lost
Where I have been, but on this coast
I feel I am a man.   70

Never did fifty things at once
Appear so lovely, never, never ;—
How tunefully the forests ring !
To hear the earth's soft murmuring
Thus could I hang for ever !   75

"Shame on you !" cried my little Boat,
"Was ever such a homesick Loon,
Within a living Boat to sit,
And make no better use of it ;
A Boat twin-sister of the crescent-moon ! 80

Ne'er in the breast of full-grown Poet
Fluttered so faint a heart before;—
Was it the music of the spheres
That overpowered your mortal ears?
—Such din shall trouble them no more.   85

These nether precincts do not lack
Charms of their own;—then come with me,
I want a comrade, and for you
There's nothing that I would not do;
Nought is there that you shall not see.   90

Haste! and above Siberian snows
We'll sport amid the boreal morning;
Will mingle with her lustres gliding
Among the stars, the stars now hiding,
And now the stars adorning.   95

I know the secrets of a land
Where human foot did never stray;
Fair is that land as evening skies,
And cool, though in the depth it lies
Of burning Africa.   100

Or we'll into the realm of Faery,
Among the lovely shades of things;
The shadowy forms of mountains bare,
And streams, and bowers, and ladies fair,
The shades of palaces and kings!   105

Or, if you thirst with hardy zeal
Less quiet regions to explore,
Prompt voyage shall to you reveal
How earth and heaven are taught to feel
The might of magic lore!"   110

"My little vagrant Form of light,
My gay and beautiful Canoe,
Well have you played your friendly part;
As kindly take what from my heart
Experience forces—then adieu!   115

Temptation lurks among your words;
But, while these pleasures you're pursuing
Without impediment or let,
No wonder if you quite forget
What on the earth is doing.   120

There was a time when all mankind
Did listen with a faith sincere
To tuneful tongues in mystery versed;
Then Poets fearlessly rehearsed
The wonders of a wild career.   125

Go—(but the world's a sleepy world,
And 'tis, I fear an age too late)
Take with you some ambitious Youth!
For, restless Wanderer! I, in truth,
Am all unfit to be your mate.   130

Long have I loved what I behold,
The night that calms, the day that cheers;
The common growth of mother-earth
Suffices me—her tears, her mirth,
Her humblest mirth and tears.   135

The dragon's wing, the magic ring,
I shall not covet for my dower,
If I along that lowly way
With sympathetic heart may stray,
And with a soul of power.   140

These given, what more need I desire
To stir, to soothe, or elevate?
What nobler marvels than the mind
May in life's daily prospect find,
May find or there create?   145

A potent wand doth Sorrow wield;
What spell so strong as guilty Fear!
Repentance is a tender Sprite;
If aught on earth have heavenly might,
'Tis lodged within her silent tear.   150

But grant my wishes,—let us now
Descend from this ethereal height;
Then take thy way, adventurous Skiff,
More daring far than Hippogriff,
And be thy own delight!   155

To the stone-table in my garden,
Loved haunt of many a summer hour,
The Squire is come: his daughter Bess
Beside him in the cool recess
Sits blooming like a flower.   160

With these are many more convened;
They know not I have been so far;—
I see them there, in number nine,
Beneath the spreading Weymouth-pine!
I see them—there they are!   165

There sits the Vicar and his Dame;
And there my good friend, Stephen Otter;
And, ere the light of evening fail,
To them I must relate the Tale
Of Peter Bell the Potter."   170

Off flew the Boat—away she flees,
Spurning her freight with indignation!
And I, as well as I was able,
On two poor legs, toward my stone-table
Limped on with sore vexation.   175

"O, here he is!" cried little Bess—
She saw me at the garden-door;
"We've waited anxiously and long,"
They cried, and all around me throng,
Full nine of them or more!   180

"Reproach me not—your fears be still—
Be thankful we again have met;—
Resume, my Friends! within the shade
Your seats, and quickly shall be paid
The well-remembered debt."   185

I spake with faltering voice, like one
Not wholly rescued from the pale
Of a wild dream, or worse illusion;
But straight, to cover my confusion,
Began the promised Tale.   190

PART FIRST.

ALL by the moonlight river side
Groaned the poor Beast—alas! in vain;
The staff was raised to loftier height,
And the blows fell with heavier weight
As Peter struck—and struck again.   195

"Hold!" cried the Squire, "against the rules
Of common sense you're surely sinning;
This leap is for us all too bold;
Who Peter was, let that be told,
And start from the beginning."   200

———" A Potter,[1] Sir, he was by trade,"
Said I, becoming quite collected;
" And wheresoever he appeared,
Full twenty times was Peter feared
For once that Peter was respected.   205

He, two-and-thirty years or more,
Had been a wild and woodland rover;
Had heard the Atlantic surges roar
On farthest Cornwall's rocky shore,
And trod the cliffs of Dover.   210

And he had seen Caernarvon's towers,
And well he knew the spire of Sarum;
And he had been where Lincoln bell
Flings o'er the fen that ponderous knell—
A far-renowned alarum.   215

At Doncaster, at York, and Leeds,
And merry Carlisle had he been;
And all along the Lowlands fair,
All through the bonny shire of Ayr;
And far as Aberdeen.   220

And he had been at Inverness;
And Peter, by the mountain-rills,
Had danced his round with Highland lasses;
And he had lain beside his asses
On lofty Cheviot Hills: 225

And he had trudged through Yorkshire dales,
Among the rocks and winding *scars;*
Where deep and low the hamlets lie
Beneath their little patch of sky
And little lot of stars: 230

[1] In the dialect of the North, a hawker of earthenware is thus designated.

And all along the indented coast,
Bespattered with the salt-sea foam;
Where'er a knot of houses lay
On headland, or in hollow bay;—
Sure never man like him did roam!   235

As well might Peter in the Fleet
Have been fast bound, a begging debtor;—
He travelled here, he travelled there;—
But not the value of a hair
Was heart or head the better.   240

He roved among the vales and streams,
In the green wood and hollow dell;
They were his dwellings night and day,—
But nature ne'er could find the way
Into the heart of Peter Bell.   245

In vain, through every changeful year,
Did Nature lead him as before;
A primrose by a river's brim
A yellow primrose was to him,
And it was nothing more.   250

Small change it made in Peter's heart
To see his gentle panniered train
With more than vernal pleasure feeding,
Where'er the tender grass was leading
Its earliest green along the lane.   255

In vain, through water, earth, and air,
The soul of happy sound was spread,
When Peter on some April morn,
Beneath the broom or budding thorn,
Made the warm earth his lazy bed.   260

At noon, when, by the forest's edge
He lay beneath the branches high,
The soft blue sky did never melt
Into his heart; he never felt
The witchery of the soft blue sky!   265

On a fair prospect some have looked
And felt, as I have heard them say,
As if the moving time had been
A thing as steadfast as the scene
On which they gazed themselves away.   270

Within the breast of Peter Bell
These silent raptures found no place;
He was a Carl as wild and rude
As ever hue-and-cry pursued,
As ever ran a felon's race.   275

Of all that lead a lawless life,
Of all that love their lawless lives,
In city or in village small,
He was the wildest far of all;—
He had a dozen wedded wives.   280

Nay, start not!—wedded wives—and twelve!
But how one wife could e'er come near him,
In simple truth I cannot tell;
For, be it said of Peter Bell,
To see him was to fear him.   285

Though Nature could not touch his heart
By lovely forms, and silent weather,
And tender sounds, yet you might see
At once that Peter Bell and she
Had often been together.   290

A savage wildness round him hung
As of a dweller out of doors;
In his whole figure and his mien
A savage character was seen
Of mountains and of dreary moors.   295

To all the unshaped half-human thoughts
Which solitary Nature feeds
'Mid summer storms or winter's ice,
Had Peter joined whatever vice
The cruel city breeds.   300

His face was keen as is the wind
That cuts along the hawthorn-fence;
Of courage you saw little there,
But, in its stead, a medley air
Of cunning and of impudence.   305

He had a dark and sidelong walk,
And long and slouching was his gait;
Beneath his looks so bare and bold,
You might perceive, his spirit cold
Was playing with some inward bait.   310

His forehead wrinkled was and furred;
A work, one half of which was done
By thinking of his 'whens' and 'hows;'
And half, by knitting of his brows
Beneath the glaring sun.   315

There was a hardness in his cheek,
There was a hardness in his eye,
As if the man had fixed his face,
In many a solitary place,
Against the wind and open sky!"   320

ONE NIGHT, (and now, my little Bess!
We've reached at last the promised Tale;)
One beautiful November night,
When the full moon was shining bright
Upon the rapid river Swale,   325

Along the river's winding banks
Peter was travelling all alone;—
Whether to buy or sell, or led
By pleasure running in his head,
To me was never known.   330

He trudged along through copse and brake,
He trudged along o'er hill and dale;
Nor for the moon cared he a tittle,
And for the stars he cared as little,
And for the murmuring river Swale.   335

But, chancing to espy a path
That promised to cut short the way;
As many a wiser man hath done,
He left a trusty guide for one
That might his steps betray.   340

To a thick wood he soon is brought
Where cheerily his course he weaves,
And whistling loud may yet be heard,
Though often buried, like a bird
Darkling, among the boughs and leaves.   345

But quickly Peter's mood is changed,
And on he drives with cheeks that burn
In downright fury and in wrath;—
There's little sign the treacherous path
Will to the road return!   350

The path grows dim, and dimmer still
Now up, now down, the Rover wends,
With all the sail that he can carry,
Till brought to a deserted quarry—
And there the pathway ends.   355

He paused—for shadows of strange shape,
Massy and black, before him lay;
But through the dark, and through the cold,
And through the yawning fissures old,
Did Peter boldly press his way   360

Right through the quarry;—and behold
A scene of soft and lovely hue!
Where blue and grey, and tender green,
Together make as sweet a scene
As ever human eye did view.   365

Beneath the clear blue sky he saw
A little field of meadow ground;
But field or meadow name it not;
Call it of earth a small green plot,
With rocks encompassed round.   370

The Swale flowed under the grey rocks,
But he flowed quiet and unseen;—
You need a strong and stormy gale
To bring the noises of the Swale
To that green spot, so calm and green!   375

And is there no one dwelling here,
No hermit with his beads and glass?
And does no little cottage look
Upon this soft and fertile nook?
Does no one live near this green grass?   380

Across the deep and quiet spot
Is Peter driving through the grass—
And now has reached the skirting trees;
When, turning round his head, he sees
A solitary Ass.   385

" A prize ! " cries Peter—but he first
Must spy about him far and near :
There's not a single house in sight,
No woodman's hut, no cottage light—
Peter, you need not fear !   390

There's nothing to be seen but woods,
And rocks that spread a hoary gleam,
And this one Beast, that from the bed
Of the green meadow hangs his head
Over the silent stream.   395

His head is with a halter bound ;
The halter seizing, Peter leapt
Upon the Creature's back, and plied
With ready heels his shaggy side ;
But still the Ass his station kept.   400

Then Peter gave a sudden jerk,
A jerk that from a dungeon-floor
Would have pulled up an iron ring ;
But still the heavy-headed Thing
Stood just as he had stood before !   405

Quoth Peter, leaping from his seat,
" There is some plot against me laid ; "
Once more the little meadow-ground
And all the hoary cliffs around
He cautiously surveyed.   410

All, all is silent—rocks and woods,
All still and silent—far and near!
Only the Ass, with motion dull,
Upon the pivot of his skull
Turns round his long left ear.   415

Thought Peter, What can mean all this?
Some ugly witchcraft must be here!
—Once more the Ass, with motion dull,
Upon the pivot of his skull
Turned round his long left ear.   420

Suspicion ripened into dread;
Yet, with deliberate action slow,
His staff high-raising, in the pride
Of skill, upon the sounding hide
He dealt a sturdy blow.   425

The poor Ass staggered with the shock;
And then, as if to take his ease,
In quiet uncomplaining mood,
Upon the spot where he had stood,
Dropped gently down upon his knees;   430

As gently on his side he fell;
And by the river's brink did lie;
And, while he lay like one that mourned,
The patient Beast on Peter turned
His shining hazel eye.   435

'Twas but one mild, reproachful look,
A look more tender than severe;
And straight in sorrow, not in dread,
He turned the eye-ball in his head
Towards the smooth river deep and clear. 440

Upon the Beast the sapling rings;
His lank sides heaved, his limbs they stirred;
He gave a groan, and then another,
Of that which went before the brother,
And then he gave a third.   445

All by the moonlight river side
He gave three miserable groans;
And not till now hath Peter seen
How gaunt the Creature is,—how lean
And sharp his staring bones!   450

With legs stretched out and stiff he lay:—
No word of kind commiseration
Fell at the sight from Peter's tongue;
With hard contempt his heart was wrung,
With hatred and vexation.   455

The meagre beast lay still as death;
And Peter's lips with fury quiver;
Quoth he, "You little mulish dog,
I'll fling your carcass like a log
Head-foremost down the river!"   460

An impious oath confirmed the threat—
Whereat from the earth on which he lay
To all the echoes, south and north,
And east and west, the Ass sent forth
A long and clamorous bray!   465

This outcry, on the heart of Peter,
Seems like a note of joy to strike,—
Joy at the heart of Peter knocks;
But in the echo of the rocks
Was something Peter did not like.   470

Whether to cheer his coward breast,
Or that he could not break the chain,
In this serene and solemn hour,
Twined round him by demoniac power,
To the blind work he turned again.   475

Among the rocks and winding crags;
Among the mountains far away ;
Once more the Ass did lengthen out
More ruefully a deep-drawn shout,
The hard dry see-saw of his horrible bray !   480

What is there now in Peter's heart !
Or whence the might of this strange sound?
The moon uneasy looked and dimmer,
The broad blue heavens appeared to glimmer,
And the rocks staggered all around—   485

From Peter's hand the sapling dropped !
Threat has he none to execute ;
" If any one should come and see
That I am here, they 'll think," quoth he,
" I 'm helping this poor dying brute."   490

He scans the Ass from limb to limb,
And ventures now to uplift his eyes ;
More steady looks the moon, and clear,
More like themselves the rocks appear
And touch more quiet skies.   495

His scorn returns—his hate revives ;
He stoops the Ass's neck to seize
With malice—that again takes flight ;
For in the pool a startling sight
Meets him, among the inverted trees.   500

Is it the moon's distorted face?
The ghost-like image of a cloud?
Is it a gallows there portrayed?
Is Peter of himself afraid?
Is it a coffin,—or a shroud?   505

A grisly idol hewn in stone?
Or imp from witch's lap let fall?
Perhaps a ring of shining fairies?
Such as pursue their feared vagaries
In sylvan bower, or haunted hall?   510

Is it a fiend that to a stake
Of fire his desperate self is tethering?
Or stubborn spirit doomed to yell
In solitary ward or cell,
Ten thousand miles from all his brethren? 515

Never did pulse so quickly throb,
And never heart so loudly panted;
He looks, he cannot choose but look;
Like some one reading in a book—
A book that is enchanted.   520

Ah, well-a-day for Peter Bell!
He will be turned to iron soon,
Meet Statue for the court of Fear!
His hat is up—and every hair
Bristles, and whitens in the moon!   525

He looks, he ponders, looks again;
He sees a motion—hears a groan;
His eyes will burst—his heart will break—
He gives a loud and frightful shriek,
And back he falls, as if his life were flown! 530

PART SECOND.

WE left our Hero in a trance,
Beneath the alders, near the river;
The Ass is by the river-side,
And, where the feeble breezes glide,
Upon the stream the moonbeams quiver.   535

A happy respite! but at length
He feels the glimmering of the moon;
Wakes with glazed eye, and feebly sighing—
To sink, perhaps, where he is lying,
Into a second swoon!   540

He lifts his head, he sees his staff;
He touches—'tis to him a treasure!
Faint recollection seems to tell
That he is yet where mortals dwell—
A thought received with languid pleasure!   545

His head upon his elbow propped,
Becoming less and less perplexed,
Sky-ward he looks—to rock and wood—
And then—upon the glassy flood
His wandering eye is fixed.   550

Thought he, that is the face of one
In his last sleep securely bound!
So toward the stream his head he bent,
And downward thrust his staff, intent
The river's depth to sound.   555

Now—like a tempest-shattered bark,
That overwhelmed and prostrate lies,
And in a moment to the verge
Is lifted of a foaming surge—
Full suddenly the Ass doth rise!   560

His staring bones all shake with joy,
And close by Peter's side he stands:
While Peter o'er the river bends,
The little Ass his neck extends,
And fondly licks his hands. 565

Such life is in the Ass's eyes,
Such life is in his limbs and ears;
That Peter Bell, if he had been
The veriest coward ever seen,
Must now have thrown aside his fears. 570

The Ass looks on—and to his work
Is Peter quietly resigned;
He touches here—he touches there—
And now among the dead man's hair
His sapling Peter has entwined. 575

He pulls—and looks—and pulls again;
And he whom the poor Ass had lost,
The man who had been four days dead,
Head-foremost from the river's bed
Uprises like a ghost! 580

And Peter draws him to dry land;
And through the brain of Peter pass
Some poignant twitches, fast and faster;
"No doubt," quoth he, "he is the Master
Of this poor miserable Ass!" 585

The meagre shadow that looks on—
What would he now? what is he doing?
His sudden fit of joy is flown,—
He on his knees hath laid him down,
As if he were his grief renewing; 590

But no—that Peter on his back
Must mount, he shows well as he can:
Thought Peter then, come weal or woe,
I'll do what he would have me do,
In pity to this poor drowned man.   595

With that resolve he boldly mounts
Upon the pleased and thankful Ass;
And then, without a moment's stay,
That earnest Creature turned away,
Leaving the body on the grass.   600

Intent upon his faithful watch,
The Beast four days and nights had past;
A sweeter meadow ne'er was seen,
And there the Ass four days had been,
Nor ever once did break his fast: 605

Yet firm his step, and stout his heart;
The mead is crossed—the quarry's mouth
Is reached; but there the trusty guide
Into a thicket turns aside,
And deftly ambles towards the south.   610

When hark a burst of doleful sound!
And Peter honestly might say,
The like came never to his ears,
Though he has been, full thirty years,
A rover—night and day!   615

'Tis not a plover of the moors,
'Tis not a bittern of the fen;
Nor can it be a barking fox,
Nor night-bird chambered in the rocks,
Nor wild-cat in a woody glen!   620

The Ass is startled—and stops short
Right in the middle of the thicket;
And Peter, wont to whistle loud
Whether alone or in a crowd,
Is silent as a silent cricket. 625

What ails you now, my little Bess?
Well may you tremble and look grave!
This cry—that rings along the wood,
This cry—that floats adown the flood,
Comes from the entrance of a cave: 630

I see a blooming Wood-boy there,
And if I had the power to say
How sorrowful the wanderer is,
Your heart would be as sad as his
Till you had kissed his tears away! 635

Grasping a hawthorn branch in hand,
All bright with berries ripe and red,
Into the cavern's mouth he peeps;
Thence back into the moonlight creeps;
Whom seeks he—whom?—the silent dead: 640

His father!—Him doth he require—
Him hath he sought with fruitless pains,
Among the rocks, behind the trees;
Now creeping on his hands and knees,
Now running o'er the open plains. 645

And hither is he come at last,
When he through such a day has gone,
By this dark cave to be distrest
Like a poor bird—her plundered nest
Hovering around with dolorous moan! 650

Of that intense and piercing cry
The listening Ass conjectures well;
Wild as it is, he there can read
Some intermingled notes that plead
With touches irresistible.   655

But Peter—when he saw the Ass
Not only stop but turn, and change
The cherished tenor of his pace
That lamentable cry to chase—
It wrought in him conviction strange;   660

A faith that for the dead man's sake,
And this poor slave who loved him well,
Vengeance upon his head will fall,
Some visitation worse than all
Which ever till this night befell.   665

Meanwhile the Ass to reach his home
Is striving stoutly as he may;
But, while he climbs the woody hill,
The cry grows weak—and weaker still;
And now at last it dies away.   670

So with his freight the Creature turns
Into a gloomy grove of beech,
Along the shade with footsteps true
Descending slowly, till the two
The open moonlight reach.   675

And there, along the narrow dell,
A fair smooth pathway you discern,
A length of green and open road—
As if it from a fountain flowed—
Winding away between the fern.   680

The rocks that tower on either side
Build up a wild fantastic scene;
Temples like those among the Hindoos,
And mosques, and spires, and abbey-windows,
And castles all with ivy green!   685

And while the Ass pursues his way
Along this solitary dell,
As pensively his steps advance,
The mosques and spires change countenance,
And look at Peter Bell!   690

That unintelligible cry
Hath left him high in preparation,—
Convinced that he, or soon or late,
This very night will meet his fate—
And so he sits in expectation!   695

The strenuous Animal hath clomb
With the green path; and now he wends
Where, shining like the smoothest sea,
In undisturbed immensity
A level plain extends.   700

But whence this faintly-rustling sound
By which the journeying pair are chased?
—A withered leaf is close behind,
Light plaything for the sportive wind
Upon that solitary waste.   705

When Peter spied the moving thing,
It only doubled his distress;
" Where there is not a bush or tree,
The very leaves they follow me—
So huge hath been my wickedness! "   710

To a close lane they now are come,
Where, as before, the enduring Ass
Moves on without a moment's stop,
Nor once turns round his head to crop
A bramble-leaf or blade of grass.   715

Between the hedges as they go,
The white dust sleeps upon the lane;
And Peter, ever and anon
Back-looking, sees, upon a stone,
Or in the dust, a crimson stain.   720

A stain—as of a drop of blood
By moonlight made more faint and wan;
Ha! why these sinkings of despair?
He knows not how the blood comes there—
And Peter is a wicked man.   725

At length he spies a bleeding wound,
Where he had struck the Ass's head;
He sees the blood, knows what it is,—
A glimpse of sudden joy was his,
But then it quickly fled;   730

Of him whom sudden death had seized
He thought,—of thee, O faithful Ass!
And once again those ghastly pains,
Shoot to and fro through heart and reins,
And through his brain like lightning pass. 735

PART THIRD.

I 'VE heard of one, a gentle Soul,
Though given to sadness and to gloom,
And for the fact will vouch,—one night
It chanced that by a taper's light
This man was reading in his room ;   740

Bending, as you or I might bend
At night o'er any pious book,
When sudden blackness overspread
The snow-white page on which he read,
And made the good man round him look. 745

The chamber walls were dark all round,—
And to his book he turned again ;
—The light had left the lonely taper,
And formed itself upon the paper
Into large letters—bright and plain !   750

The godly book was in his hand—
And on the page, more black than coal,
Appeared, set forth in strange array,
A *word*—which to his dying day
Perplexed the good man's gentle soul.   755

The ghostly word, thus plainly seen,
Did never from his lips depart ;
But he hath said, poor gentle wight !
It brought full many a sin to light
Out of the bottom of his heart.   760

Dread Spirits ! to confound the meek
Why wander from your course so far,
Disordering colour, form, and stature !
—Let good men feel the soul of nature,
And see things as they are.   765

Yet, potent Spirits! well I know,
How ye, that play with soul and sense,
Are not unused to trouble friends
Of goodness, for most gracious ends—
And this I speak in reverence!   770

But might I give advice to you,
Whom in my fear I love so well;
From men of pensive virtue go,
Dread Beings! and your empire show
On hearts like that of Peter Bell.   775

Your presence often have I felt
In darkness and the stormy night;
And with like force, if need there be,
Ye can put forth your agency
When earth is calm, and heaven is bright. 780

Then coming from the wayward world,
That powerful world in which ye dwell,
Come, Spirits of the Mind! and try,
To-night, beneath the moonlight sky,
What may be done with Peter Bell!   785

—O, would that some more skilful voice
My further labour might prevent!
Kind Listeners, that around me sit,
I feel that I am all unfit
For such high argument.   790

I've played, I've danced, with my narration;
I loitered long ere I began:
Ye waited then on my good pleasure;
Pour out indulgence still, in measure
As liberal as ye can!   795

Our Travellers, ye remember well,
Are thridding a sequestered lane;
And Peter many tricks is trying,
And many anodynes applying,
To ease his conscience of its pain.   800

By this his heart is lighter far;
And, finding that he can account
So snugly for that crimson stain,
His evil spirit up again
Does like an empty bucket mount.   805

And Peter is a deep logician
Who hath no lack of wit mercurial;
" Blood drops—leaves rustle—yet," quoth he,
" This poor man never but for me
Could have had Christian burial.   810

And, say the best you can, 'tis plain,
That here has been some wicked dealing;
No doubt the devil in me wrought;
I 'm not the man who could have thought
An Ass like this was worth the stealing!" 815

So from his pocket Peter takes
His shining horn tobacco-box;
And in a light and careless way,
As men who with their purpose play,
Upon the lid he knocks.   820

Let them whose voice can stop the clouds,
Whose cunning eye can see the wind,
Tell to a curious world the cause
Why, making here a sudden pause,
The Ass turned round his head and *grinned.* 825

Appalling process! I have marked
The like on heath, in lonely wood;
And, verily, have seldom met
A spectacle more hideous—yet
It suited Peter's present mood.　　　830

And, grinning in his turn, his teeth
He in jocose defiance showed—
When, to upset his spiteful mirth,
A murmur, pent within the earth,
In the dead earth beneath the road,　　835

Rolled audibly! it swept along,
A muffled noise—a rumbling sound!—
'Twas by a troop of miners made,
Plying with gunpowder their trade,
Some twenty fathoms underground.　　840

Small cause of dire effect! for, surely,
If ever mortal, King or Cotter,
Believed that earth was charged to quake
And yawn for his unworthy sake,
'Twas Peter Bell the Potter.　　845

But as an oak in breathless air
Will stand though to the centre hewn;
Or as the weakest things, if frost
Have stiffened them, maintain their post;
So he, beneath the gazing moon!—　　850

The Beast bestriding thus, he reached
A spot where, in a sheltering cove,
A little chapel stands alone,
With greenest ivy overgrown,
And tufted with an ivy grove;　　855

Dying insensibly away
From human thoughts and purposes,
It seemed—wall, window, roof and tower—
To bow to some transforming power,
And blend with the surrounding trees.   860

As ruinous a place it was,
Thought Peter, in the shire of Fife
That served my turn, when following still ·
From land to land a reckless will
I married my sixth wife!   865

The unheeding Ass moves slowly on,
And now is passing by an inn
Brim-full of a carousing crew,
That make, with curses not a few,
An uproar and a drunken din.   870

I cannot well express the thoughts
Which Peter in those noises found ;—;
A stifling power compressed his frame,
While-as a swimming darkness came
Over that dull and dreary sound.   875

For well did Peter know the sound;
The language of those drunken joys
To him, a jovial soul, I ween,
But a few hours ago, had been
A gladsome and a welcome noise.   880

Now, turned adrift into the past,
He finds no solace in his course;
Like planet-stricken men of yore,
He trembles, smitten to the core
By strong compunction and remorse.   885

But, more than all, his heart is stung
To think of one, almost a child;
A sweet and playful Highland girl,
As light and beauteous as a squirrel,
As beauteous and as wild!   890

Her dwelling was a lonely house,
A cottage in a heathy dell;
And she put on her gown of green,
And left her mother at sixteen,
And followed Peter Bell.   895

But many good and pious thoughts
Had she; and, in the kirk to pray,
Two long Scotch miles, through rain or snow,
To kirk she had been used to go,
Twice every Sabbath-day.   900

And, when she followed Peter Bell,
It was to lead an honest life;
For he, with tongue not used to falter,
Had pledged his troth before the altar
To love her as his wedded wife.   905

A mother's hope is hers;—but soon
She drooped and pined like one forlorn;
From Scripture she a name did borrow;
Benoni, or the child of sorrow,
She called her babe unborn.   910

For she had learned how Peter lived,
And took it in most grievous part;
She to the very bone was worn,
And, ere that little child was born,
Died of a broken heart.   915

And now the Spirits of the Mind
Are busy with poor Peter Bell;
Upon the rights of visual sense
Usurping, with a prevalence
More terrible than magic spell. 920

Close by a brake of flowering furze
(Above it shivering aspens play)
He sees an unsubstantial creature,
His very self in form and feature,
Not four yards from the broad highway: 925

And stretched beneath the furze he sees
The Highland girl—it is no other;
And hears her crying as she cried,
The very moment that she died.
"My mother! oh my mother!" 930

The sweat pours down from Peter's face,
So grievous is his heart's contrition;
With agony his eye-balls ache
While he beholds by the furze-brake
This miserable vision! 935

Calm is the well-deserving brute,
His peace hath no offence betrayed;
But now, while down that slope he wends,
A voice to Peter's ear ascends,
Resounding from the woody glade: 940

The voice, though clamorous as a horn
Re-echoed by a naked rock,
Comes from that tabernacle—List!
Within, a fervent Methodist
Is preaching to no heedless flock! 945

"Repent! repent!" he cries aloud,
"While yet ye may find mercy;—strive
To love the Lord with all your might;
Turn to him, seek him day and night,
And save your souls alive!   950

Repent! repent! though ye have gone,
Through paths of wickedness and woe,
After the Babylonian harlot;
And though your sins be red as scarlet,
They shall be white as snow!"   955

Even as he passed the door, these words
Did plainly come to Peter's ears;
And they such joyful tidings were,
The joy was more than he could bear!—
He melted into tears.   960

Sweet tears of hope and tenderness!
And fast they fell, a plenteous shower!
His nerves, his sinews seemed to melt;
Through all his iron frame was felt
A gentle, a relaxing, power!   965

Each fibre of his frame was weak;
Weak all the animal within;
But, in its helplessness, grew mild
And gentle as an infant child,
An infant that has known no sin.   970

'Tis said, meek Beast! that, through Heaven's
    grace,
He not unmoved did notice now
The cross upon thy shoulder scored,
For lasting impress, by the Lord
To whom all human-kind shall bow;   975

Memorial of his touch—that day
When Jesus humbly deigned to ride,
Entering the proud Jerusalem,
By an immeasurable stream
Of shouting people deified!   980

Meanwhile the persevering Ass
Turned towards a gate that hung in view
Across a shady lane; his chest
Against the yielding gate he pressed
And quietly passed through.   985

And up the stony lane he goes;
No ghost more softly ever trod;
Among the stones and pebbles he
Sets down his hoofs inaudibly,
As if with felt his hoofs were shod.   990

Along the lane the trusty Ass
Went twice two hundred yards or more,
And no one could have guessed his aim,—
Till to a lonely house he came,
And stopped beside the door.   995

Thought Peter, 'tis the poor man's home!
He listens—not a sound is heard
Save from the trickling household rill;
But, stepping o'er the cottage-sill,
Forthwith a little Girl appeared.   1000

She to the Meeting-house was bound
In hopes some tidings there to gather:
No glimpse it is, no doubtful gleam;
She saw—and uttered with a scream,
" My father! here's my father!"   1005

The very word was plainly heard,
Heard plainly by the wretched Mother—
Her joy was like a deep affright:
And forth she rushed into the light
And saw it was another!   1010

And instantly upon the earth,
Beneath the full moon shining bright,
Close to the Ass's feet she fell;
At the same moment Peter Bell
Dismounts in most unhappy plight.   1015

As he beheld the Woman lie
Breathless and motionless, the mind
Of Peter sadly was confused;
But, though to such demands unused,
And helpless almost as the blind,   1020

He raised her up; and while he held
Her body propped against his knee,
The Woman waked—and when she spied
The poor Ass standing by her side,
She moaned most bitterly.   1025

"Oh! God be praised—my heart's at ease—
For he is dead—I know it well!"
—At this she wept a bitter flood;
And, in the best way that he could,
His tale did Peter tell.   1030

He trembles—he is pale as death;
His voice is weak with perturbation;
He turns aside his head, he pauses;
Poor Peter from a thousand causes
Is crippled sore in his narration.   1035

At length she learned how he espied
The Ass in that small meadow-ground;
And that her Husband now lay dead,
Beside that luckless river's bed
In which he had been drowned.   1040

A piercing look the Widow cast
Upon the Beast that near her stands;
She sees 'tis he, that 'tis the same;
She calls the poor Ass by his name,
And wrings, and wrings her hands.   1045

"O wretched loss—untimely stroke!
If he had died upon his bed!
He knew not one forewarning pain;
He never will come home again—
Is dead, for ever dead!"   1050

Beside the Woman Peter stands;
His heart is opening more and more;
A holy sense pervades his mind;
He feels what he for human-kind
Had never felt before.   1055

At length, by Peter's arm sustained,
The Woman rises from the ground—
"Oh, mercy! something must be done,
My little Rachel, you must run,—
Some willing neighbour must be found.   1060

Make haste—my little Rachel—do,
The first you meet with—bid him come,
Ask him to lend his horse to-night,
And this good Man, whom Heaven requite,
Will help to bring the body home."   1065

Away goes Rachel weeping loud;—
An Infant, waked by her distress,
Makes in the house a piteous cry;
And Peter hears the Mother sigh,
" Seven are they, and all fatherless!"   1070

And now is Peter taught to feel
That man's heart is a holy thing;
And Nature, through a world of death,
Breathes into him a second breath,
More searching than the breath of spring. 1075

Upon a stone the Woman sits
In agony of silent grief—
From his own thoughts did Peter start;
He longs to press her to his heart,
From love that cannot find relief.   1080

But roused, as if through every limb
Had past a sudden shock of dread,
The Mother o'er the threshold flies,
And up the cottage stairs she hies,
And on the pillow lays her burning head. 1085

And Peter turns his steps aside
Into a shade of darksome trees,
Where he sits down, he knows not how,
With his hands pressed against his brow,
His elbows on his tremulous knees.   1090

There, self-involved, does Peter sit
Until no sign of life he makes,
As if his mind were sinking deep
Through years that have been long asleep!
The trance is passed away—he wakes;   1095

He lifts his head—and sees the Ass
Yet standing in the clear moonshine;
"When shall I be as good as thou?
Oh! would, poor beast, that I had now
A heart but half as good as thine!"   1100

But *He*—who deviously hath sought
His Father through the lonesome woods,
Hath sought, proclaiming to the ear
Of night his grief and sorrowful fear—
He comes, escaped from fields and floods;—   1105

With weary pace is drawing nigh;
He sees the Ass—and nothing living
Had ever such a fit of joy
As hath this little orphan Boy,
For he has no misgiving!   1110

Forth to the gentle Ass he springs,
And up about his neck he climbs;
In loving words he talks to him,
He kisses, kisses face and limb,—
He kisses him a thousand times!   1115

This Peter sees, while in the shade
He stood beside the cottage-door;
And Peter Bell, the ruffian wild,
Sobs loud, he sobs even like a child,
"Oh! God, I can endure no more!"   1120

—Here ends my Tale: for in a trice
Arrived a neighbour with his horse;
Peter went forth with him straightway;
And, with due care, ere break of day,
Together they brought back the Corse.   1125

II.   S

And many years did this poor Ass,
Whom once it was my luck to see
Cropping the shrubs of Leming-Lane,
Help by his labour to maintain
The Widow and her family.   1130

And Peter Bell, who, till that night,
Had been the wildest of his clan,
Forsook his crimes, renounced his folly,
And, after ten months' melancholy,
Became a good and honest man.   1135

                                        1798.

NOTES.

A Morning Exercise (page 3).

Written at Rydal Mount. I could wish the last five stanzas of this to be read with the poem addressed to the skylark.—I. F.

Dated by Wordsworth 1828 ; first published 1832. The last stanza but two ("To the last point of vision") was transferred in 1845 to its present position from the poem (first printed 1827, written 1825), "To a Skylark," beginning "Ethereal minstrel! pilgrim of the sky!" The other changes are slight. In line 20 "grief" (1836) was " griefs" (1832). Lines 51, 52 (1836); in 1832 :

" The harmony that thou best lovest to make
Where earth resembles most his blank domain !"—ED.

A Flower Garden (page 5).

Planned by my friend, Lady Beaumont, in connection with the garden at Coleorton.—I. F.

Dated by Wordsworth 1824; first published 1827 with the title "A Flower Garden," the place being first named in 1836. Lines 26-29 (1836); previously :

" So subtly is the eye beguiled
It sees not nor suspects a Bound,
No more than in some forest wild ;
Free as the light in semblance—crost "—ED.

" A whirl-blast from behind the hill " (page 7).

Observed in the holly-grove at Alfoxden, where these verses were written in the spring of 1799. I had the pleasure of again seeing, with dear friends, this grove in unimpaired beauty forty-one years after.—I. F.

Written 1798 ; first published 1800. Wordsworth

says that the verses were written in the holly-grove at
Alfoxden in the spring of 1799; but he left Alfoxden for
Germany in 1798, and the date 1799 is erroneous. We
read in Dorothy Wordsworth's Journal, March 18,
1798, "On our return [from Nether Stowey to Alfoxden],
sheltered under the hollies during a hailshower. The
withered leaves danced with the hailstones. William
wrote a description of the storm"—probably this poem.
It was altered 1 August, 1800, as noted in Dorothy's
Journal. Two judicious omissions were made from the
1800 text. After l. 22 these four lines closing the poem
are found, 1800-1805:

> "Oh! grant me Heaven a heart at ease
> That I may never cease to find,
> Even in appearances like these
> Enough to nourish and to stir my mind!"
> (Omitted 1815.)

In edd. 1800-1815, between l. 10 and l. 11, came the line
(omitted 1820):

> "You could not lay a hair between:"

Ll. 21, 22 (1815); previously:

> "And all these leaves, that jump and spring,
> Were each a joyous living thing."—ED.

The Waterfall and the Eglantine (page 8).

Suggested nearer to Grasmere, on the same mountain
track as that referred to in the following Note. The
eglantine remained many years afterwards, but is now
gone.—I. F.

Dated by Wordsworth 1800; first published 1800.
Wordsworth's statement in the Fenwick note, together
with the date of his arrival at Grasmere and that of pub-
lication, establishes the date given as correct. The exact
spot can be determined: "the Eglantine grew on the
little brook that runs past two cottages (close to the path
under Nab Scar)."—Knight. Here on Aug. 23, 1802,
while Wordsworth was left "sitting on the stones, feast-
ing with silence," Dorothy and S. T. Coleridge "sat down
upon a rocky seat—a couch it might be, under the bower
of William's eglantine, Andrew's Broom."—Dorothy's
Journal.

Ll. 52, 53 gave Wordsworth considerable trouble:

" The stream came thundering down the dell
And gallop'd loud and fast;" (1800)

" The Torrent thundered down the dell
With unabating haste;" (1815)

" The Torrent thundered down the dell
With aggravated haste;" (1827)

" The stream came thundering down the dell
With aggravated haste;" (1836)

The present reading is of 1842. Boldness in these readings was followed by tameness, by infelicity, and finally by felicity.

In l. 2 "angry" (1836) replaced "thundering." Lines 5, 6 (1820); previously:

" A falling Water swoln with snows
Thus spake to a poor Briar-rose,"

In l. 23 " sequestered" (1820) replaced " natal," which was hardly applicable to the torrent. Did l. 15, " The Flood was tyrannous and strong," suggest a reading for the later text of " The Ancient Mariner ?"

" And now the Storm-blast came and he
Was tyrannous and strong."—ED.

The Oak and the Broom (page 10).

Suggested upon the mountain pathway that leads from Upper Rydal to Grasmere. The ponderous block of stone which is mentioned in the poem remains, I believe, to this day, a good way up Nab-Scar. Broom grows under it, and in many places on the side of the precipice.—I. F.

Dated by Wordsworth 1800; first published 1800. The same evidence given in note on " The Waterfall and the Eglantine" proves that the date is correct. Crabb Robinson (" Diary," Sept. 11, 1816), recording Words-worth's conversation, writes: " The fable of *The Oak and the Broom* proceeded from his beholding a rose in just such a situation as he described the broom to be in." The changes of text are not extensive. In l. 6 " roaring" (1820) replaced " thundering." L. 19, " a giant and a sage" (1815) was an improvement on " half giant and half sage" (1800-1805). Ll. 36, 37 (1820) replaced:

"It came, you know, with fire and smoke
And hitherward it bent [hither did it bend, 1800]
    its way." (1802-5.)

Ll. 41-44 (1836) replaced:

"The Thing had better been asleep,
Whatever thing it were,
Or Breeze, or Bird, or Dog, or Sheep,
That first did plant you there," (1802)

of which reading the third line varied from 1800: "Or Breeze, or Bird, or fleece of Sheep."

Ll. 75, 76 (1815) replace (the broom being a plant of summer bloom):

"The Spring for me a garland weaves
Of yellow flowers and verdant leaves." (1800-1805.)

L. 100 (1815) is probably intended as another correction in Natural History, the broom not flowering, and so not affording honey, in March:

"Two stripling bees
To feed and murmur there." (1800-1805.)—ED.

To a Sexton (page 14).

Written in Germany.—I. F.

Dated by Wordsworth 1799; first published 1800. Having been written in Germany, it belongs to the early part of the year. In l. 23 "Thou, too heedless," (1845) replaced "Thou, old Grey-Beard" (1800-1843).—ED.

To the Daisy (page 15).

This poem, and two others to the same flower, were written in the year 1802; which is mentioned, because in some of the ideas, though not in the manner in which those ideas are connected, and likewise even in some of the expressions, there is a resemblance to passages in a poem (lately published) of Mr. Montgomery's, entitled "A Field Flower." This being said, Mr. Montgomery will not think any apology due to him; I cannot, however, help addressing him in the words of the Father of English Poets.

"Though it happe me to rehersin
That ye han in your freshe songis saied,

Forberith me, and beth not ill apaied,
Sith that ye se I doe it in the honour
Of Love, and eke in service of the Flour."
1807.—W. W.

This and the two following were composed in the
orchard, Town-end, Grasmere, where the bird was often
seen as here described.—I. F.

Dated by Wordsworth 1802; first published 1807.
This is one of three poems to the Daisy published in
the volumes of 1807. In edd. 1836-49 Wordsworth
assigned this poem to 1802; the poem, " To the Same
Flower," beginning " With little here to do and see," to
1805; and the poem, " To the Daisy " (transferred in
1836 from " Poems of the Fancy " to " Poems of Senti-
ment and Reflection "), beginning " Bright Flower! whose
home is everywhere," to 1803. But it is certain that the
three poems belong to 1802. (1) In the Fenwick note to
" Bright Flower!" Wordsworth says that they were all
" composed at Townend, Grasmere, *during the earlier
part of my residence there;*" (2) in a footnote of the
Poems, 1807, ii. 93, he says (of " With little here to do
and see," and " Bright Flower!"): '' The two following
Poems were overflowings of the mind in composing the
one which stands first in the first volume " (*i.e.*, " In youth
from rock to rock I went "); (3) the note of 1807 printed
above fixes the date. The quotation from Wither was
prefixed in 1815. In that year and in 1827 a few changes
of the 1807 text were effected; the principal rehandling
was in 1836. Lines 7, 8 are a return (1843) to the 1807
text; in 1836:

" And Nature's love of thee partake,
Her much-loved Daisy!"

Lines 9-12 (1836); previously:

" When soothed a while by milder airs,
Thee Winter in the garland wears
That thinly shades his few grey hairs;
Spring cannot shun thee; " (1807.)

" When Winter decks his few grey hairs
Thee in the scanty wreath he wears;
Spring parts the clouds with softest airs,
That she may sun thee; " (1827.)

Lines 19-21 (1836) stood thus in 1807 :

> "If welcome [welcom'd 1815, 1820] once thou
> count'st it gain ;
> Thou art not daunted,
> Nor car'st if thou be set at naught ; "

Lines 57-64 stood thus in 1807 :

> " When, smitten by the morning ray,
> I see thee rise alert and gay,
> Then, chearful Flower! my spirits play
> With kindred motion :
> At dusk, I've seldom mark'd thee press
> The ground, as if in thankfulness,
> Without some feeling, more or less,
> Of true devotion."

The first two lines of this stanza were altered to the
present text in 1836 ; the last four lines in 1815. The
last stanza of the poem dates from 1836. The text of
1807, containing a memorable phrase, " bold lover of the
sun," was as follows :

> " Child of the Year! that round dost run
> Thy course, bold lover of the sun,
> And chearful when the day's begun
> As morning Leveret,
> Thou long the Poet's praise shalt gain ;
> Thou wilt be more belov'd by men
> In times to come ; thou not in vain
> Art Nature's Favourite."

Altered in 1815 to :

> " Thy long-lost praise thou shalt regain ;
> Dear shalt thou be to future men
> As in old time ; "—ED.

To the Same Flower (*page* 18).

Written 1802, dated erroneously by Wordsworth 1805
(see note to preceding poem) ; first published 1807. The
changes of text are slight. Line 3 (1845) was :

> " Sweet Daisy! oft I talk to thee," (1807-32.)

> " Yet once again I talk to thee." (1836-43.)

Lines 9, 10 (1820) were previously :

> " Oft do I sit by thee at ease,
> And weave a web of similies." (*sic*)

In l. 41 "Bright" (1836) replaced "Sweet."—ED.

The Green Linnet (*page* 20).

Dated by Wordsworth 1803; first published 1807. The first and last stanzas were rehandled; the intermediate stanzas left untouched (except l. 25, "Upon", 1845, for earlier "Amid"). The first stanza dates from 1815 (with "flowers and birds," 1815-20, in line 7 for the present "birds and flowers," 1827-49); in 1807 it ran :

> " The May is come again :—how sweet
> To sit upon my Orchard-seat !
> And Birds and Flowers once more to greet,
>   My last year's Friends together :
> My thoughts they all by turns employ ;
> A whispering Leaf is now my joy,
> And then a Bird will be the toy
>   That doth my fancy tether."

The last stanza was retouched in 1820, 1827, 1832, 1843, 1845 :

> " While thus before my eyes he gleams,
> A Brother of the Leaves he seems ;
> When in a moment forth he teems
>   His little song in gushes :
> And if it pleas'd him to disdain
> And mock the Form which he did feign,
> While he was dancing with the train
>   Of Leaves among the bushes." (1807.)

Line 6 of this stanza became in 1820 : " The voiceless Form he chose to feign." The present text of the stanza was reached in 1827 with the exception of its first two lines. The several forms of these lines were :

> " My sight he dazzles, half deceives,
> A bird so like the dancing Leaves." (1827.)

> " My dazzled sight the Bird deceives
> A Brother of the dancing leaves." (1832-36.)

> " The Bird my dazzled sight deceives
> A Brother of the dancing leaves." (1843.)

> "My dazzled sight he oft deceives
> A Brother of the dancing leaves." (1845.)

Dorothy Wordsworth, in her Journal, May 28, 1802, thus describes the birds in the orchard : " We sate in the orchard . . . The young bulfinches, in their party-coloured raiment, bustle about among the blossoms, and poise themselves like wire-dancers or tumblers, shaking the twigs and dashing off the blossoms." See also in " The Kitten and the Falling Leaves " the passage beginning " Where is he the giddy Sprite ? "—ED.

To a Skylark (page 21).

Dated by Wordsworth 1805; first published 1807. The following note from Wordsworth's MS. is given by Knight : " Rydal Mount, 1825, where there are no sky-larks; but the poet is everywhere." Down to l. 25 the present text differs little from 1807 : l. 5 (1827) was pre-viously " With clouds and sky about thee ringing;" l. 10 (1815) had in 1807 " soul" for " wings;" l. 14 (1832) was previously " Up with me, up with me, high and high." After l. 25 ("Joy and jollity be with us both!") followed in 1807 :

> " Hearing thee, or else some other,
>   As merry a Brother,
> I on the earth will go plodding on,
> By myself, chearfully, till the day is done."

And so the poem ended. In 1820 for these lines was substituted the following :

> " What though my course be rugged and uneven,
> To prickly moors and dusty ways confined,
> Yet hearing thee, or others of thy kind,
> As full of gladness and as free of heaven,
> I on the earth will go plodding on,
> By myself, cheerfully, till the day is done."

In 1827 the first seven lines of the poem were given (to " The spot that seems so," &c.,) ; from l. 8 to l. 25 was omitted ; and the last six lines of the present text, placed immediately after the first seven lines, completed the poem. In 1832 the omitted lines, 8-25, were restored. —ED.

To the small Celandine (page 22).

Written at Town-end, Grasmere. It is remarkable that this flower, coming out so early in the spring as it does, and so bright and beautiful, and in such profusion, should not have been noticed earlier in English verse. What adds much to the interest that attends it is its habit of shutting itself up and opening out according to the degree of light and temperature of the air.—I. F.

Written April 30, 1802; erroneously dated by Wordsworth 1803; first published 1807. Dorothy Wordsworth writes in her Journal, April 30, 1802: "We came into the orchard directly after breakfast and sat there. The lake was calm, the sky cloudy. William began to write the poem of the Celandine . . . I walked backwards and forwards with William. He repeated his poem to me. Then he got to work again, and would not give over." In l. 16 "sage" (1836) replaces "great." In l. 27 "her" (1836) replaces "its." In 1836-43, after l. 40 is given a stanza transferred in 1845-49 to the next following poem, "To the Same Flower," the stanza beginning "Drawn by what peculiar spell;" it may be given here with its earlier readings (1836-43):

> "Drawn by what peculiar spell,
> By what charm for sight or smell,
> Do those wingèd dim-eyed creatures,
> Labourers sent from waxen cells,
> Settle on thy brilliant features,
> In neglect of buds and bells
> Opening daily at thy side,
> By the season multiplied?"

Line 58 (1836) was previously "Scorned and slighted upon earth." Lines 61, 62 (1836) were previously:

> "Singing at my heart's command,
> In the lanes my thoughts pursuing."—ED.

To the Same Flower (page 25).

Written May 1, 1802; erroneously dated by Wordsworth 1803; first published 1807. In Dorothy Wordsworth's Journal, May 1, 1802, we find: "William wrote the Celandine, second part" (Knight's "Wordsworth," ii., 272). In l. 14 "rising sun" (1836) was previously "risen sun." In l. 38 "sheltering" (1832) was previously "shelter'd." A like change of the same word was made (1836) in "Goody Blake." L. 39 (1845) was previously "Bright as any of the train." For the transfer of the sixth stanza and its earlier readings see note on preceding poem, "To the small Celandine." Lines 51-53 in 1807 ran :

> "Let, as old Magellen [Magellan, 1815] did,
> Others roam about the sea ;
> Build who will a pyramid."

> "Let, with bold advent'rous skill,
> Others thrid the polar sea ;
> Rear a pyramid who will." (1820.)

> "Let the bold Adventurer thrid
> In his bark the polar sea ;
> Rear who will a pyramid ;" (1827.)

"Discoverer" replaced "Adventurer" in 1845. Words-worth promised Barron Field that "Old Magellan" should be restored, but the promise was not fulfilled.—ED.

The Seven Sisters (page 27).

The story of this poem is from the German of Frederica Brun.— W. W.

Written 1800 ; in Dorothy Wordsworth's Journal, Aug. 17, 1800, we find : "William read us 'The Seven Sisters ;'" erroneously dated by Wordsworth 1804 (in edd. 1836-43) and 1803 (in edd. 1845-49) ; first published 1807. Text unchanged except in l. 3, "You" (1836) for the earlier "I." Friderike Brun, from whom the story is derived, lived from 1765 to 1835. The name Binnorie is found in the well-known ballad, "The twa' sisters of Binnorie."—ED.

"Who fancied what a pretty sight" (page 29).

Dated by Wordsworth 1803 ; first published 1807, in the group, "Moods of my own Mind." The only changes of text are in l. 8, "gentle" (1836) for the earlier "love-sick," and l. 14, "each and all," 1827 reverting to 1807, after "each or all" of edd. 1815-20.—ED.

The Redbreast chasing the Butterfly (page 30).

Observed, as described, in the then beautiful orchard, Town-end, Grasmere.—I. F.

Written April 18, 1802 ; erroneously dated by Words-worth 1806 ; first published 1807 with the title, "The Redbreast and the Butterfly." In Dorothy Wordsworth's Journal, April 18, 1802 (Sunday), we find : " A mild grey morning with rising vapours.   We sate in the orchard.   William wrote the poem on ' The Robin and the Butterfly' . . . William met me at Rydal with the conclusion of the poem to the Robin.   I read it to him in bed. We left out some lines."   It is perhaps worth noting that in l. 9 " the bird that " (1849) was preceded by "the Bird, whom " (1807-20), " the Bird, who " (1827-1845). In 1807, after l. 19 occurred the line, " His little heart is throbbing," omitted 1815 ; and, rhyming with this, after l. 20 came the line, " Our consecrated Robin !" omitted 1815.   After l. 34, in 1807 occurred the line (omitted 1815), " Like the hues of thy breast."   Lines 35, 36 (1815) were in 1807 :

> " His beautiful wings in crimson are drest,
> A brother he seems of thine own."

In the text of 1832 is found :

> " His beautiful bosom is drest
> In crimson as bright as thine own ; "

but in the errata of that edition the reading is cancelled and the text of 1815 is retained.

The footnote reference to "Paradise Lost " was added in 1815 under interesting circumstances detailed by De Quincey (see Masson's edition, iii. 26-29).—ED.

Song for the Spinning Wheel (page 31).

The belief on which this is founded I have often heard expressed by an old neighbour of Grasmere.—I F.

Dated by Wordsworth 1812 ; first published 1820.   In l. 8 " Couch " (1827) replaced " Rest."   Lines 11, 12 (1832), previously

> " With a motion smooth and fine
> Gathers "   (1820.)

> " Runs with motion smooth and fine
> Gathering "   (1827.)

Professor Knight notes that " It was for Sarah Hutchinson that this song was written."   Cf. Miscellaneous Sonnets, i. 20 (" To S. H.").—ED.

Hint from the Mountains (page 32).

Bunches of fern may often be seen wheeling about in the wind as here described.   The particular bunch that

suggested these verses was noticed in the Pass of Dunmail
Raise. The verses were composed in 1817, but the appli-
cation is for all times and places.—I. F.

Dated by Wordsworth 1817; first published 1820. The
present text dates from 1827. In 1820 l. 1 was " Stranger,
'tis a sight of pleasure ;" in l. 17 the first word was
" Traveller"; l. 22 was " See, when Commonwealth-
vexations"; and ll. 25-28 ran thus:

> " Such it is, and not a Haggard
> Soaring on undaunted wing ;
> 'Tis by nature dull and laggard,
> A poor helpless Thing."—ED.

On Seeing a Needle-case, &c. (page 33).

Dated by Wordsworth 1827; first published 1827.
" E. M. S." of the title is Southey's daughter, Edith
May. Text unchanged, except l. 12, " Such honour "
(1845) for " Like station" (1827); and in the last line
but one " shine " (1832); " shines" (1827).—ED.

To a Lady (page 35).

Dated conjecturally 1845; first published 1845. Text
unaltered.—ED.

Glad sight, &c. (page 36).

Dated conjecturally 1845; first published 1845. Text
unaltered.—ED.

The Contrast (page 37.)

The parrot belonged to Mrs. Luff while living at Fox-
Ghyll. The wren was one that haunted for many years
the summer-house between the two terraces at Rydal
Mount.—I. F.

Dated by Wordsworth 1825; first published 1827,
with the title " The Contrast;" present title, 1832. Text
unaltered, except in l. 39, " Proof that " (1836), previously
" That tells."—ED.

The Danish Boy (page 39.)

Written in Germany. It was entirely a fancy; but
intended as a prelude to a ballad-poem never written.
—I. F.

Dated by Wordsworth 1799 ; and (having been written in Germany) early in that year; first published 1800. Named, 1800-1832, " A Fragment." In 1827 the following note is given: " These stanzas were designed to introduce a Ballad upon the Story of a Danish Prince who had fled from Battle, and, for the sake of the valuables about him, was murdered by the Inhabitant of a Cottage in which he had taken refuge. The House fell under a curse, and the Spirit of the Youth, it was believed, haunted the Valley where the crime had been committed." The most important of many changes of text is the omission (1802) of a stanza, placed between the present st. iv and st. v, and found only in 1800 :

> " When near this blasted tree you pass,
> Two sods are plainly to be seen
> Close at its root, and each with grass
> Is cover'd fresh and green.
> Like turf upon a new-made grave
> These two green sods together lie,
> Nor heat, nor cold, nor rain, nor wind
> Can these two sods together bind,
> Nor sun, nor earth, nor sky,
> But side by side the two are laid,
> As if just sever'd by the spade."

In 1802, noticing that the Spirit wearing " a royal vest of fur " could not well be a shepherd or a herd-boy, Wordsworth reversed the sense of ll. 25, 26 in the earlier text :

> " A piping Shepherd he might be,
> A Herd-boy of the wood." (1800.)

In l. 8 " lonely " (1836) replaced " cottage." Lines 13-15 in 1800 ran :

> " He sings his blithest and his best;
> But in this lonesome nook the bird
> Did never build his nest."

In 1820 the bird becomes feminine, l. 13 : " She sings, regardless of her rest," and l. 15, " her nest."

In 1827 l. 13 assumed its present form.

L. 17 (1827) replaced " The bees borne on the breezy air"; and also in 1827 l. 20 replaces " Nor ever linger there." Ll. 35-37 (1836); previously:

> " He rests his harp upon his knee,
> And there in a forgotten tongue
> He warbles melody."

L. 38 (1820); previously:

"Of flocks and herds both far and near," (1800)
"Of flocks upon the neighbouring hills," (1802)

for the singular "hill" agrees better with the seclusion
of the Spirit's dell.   So late as 1845 a touch was added,
in l. 43, "he sings alone" replaced "he sits alone"
(1800-1843).—ED.

Song for the Wandering Jew (page 41).

Dated by Wordsworth 1800; first published 1800. The
present text and arrangement of stanzas is that of 1836.
In 1800 the poem consisted of five of the present seven
stanzas, with different readings and in a different order,
viz., stanzas 1, 3, 5, 4, 7 (in the order here given).   In
1827 the order was 1, 2, 3, 5, 4, 6, 7, the added stanzas
appearing first in this edition.   In 1836 stanzas 4 and 5
assume their present position.   The text of st. 1 is
unchanged; that of the last stanza is identical with 1800;
but 1815-1820 read:

"Never—never does the trouble
Of the Wanderer leave my soul."

Stanzas 2 and 6, added in 1827, were not altered.   In
stanza 5 the sex of the raven became feminine in 1827
("she" and "her" in l. 3 of st. 5 replacing "he" and
"his"); and in l. 4 of the same stanza "In" (1815)
replaces "On."   Stanzas 3 and 4 in 1800 stood thus:

"Though almost with eagle pinion
O'er the rocks the Chamois roam,
Yet he has some small dominion
Which no doubt he calls his home.

"Though the Sea-horse in the ocean
Own no dear domestic cave;
Yet he slumbers without motion
On the calm and silent wave."

Some variations in these stanzas are found in 1815;
the present text of st. 3 was attained in 1827, and that of
st. 4, which in 1827 exhibits new variations, was reached
in 1836.—ED.

Stray Pleasures (page 42).

Suggested on the Thames by the sight of one of those
floating mills that used to be seen there.   This I noticed

-on the Surrey side between Somerset House and Black-friars Bridge. Charles Lamb was with me at the time; and I thought it remarkable that I should have to point out to *him*, an idolatrous Londoner, a sight so interesting as the happy group dancing on the platform. Mills of this kind used to be, and perhaps still are, not uncommon on the Continent. I noticed several upon the river Saone in the year 1790, particularly near the town of Chalons, where my friend Jones and I halted a day when we crossed France; so far on foot: there we embarked and floated down to Lyons.—I. F.

Dated by Wordsworth 1806; first published 1807. It bore no title until 1820. Text unchanged except in l. 2, " that " (1827) for the earlier " which," and in l. 5 " gives room " (1820) for the earlier " there's room."—ED.

The Pilgrim's Dream (*page* 43).

I distinctly recollect the evening when these verses were suggested in 1818. It was on the road between Rydal and Grasmere, where glow-worms abound. A star was shining above the ridge of Loughrigg Fell, just opposite. I remember a critic, in some review or other, crying out against this piece. " What so monstrous," said he, " as to make a star talk to a glow-worm ! " Poor fellow ! we know from this sage observation what the " primrose on the river's brim " was to him.—I. F.

Dated by Wordsworth 1818; first published 1820. Changes of text are few. Line 21 (1827) was in 1820: " And *That* whose radiance gleam'd from far;" in l. 25 " humble " (1845) replaced " humbler "; l. 41 " But " (1827) replaced " Yet "; and l. 45 (1827) was in 1820: " But it behoves that thou shouldst know."—ED.

The Poet and the caged Turtledove (*page* 46).

Written at Rydal Mount. This dove was one of a pair that had been given to my daughter by our excellent friend, Miss Jewsbury, who went to India with her husband, Mr. Fletcher, where she died of cholera. The dove survived its mate many years, and was killed, to our great sorrow, by a neighbour's cat that got in at the window and dragged it partly out of the cage. These verses were composed extempore, to the letter, in the Terrace Summer-house before spoken of. It was the

T

habit of the bird to begin cooing and murmuring when-
ever it heard me making my verses.—I. F.

Dated by Wordsworth 1830; first published 1835.
Text unchanged. Prof. Knight says : " In a MS. letter
to Sir George Beaumont I find the poem entitled,
'Twenty Minutes Exercise on the Terrace last night, but
scene within doors.'" If the date 1830 be correct, this
letter must be to the younger Sir G. Beaumont, the elder
having died in Feb. 1827.—ED.

A Wren's Nest (page 47).

Written at Rydal Mount. This nest was built, as
described, in a tree that grows near the pool in Dora's
field next the Rydal Mount garden.—I. F.

Dated by Wordsworth 1833; first published 1835.
Text unchanged.—ED.

Love lies Bleeding (page 50).

It has been said that the English, though their country
has produced so many great poets, is now the most un-
poetical nation in Europe. It is probably true ; for they
have more temptation to become so than any other
European people. Trade, commerce, and manufactures,
physical science, and mechanic arts, out of which so much
wealth has arisen, have made our countrymen infinitely
less sensible to movements of imagination and fancy than
were our forefathers in their simple state of society. How
touching and beautiful were, in most instances, the names
they gave to our indigenous flowers, or any other they
were familiarly acquainted with!—Every month for
many years have we been importing plants and flowers
from all quarters of the globe, many of which are spread
through our gardens, and some perhaps likely to be met
with on the few Commons which we have left. Will
their botanical names ever be displaced by plain English
appellations, which will bring them home to our hearts by
connection with our joys and sorrows ? It can never be,
unless society treads back her steps towards those simpli-
cities which have been banished by the undue influence of
towns spreading and spreading in every direction, so that
city-life with every generation takes more and more the
lead of rural. Among the ancients, villages were
reckoned the seats of barbarism. Refinement, for the
most part false, increases the desire to accumulate

wealth; and while theories of political economy are boastfully pleading for the practice, inhumanity pervades all our dealings in buying and selling. This selfishness wars against disinterested imagination in all directions, and, evils coming round in a circle, barbarism spreads in every quarter of our island. Oh for the reign of justice, and then the humblest man among us would have more power and dignity in and about him than the highest have now.—I. F.

Neither this nor the poem which immediately follows, " Companion to the Foregoing," is dated by Wordsworth; we date both conjecturally 1845 ; first published 1845. Text unchanged.—ED.

Rural Illusions (page 52).

Written at Rydal Mount. Observed a hundred times in the grounds there.—I. F.

Dated by Wordsworth 1832; first published 1835. No change of text except l. 15 (1836); in 1835, " Which sprinkles here these tiny flowers."—ED.

The Kitten and Falling Leaves (page 53).

Seen at Town-end, Grasmere. The elder-bush has long since disappeared : it hung over the wall near the cottage; and the kitten continued to leap up, catching the leaves as here described. The infant was Dora.—I. F.

Dated by Wordsworth 1804 ; first published 1807. There is one interesting change of text; in 1849 Wordsworth, after his daughter's death in July, 1847, seemed to wish to acknowledge the connection of this poem with her infancy, and in l. 104 changed " Laura's " (1807-1843) to " Dora's." See note on title of the next poem. L. 69 (1836), previously, " Hung with head towards the ground." In Crabb Robinson's " Diary," Sept. 11, 1816, " He [Wordsworth] quoted some of . . . ' The Kitten and the Falling Leaves ' to show he had connected even the kitten with the great, awful, and mysterious powers of nature."—ED.

Address to my Infant Daughter Dora (page 57).

Written Sept. 16, 1804 ; first published 1815. Text unchanged. The name " Dora " was added to the title in 1849, after Dora's death. See note on " The Kitten and the Falling Leaves."—ED.

The Waggoner (*page* 60).

Several years after the event that forms the subject of the poem, in company with my friend, the late Mr. Coleridge, I happened to fall in with the person to whom the name of Benjamin is given. Upon our expressing regret that we had not, for a long time, seen upon the road either him or his waggon, he said:—"They could not do without me; and as to the man who was put in my place, no good could come out of him; he was a man of no *ideas*."

The fact of my discarded hero's getting the horses out of a great difficulty with a word, as related in the poem, was told me by an eye-witness.—W. W.

Written at Town-end, Grasmere. The characters and story from fact.—I. F.

" *The buzzing dor-hawk, round and round, is wheeling* "
(*page* 60).

When the poem was first written the note of the bird was thus described:

> " The Night-hawk is singing his frog-like tune,
> Twirling his watchman's rattle about—"

but from unwillingness to startle the reader at the outset by so bold a mode of expression, the passage was altered as it now stands.—W. W.

After the line, " *Can any mortal clog come to her,*" (p. 74) followed in the MS. an incident which has been kept back. Part of the suppressed verses shall here be given as a gratification of private feeling, which the well-disposed reader will find no difficulty in excusing. They are now printed for the first time.

> " Can any mortal clog come to her ?
> It can : . . .

> *   *   *   *

> But Benjamin, in his vexation,
> Possesses inward consolation;
> He knows his ground, and hopes to find
> A spot with all things to his mind,
> An upright mural block of stone,
> Moist with pure water trickling down.

A slender spring ; but kind to man
It is, a true Samaritan;
Close to the highway, pouring out
Its offering from a chink or spout ;
Whence all, howe'er athirst, or drooping
With toil, may drink, and without stooping.

Cries Benjamin " Where is it, where ?
Voice it hath none, but must be near."
—A star, declining towards the west,
Upon the watery surface threw
Its image tremulously imprest,
That just marked out the object and withdrew :
Right welcome service ! . . .

    *   *   *   *   *   *

                    Rock of Names !
Light is the strain, but not unjust
To Thee and Thy memorial-trust
That once seemed only to express
Love that was love in idleness;
Tokens, as year hath followed year
How changed, alas, in character !
For they were graven on thy smooth breast
By hands of those my soul loved best ;
Meek women, men as true and brave
As ever went to a hopeful grave :
Their hands and mine, when side by side
With kindred zeal and mutual pride,
We worked until the Initials took
Shapes that defied a scornful look.—
Long as for us a genial feeling
Survives, or one in need of healing,
The power, dear Rock, around thee cast,
Thy monumental power, shall last
For me and mine ! O thought of pain,
That would impair it or profane !
Take all in kindness then, as said
With a staid heart but playful head ;
And fail not Thou, loved Rock ! to keep
Thy charge when we are laid asleep."—W. W.

Dated by Wordsworth 1805; first published 1819. It
was classed in 1820, 1832, 1845, 1849 among "Poems of
the Fancy;" in 1827 among "Poems founded on the
Affections;" in 1836, 1843 not classed, but placed between
" Poems founded on the Affections " and " Poems of the

Fancy." The central fact about the text is that after
some slight changes in earlier editions, Wordsworth
altered it materially in 1836; and in many instances
returned in 1845-49 to the readings of 1819.

CANTO I.

Ll. 3-6 now as in 1819, were altered in 1820 and 1836:

" The dor-hawk, solitary bird,
Round the dim crags on heavy pinions wheeling,
Buzzes incessantly, a tiresome tune;
That constant voice is all that can be heard
In silence deeper far than that of deepest noon!"
(1820.)

Of this version the third and fourth lines became in
1836:

" With untired voice sings an unvaried tune;
Those burring notes are all that can be heard."

Ll. 7-12, now as in 1819, were expanded thus in 1836:

" Now that the children's busiest schemes
Do all lie buried in blank sleep,
Or only live in stirring dreams,
The glow-worms fearless watch may keep;
Rich prize as their bright lamps would be,
They shine a quiet company,
On mossy bank by cottage-door,
As safe as on the loneliest moor.
In hazy straits the clouds between,
And in their stations twinkling not,
Some thinly-sprinkled stars are seen,
Each changed into a pallid spot."

The lines in 1819-27 corresponding to ll. 13, 14 (now
as in 1836) followed the present l. 19:

" The mountains rise to wonderous height,
And in the heavens there is [hangs, 1827 a
weight;" (1820.)

In l. 17 " tired" (1819) became " faint" in 1836; and
l. 20, " the dews" (1819) became " welcome dews"
(1836).

For ll. 32-37, now as in 1819, the following appeared
in 1836:

> "Listen! you can hardly hear!
> Now he has left the lower ground,
> And up the hill his course is bending,
> With many a stop and stay ascending;"—

L. 41, "so" (1836), "now" (1819-32); l. 44, "recover-
ing" (1836), "gathering" (1819-32).

Ll. 50, 51 (now as in 1819) were in 1836:

> "No;—him infirmities beset,
> But danger is not near him yet;"

L. 71, "walks" (1836-49), "is" (1819-32); l. 83,
"right well" (1836-49), "full well" (1819-32).

For ll. 89, 90 (1836) stood in 1819:

> "Uncouth although the object be,
> An image of perplexity;
> Yet not the less it is our boast,
> For it was painted by the Host;"

L. 94, "sing" (1827), "frame" (1819)
L. 111 (1836) was previously, "And never was my
heart more light."
L. 113, "has blest" (1836), "will bless" (1819).
L. 114, "content" (1836), "delight" (1819). L. 120,
"full proof" (1836), "good proof" (1819).
Ll. 121-123 (1836); previously:

> "One day, when ye were vex'd and strain'd—
> Entrusted to another's care,
> And forced unworthy stripes to bear."

Ll. 124-128 (1836); previously:

> "Here was it—on this rugged spot
> Which now contented with our lot
> We climb—that piteously abused
> Ye plung'd in anger and confused."

L. 131, "that" (1836), "your" (1819).
L. 133, "Ye pulled together" (1836); "The ranks
were taken" (1819).
L. 139, now as in 1819; in 1836, "Our road be narrow,
steep, and rough."
L. 156, "rain-drops on" (1836), "drops upon" (1819).

Ll. 158, 159 (1836) were previously:

> "He starts—and, at the admonition
> Takes a survey of his condition."

L. 164 (1836); previously: "A huge and melancholy room."

L. 173, "aloft" (1836); "on high" (1819).

Ll. 184-187 (1836) were added in 1820, with "sounded through the trees" in l. 185, and "Was felt throughout the region bare," as l. 187.

L. 197 (1836); previously: "By peals of thunder, clap on clap!"

Ll. 198, 199 (1836); previously:

> "And many a terror-striking flash;—
> And somewhere, as it seems, a crash."

L. 201, "sullen" (1820); "rattling" (1819).

Ll. 225-228 (1836); previously:

> "The voice, to move commiseration,
> Prolong'd its earnest supplication—
> 'This storm that beats so furiously—
> This dreadful place! oh pity me!'
> While this was said, with sobs between,
> And many tears, by one unseen;"

L. 232, "without a question" (1836), previously, "without further question." Ed. 1836 reverses the lines 232, 233, reading:

> "And, kind to every way-worn rover,
> Benjamin, without a question,"

ed. 1845 reverts to the 1819 order.

L. 252, "terror" (1820), "trouble" (1819).

Ll. 264, 265 (1845), in 1819-32:

> "And to a little tent hard by
> Turns the rough Sailor instantly."

Expanded in 1836:

> "And to his tent-like domicile,
> Built in a nook with cautious skill,
> The Sailor turns, well pleased to spy
> His shaggy friend who stood hard by
> Drenched—and, more fast than with a tether,
> Bound to the nook by that fierce weather,
> Which caught the vagrants unaware:"

L. 269, "Tempted" (1836); "Had tempted" (1819).

CANTO II.

Ll. 14, 15 (1836); previously:

" Proceeding with an easy mind;
While he, who had been left behind,"

Ll. 25-28 (1820); in 1819 thus:

" Who neither heard nor saw—no more
Than if he had been deaf and blind,
Till, startled by the Sailor's roar,
He hears a sound and sees the light,"

Ll. 44-46 now as in 1819; in 1836-43:

".   .   .   dance, boys, dance
Rare luck for us! my honest soul,
I'll treat thee to a friendly bowl!"

Ll. 74, 75 (1836); previously:

" To *seek* for thoughts of painful cast,
If such be the amends at last."

L. 76, " say " (1836); " think " (1819).
L. 78, " of all," as in 1819; " among " (1836).
Ll. 80-83, now as in 1819; in 1836-1843:

" And happiest far is he, the One
No longer with himself at strife,
A Cæsar past the Rubicon!
The Sailor, Man by nature gay,
Found not a scruple in *his* way;"

Ll. 87, 88 (1836); previously:

" Deems that she is happier, laid
Within that warm and peaceful bed;"

Ll. 92, 93 (1845).   In 1819-32:

" With bowl in hand,
(It may not stand)
Gladdest of the gladsome band,"

In 1836-43:

" With bowl that sped from hand to hand,
Refreshed, brimful of hearty fun,
The gladdest of the gladsome band."

L. 96 (1836); previously, " They hear—when every fit is o'er."

L. 144, " marvellous " (1836); "wondrous" (1819).

CANTO III.

Ll. 60-63 (1836); previously:

" (The Mastiff not well pleased to be
So very near such company.)"

L. 85, "stems" (1836); " sails" (1819).
L. 121, " Upon" (1836); " On " (1819).
L. 129, " at the top" (1836); " in the height " (1819).
L. 136, " wheels " (1836); " wheel'd" (1819).

CANTO IV.

L. 23, " while she roves" (1827); "rambling on " (1819-1820).

L. 68, "lost amid a" (1845, as in 1819); "hidden by the " (1836-43).

Ll. 75-82 (1845). These lines are based on lines added in 1836, in which the remorseful interpretation of nature was made common to the Sailor and Benjamin; in 1845 "his" is substituted for " their" in ll. 77-82; and 75, 76 were altered from the reading:

" Say more : for by that power a vein
Seems opened of brow-saddening pain :" (1836-43.)

L. 83 (1845). See last note.

" They are drooping, weak and dull ;" (1819.)

"Drooping are they, and weak and dull ;" (1836.)

L. 88 (1836). The reading of 1819 : " Knowing that there's cause," was changed in 1827 to " Knowing there is cause."

Ll. 89, 90 (1845) :

" They are labouring to avert
At least a portion of the blame " (1819.)

" They now are labouring to avert
(Kind creatures !) something of the blame," (1836.)

Ll. 91-93 (1836). In 1819 : " Which full surely will

alight", with " faults," instead of " failings " in l. 93, and
" they love the best."

L. 104, " Blend " (1836), " Blends " (1819).

Ll. 108-113 (1845) gave Wordsworth many poetic
pains. The readings are :

> " Never, surely, old Apollo,
> He, or other God as old,
> Of whom in story we are told,
> Who had a favourite to follow
> Through a battle or elsewhere,
> Round the object of his care,
> In a time of peril, threw
> Veil of such celestial hue ;" (1819-27.)

> " Never Venus or Apollo,
> Pleased a favourite chief to follow
> Through accidents of peace or war,
> In a time of peril threw,
> Round the object of his care,
> Veil of such celestial hue ; " (1832.)

> " Never golden-haired Apollo,
> Nor blue-eyed Pallas, nor the Idalian Queen,
> When each was pleased some favourite chief to follow
> Through accidents of peace or war,
> In a perilous moment threw
> Around the object of celestial care
> A veil so rich to mortal view." (1836-43.)

Professor Knight gives yet another version from MS.

L. 125, " And " (1836), " Or " (1829); l. 128 (1845
returning to 1819), " If, as he cannot but forbode "
(1836); l. 129 " been loitering " (1836), " loitered "
(1819); l. 130 " His fears, his doubts " (1836), " His
doubts—his fears " (1819).

L. 213 (1827); previously two lines :

> " Sometimes, as in the present case,
> Will show a more familiar face;" (1819.)

> " Or, proud all rivalship to chase,
> Will haunt me with familiar face;" (1820.)

L. 253, " windows " (1836), " window " (1819).

Professor Knight traces the journey of the Waggoner
from Rydal to Keswick. " The Cherry Tree Tavern,
where the ' village Merry-night' was being celebrated,

still stands on the eastern or Helvellyn side of the road.
It is now a farm-house."

The Rock of Names, of which the passage given from
MS. in Wordsworth's note tells, is at Thirlmere, "on the
right hand of the road a short way past Waterhead." On
it were carved the initials of William Wordsworth, Mary
Hutchinson, Dorothy Wordsworth, S. T. Coleridge, John
Wordsworth, Sara Hutchinson. (See Knight's "The
English Lake District," ed. 1891, p. 218.)

" The master of the Waggon," writes Southey ("Life
and Correspondence," iv. 348), " was my poor landlord
Jackson; and the cause of his exchanging it for the one-
horse cart was just as is represented in the poem; nobody
but Benjamin could manage it upon these hills, and
Benjamin could not resist the temptations by the way-
side." For an account by S. T. Coleridge of Jackson's
excellence of character and his love of learning see " Life
and Correspondence of Southey," by his son, ii. 147, 148.
In Reminiscences by the Hon. Mr. Justice Coleridge,
printed in the Bishop of Lincoln's " Memoirs of Words-
worth " (ii. 310), he writes (1836): " ' The Waggoner '
seems a very favourite poem of his [Wordsworth's] . . .
He said his object in it had not been understood. It was
a play of the fancy on a domestic incident and lowly
character: he wished by the opening descriptive lines to
put his reader into the state of mind in which he wished
it to be read. If he failed in doing that, he wished him
to lay it down."—ED.

There was a Boy (page 86).

Written in Germany. This is an extract from the
poem on my own poetical education. This practice of
making an instrument of their own fingers is known to
most boys, though some are more skilful at it than others.
William Raincock of Rayrigg, a fine spirited lad, took the
lead of all my schoolfellows in this art.—I. F.

Written 1798; first published 1800. The poem,
written in Germany, was sent to Coleridge at Ratzeburg;
Coleridge, on Dec. 10, 1798, acknowledged its arrival:
" That

> ' Uncertain heaven received
> Into the bosom of the steady lake '

I should have recognized anywhere; and had I met these
lines running wild in the deserts of Arabia, I should have

instantly screamed out 'Wordsworth!'" " Memoirs of Wordsworth," i. 137. This poem forms part of the Fifth Book of " The Prelude." The most important change was effected in 1805. In 1800-1802 the fact of the boy's death is told in the closing line, after the mention of his grave : the line is bare and heavy with monosyllables :

" Mute—for he died when he was ten years old."

In 1805 the present text was substituted; the fact of the boy's death is stated in two lines inserted after l. 25 :

" This Boy was taken from his Mates, and died
In childhood, ere he was ten years old."

The mention of the grave is reserved for the closing line of the poem. The words, " ten years old," became in 1815 " full twelve years old." Lines 28, 29 date from 1845 : the readings of 1800 and 1843 are identical:

" Fair are the woods, and beauteous is the spot,
The vale where he was born ; the church-yard hangs."

The readings of 1827 and of " The Prelude " agree :

" Fair is the spot, most beautiful the vale
Where he was born ; the grassy church-yard hangs."

Lines 31-33 were in 1800 :

" And there, along that bank, when I have pass'd
At evening, I believe, that near his grave
A full half-hour together I have stood."

In 1805 a new reading, suiting the new close, appeared :

" I believe, that oftentimes
A full half-hour," &c.

" Full half-hour " became in 1815 " long half-hour." The final text of ll. 31-33 was reached in 1836.

Changes in the earlier portion of the poem were also made. L. 3 (1815) was previously " At evening, when the stars had just begun." In l. 15, " concourse wild " (1805) happily replaced " a wild scene " (a " scene " of " din" being incorrect). Lines 16, 17 (1836) were previously :

" Of mirth and jocund din ! And, when it chanced
That pauses of deep silence mocked his skill,"

In " The Prelude " we find :

<blockquote>
" And when a lengthened pause
Of silence came, and baffled his best skill."
</blockquote>

Professor Knight errs in stating that William Rainock, referred to in the Fenwick note, was with Wordsworth at Cambridge; it was not William, but his elder brother, Fletcher Rainock, who graduated as Second Wrangler in 1790.—ED.

<h3 style="text-align:center">*To the Cuckoo* (*page* 87).</h3>

Composed in the orchard, Town-end, Grasmere.—I. F.
Written March 23-26, 1802; erroneously dated by Wordsworth 1804; first published 1807, in the group, " Moods of my own Mind." In Dorothy Wordsworth's Journal we read : " Tuesday [March 23] . . . William worked at the Cuckoo poem ;" and the same entry occurs on Friday, March 26, 1802. On May 1, 1802, she " heard the cuckoo." On May 14 she notes, " William tired himself with seeking an epithet for the cuckoo." On June 3, " The cuckoo sang in Easedale; after dinner we read, the life and some of the writings of poor Logan." Logan disputes with Michael Bruce the authorship of a well-known poem " To the Cuckoo." In his " Guide to the Lakes," Wordsworth writes : " There is also an imaginative influence in the voice of the cuckoo, when the voice has taken possession of a deep mountain valley." The second stanza affords an excellent example of the attainment of simplicity and beauty through elaboration. It is worth giving the several forms :

<blockquote>
" While I am lying on the grass,
I hear thy restless shout :
From hill to hill it seems to pass,
About, and all about !" (1807.)
</blockquote>

<blockquote>
" While I am lying on the grass
Thy loud note smites my ear !—
From hill to hill it seems to pass,
At once far off and near !" (1815.)
</blockquote>

Line 3 of this stanza became :

<blockquote>
" It seems to fill the whole air's space " (1820.)
</blockquote>

<blockquote>
" While I am lying on the grass,
Thy twofold shout I hear,
</blockquote>

That seems to fill the whole air's space,
As loud far off as near." (1827-1843.)

The final text was at length attained in 1845. When Barron Field objected to " As loud far off as near," Wordsworth wrote: " Restore ' At once far off and near." The alteration was made in consequence of my noticing one day that the voice of a cuckoo, which I had heard from a tree at a great distance, did not seem any louder when I approached the tree." Stanza 3 was also re-handled: originally it stood :

" To me, no Babbler with a tale
Of sunshine and of flowers,
Thou tellest, Cuckoo ! in the vale
Of visionary hours." (1807.)

" I hear thee babbling to the Vale
Of sunshine and of flowers ;
And [But 1820] unto me thou bring'st a tale
Of visionary hours." (1815.)

The final text of this stanza was attained in 1827.—Ed.

A Night-piece (page 88).

Composed on the road between Nether Stowey and Alfoxden, extempore. I distinctly recollect the very moment when I was struck, as described,—" He looks up —the clouds are split," etc.—I. F.
Dated by Wordsworth 1798; first published 1815. Text unchanged. The precise date is doubtless Jan. 25, 1798, for the entry in Dorothy Wordsworth's Journal of that date describes the same phenomena of the sky in language, which, if the Fenwick note be correct, was derived from Wordsworth's extempore verses.—Ed.

Airey Force Valley (page 89).

Date uncertain ; first published 1842 in " Poems Chiefly of Early and Late Years." Text unchanged.—Ed.

Yew Trees (page 90).

Written at Grasmere. These yew-trees are still standing, but the spread of that at Lorton is much diminished by mutilation. I will here mention that a little way up the hill, on the road leading from Rosthwaite to Stonethwaite (in Borrowdale), lay the trunk of a yew-tree, which appeared as you approached, so vast was its diameter, like the entrance of a cave, and not a small one. Calculating upon what I have observed of the slow growth of this tree in rocky situations, and of its durability, I have often thought that the one I am describing must have been as old as the Christian era. The tree lay in the line of a fence. Great masses of its ruins were strewn about, and some had been rolled down the hillside and lay near the road at the bottom. As you approached the tree, you were struck with the number of shrubs and young plants, ashes, etc., which had found a bed upon the decayed trunk and grew to no inconsiderable height, forming as it were a part of the hedgerow. In no part of England, or of Europe, have I ever seen a yew-tree at all approaching this in magnitude, as it must have stood. By the bye, Hutton, the old Guide, of Keswick, had been so impressed with the remains of this tree that he used gravely to tell strangers that there could be no doubt of its having been in existence before the flood. —I. F.

Dated by Wordsworth 1803; first published 1815. Text unchanged. Wordsworth named *A Night Piece* and *Yew Trees* as amongst the most imaginative of his poems. See " Crabb Robinson's Diary," May 9, 1815. Coleridge (Biog. Lit. ii. 177, ed. 1847) cites this poem as evidence of Wordsworth's possession of " Imagination in the highest and strictest sense of the word." " The most vigorous and solemn bit of forest landscape ever painted." Ruskin (" Mod. Painters," Part iii. sect. ii. ch. iv.). For a description of the Buttermere yews and the Lorton yew see " Crabb Robinson's Diary," Sept. 16, 20, 1816, in Knight's " Life of Wordsworth," ii. 283. Lines 23-28 were probably suggested by Virgil, " Aen." vi. 273-284.—ED.

Nutting (page 91).

Written in Germany; intended as part of a poem on my own life, but struck out as not being wanted there. Like most of my schoolfellows I was an impassioned nutter. For this pleasure, the vale of Esthwaite, abounding in coppice-wood, furnished a very wide range. These verses arose out of the remembrance of feelings I had often had when a boy, and particularly in the extensive woods that still stretch from the side of Esthwaite Lake

towards Graythwaite, the seat of the ancient family of
Sandys.—I. F.

Written 1799; first published 1800. Written, Words-
worth says, in Germany; and intended for "The
Prelude," which was begun while Wordsworth was
abroad. Line 2 was inserted 1802, and l. 4 in 1827, the
reading of l. 5 previous to that date being, "When forth
I sallied from our cottage-door." Originally to this line a
note (1800-1815) was appended: "The house at which I
was boarded during the time I was at school." The
"huge wallet" is of 1815; previously, "And with a
wallet." L. 7 (1815), "I turn'd my steps" (1800). L. 8
(1836), "Towards the distant woods" (1800-1832). The
boy's dress, ll. 8-10 (1815) was originally (1800-5):

> " of Beggar's weeds
> Put on for the occasion, by advice
> And exhortation of my frugal Dame.
> Motley accoutrements!" [accoutrement 1802-1805.]

The scene was enriched with matted ferns and tangled
thickets, ll. 14-16 in 1836; previously:

> " Among the woods
> And o'er the pathless rocks, I forc'd my way
> Until, at length, I came."

"Tempting clusters" (1845) were previously "milk-
white clusters;" again, in 1845, "saw" was introduced
in l. 53, perhaps to lessen the stress on "the" which
precedes "intruding"; and in the same year in l. 36
"under" replaced "beneath", perhaps to vary from l. 25
and l. 29. The "mutilated bower," l. 50, dates from
1836; previously, "Even then, when from the bower I
turned away," the three opening words of which line were
too much akin in sound.—ED.

The Simplon Pass (page 93).

Written most probably in 1804, but possibly in 1799,
which date is given by Wordsworth; first published
1845. This is a passage from "The Prelude," B. vi., in
which he writes (l. 48):

> " Four years and thirty, told this very week,
> Have I been now a sojourner on earth."

The time spoken of in the passage is 1790, when, with

his friend Jones, Wordsworth crossed the Alps.   In l. 2
for " Pass " we find in " The Prelude " " strait "; and in
l. 4 for " step " we find " pace."   The date 1799 was
probably given as that when " The Prelude " was begun.
—ED.

She was a Phantom of delight (page 94).

Written at Town-end, Grasmere.   The germ of this
poem was four lines composed as a part of the verses on
the Highland Girl.   Though beginning in this way, it
was written from my heart, as is sufficiently obvious.—
I. F.

Dated by Wordsworth 1804; first published 1807.
The " germ of the poem," as Wordsworth expresses it,
belongs to 1803, the date of " To a Highland Girl."   In
the Hon. Justice Coleridge's reminiscences of Wordsworth
(" Memoirs," ii. 306) we read : " ' She was a phantom
of delight ' he [Wordsworth] said was written on ' his
dear wife.' "   The lines about Mary Hutchinson in " The
Prelude," B. vi. agree with the ideal portrait here given :

> " Another maid there was, who also shed
> A gladness o'er that season, then to me
> By *her exulting outside look of youth*
> *And placid under-countenance* first endeared."

It is worth noting, however, that this poem is placed
among " Poems of the Imagination " rather than of the
" Affections."   Except in l. 24 the word " between "
(1832), previously " betwixt ", and in the last line " angelic
light " (1845) for " an angel light," 1807 (angel-light,
1836), the text is as in 1807; but in 1836 only l. 8 was,
" From May-time's brightest, liveliest dawn."   A point in
punctuation should perhaps be noticed; in l. 27 (1807),
after " A perfect Woman," a semi-colon occurred.   Com-
pare " The Prelude," xiv. l. 268 (of Mary Wordsworth):

> " She came, no more a phantom to adorn
> A moment, but an inmate of the heart,
> And yet a spirit," &c.—ED.

" O Nightingale! thou surely art " (page 95).

Written at Town-end, Grasmere.   (Mrs. W. says in a
note, " At Coleorton.")—I. F.

Dated by Wordsworth 1806; first published 1807 in
the group, " Moods of my own Mind."   Mrs. Wordsworth
corrects her husband's note, and says the poem was

written "At Coleorton." Prof. Knight argues that the date is probably 1807, for during the nightingale's song-time Wordsworth was at Coleorton, and at Grasmere there are no nightingales. But the printing of the 1807 volumes took place before the song-time of the nightingale. The poem may have been written at Coleorton in November or December 1806. The text is as in 1807; the only change ever made was the deplorable one in l. 2, found only in 1815,

> " A creature of ebullient heart."

See " Crabb Robinson's Diary," May 9, 1815, where he prophesies the restoration of " a fiery heart." In his modernization of " The Cuckoo and the Nightingale," Wordsworth departs from his original to tell of the " loud rioting " of the nightingale's voice (see " Words-worthiana," p. 27).—Ed.

" Three years she grew in sun and shower " (*page* 96).

Composed in the Hartz Forest.—I. F.
Dated by Wordsworth 1799; first published 1800. One of the Lucy poems written in Germany. In 1802 Wordsworth made two changes. Lines 7, 8 became:

> " Her Teacher I myself will be,
> She is my darling;—and with me."

This was wisely repented of in 1805. The other alteration held its ground: l. 23 assumed its present form, the earlier reading being,

> "A beauty that shall mould her form."—Ed.

A slumber did my spirit seal (*page* 97).

Written in Germany.—I. F.
Dated by Wordsworth 1799; first published 1800. Text unchanged. Another poem of the Lucy group.—Ed.

" I wandered lonely as a cloud " (*page* 97).

Written at Town-end, Grasmere. The daffodils grew, and still grow, on the margin of Ullswater, and probably may be seen to this day as beautiful in the month of March, nodding their golden heads beside the dancing and foaming waves.—I. F.
Dated by Wordsworth 1804; first published 1807.

The origin of the poem is evidently connected with a visit
to Gowbarrow Park, April 15, 1802, recorded in Dorothy
Wordsworth's Journal of that date : " When we were in
the woods beyond Gowbarrow Park, we saw a few
daffodils close to the water side. We fancied that the sea
had floated the seeds ashore, and that the little colony had
so sprung up. But as we went along there were more
and yet more ; and, at last, under the boughs of the trees,
we saw that there was a long belt of them along the
shore, about the breadth of a country turnpike road. I
never saw daffodils so beautiful. They grew among the
mossy stones, about and above them; some rested their
heads upon these stones, as on a pillow for weariness ; and
the rest tossed and reeled and danced, and seemed as if
they verily laughed with the wind that blew upon them
over the lake. They looked so gay, ever glancing, ever
changing . . . There was here and there a little knot,
and a few stragglers higher up ; but they were so few as
not to disturb the simplicity, unity, and life of that one
busy highway. We rested again and again. The bays
were stormy, and we heard the waves at different
distances, and in the middle of the water, like the sea."
The two lines,

> " They flash upon that inward eye
> Which is the bliss of solitude,"

are by Mary Wordsworth—lines which, Wordsworth
said (see his letter to Wrangham, " Memoirs," i. 183-4), " if
thoroughly felt would annihilate nine-tenths of the reviews
of the kingdom." The chief fact about the text is that
st. 2 was added in 1815, when the final state of the text
was reached. The joyous animation of the wind-tossed
flowers was more insisted on in the first version ; in l. 4
the reading was " dancing daffodils," and in l. 16 " laugh-
ing company " (Crabb Robinson lamented the change of
" laughing " to " jocund "). Lines 5, 6 in 1807 were.:

> " Along the Lake, beneath the trees,
> Ten thousand dancing in the breeze."

In 1836 (only), in l. 15 " but be " was " be but "; 1843
reverts to the reading of 1807. In 1815 Wordsworth
appended a note : " The subject of these Stanzas is rather
an elementary feeling and simple impression (approaching
to the nature of an ocular spectrum) upon the imaginative
faculty, than an *exertion* of it. The one which follows

[' Poor Susan '] is strictly a Reverie; and neither that, nor the next after it in succession, ' The Power of Music,' would have been placed here [*i e.* among " Poems of the Imagination "] except for the reason given in the foregoing note."—ED.

The Reverie of Poor Susan (page 98).

Written 1801 or 1802. This arose out of my observation of the affecting music of these birds hanging in this way in the London streets during the freshness and stillness of the Spring morning.—I. F.

Dated by Wordsworth (in edd. 1836-49) 1797; dated erroneously in the Fenwick note 1801 or 1802; the earlier date may be accepted; first published 1800, with the title " Poor Susan." See last note with reference to its being a " Reverie." In 1800 a stanza closes the poem, which was wisely omitted in 1802 and all subsequent editions:

" Poor Outcast! return—to receive thee once more
The house of thy Father will open its door,
And thou once again, in thy plain russet gown,
May'st hear the thrush sing from a tree of its own."

In l. 2 " Hangs " in 1820 replaced " There's."—ED.

Power of Music (page 99).

Taken from life.—I. F.

Dated by Wordsworth 1806; first published 1807. The poem belongs, doubtless, to Wordsworth's visit to London in the Spring and early Summer, 1806. In l. 15 " dusky-browed " (1815) replaced " dusky-faced " (1807), " face " occurring elsewhere in the same line. In l. 37 " Mark that Cripple " (1827) replaced " There's a Cripple ", and l. 39, " That Mother " replaced " A Mother."—ED.

Star-gazers (page 102).

Observed by me in Leicester Square as here described. —I. F.

Dated by Wordsworth 1806, and doubtless, like the last, and " Stray Pleasures," belonging to the London visit of that year; first published 1807. The earliest form of the poem is found accompanying a letter of Dorothy Wordsworth to Lady Beaumont, Nov. 14, 1806

("Memorials of Coleorton," i. 178-180). The only important
difference between this and the printed text is that the
seventh printed stanza precedes in the MS. the printed
sixth stanza, and the sixth has a different text in its
first and fourth lines from that printed: l. 1: "Or is it—
last unwelcome thought!—that these spectators rude";
l. 4: "Not to be lifted up at once to power and majesty."
Of a few variations of little importance between the first
and the final printed text we may note l. 16 (1827); pre-
viously:

"Do they betray us when they're seen? and are they but
    a name?"

In l. 8, "And envies him that's looking" is a reversion of
1842 to the reading of 1807, from the 1827 reading:
"Impatient till his moment comes [come 1836]."   Com-
pare with ll. 19, 20, Shelley's statement in "Julian and
Maddalo"—where he speaks of material not spiritual
voyaging—that coming homeward "always makes the
spirit tame."—ED.

Written in March (page 104).

Extempore. This little poem was a favourite with
Joanna Baillie.—I. F.
Written April 16, 1802 (Good Friday); erroneously
dated by Wordsworth 1801, and named "Written in
March"; first published 1807 in the group, "Moods of
my own Mind."   In Dorothy Wordsworth's Journal
of the date given we read: "When we came to the foot
of Brother's Water I left William sitting on the bridge
. . . When I returned I found William writing a poem
descriptive of the sights and sounds we saw and heard.
There was the gentle flowing of the stream, the glittering,
lively lake, green fields without a living creature to be
seen on them; behind us, a flat pasture with forty-two
cattle feeding . . . The people were at work ploughing,
harrowing, and sowing; lasses working, a dog barking
now and then; cocks crowing, birds twittering; the snow
in patches at the top of the highest hills . . . William
finished his poem before we got to the foot of Kirkstone."
"The bridge . . . crosses Goldrill Beck a little below
Hartsop in Patterdale" (Knight). Text unchanged.—ED.

Lyre! &c. (page 105).

Date uncertain; first published 1842, in "Poems
Chiefly of Early and Late Years." Text unchanged.—ED.

Beggars (page 106).

Written at Town-end, Grasmere. Met, and described to me by my sister, near the quarry at the head of Rydal Lake, a place still a chosen resort of vagrants travelling with their families.—I. F.

Written March 13, 14, 1802; first published 1807. Having written " Alice Fell or Poverty " on March 12, 13, Wordsworth immediately wrote " Beggars." Dorothy Wordsworth writes in her Journal : " Saturday [13th]. William finished ' Alice Fell,' and then wrote the poem of ' The Beggar Woman,' taken from a woman whom I had seen in May (now nearly two years ago) when John and he were at Gallow Hill. I sate with him at intervals all the morning, took down his stanzas, &c. . . . After tea I read to William [from the Journal] that account of the little boy belonging to the tall woman, and an unlucky thing it was, for he could not escape from those very words, and so he could not write the poem. He left it unfinished, and went tired to bed. In our walk from Rydal he had got warmed with the subject, and had half cast the poem. *Sunday Morning.*—William . . . got up at nine o'clock, but before he rose he had finished ' The Beggar Boy.' " Dorothy's record of the incident on which the poem is founded affords an interesting example of the manner in which Wordsworth dealt with his material : " *Tuesday, May 27th* [1800]. A very tall woman, tall much beyond the measure of tall women, called at the door. She had on a very long brown cloak, and a very white cap without bonnet. Her face was excessively brown, but it had plainly once been fair. She led a little barefooted child, about two years old, by the hand, and said her husband, who was a tinker, was gone before with the other children. I gave her a piece of bread. Afterwards, on my way to Ambleside, beside the bridge at Rydal, I saw her husband sitting by the roadside, his two asses feeding beside him, and the two young children at play upon the grass. The man did not beg. I passed on, and about a quarter of a mile further, I saw two boys before me, one about ten, the other about eight years old, at play chasing a butterfly. They were wild figures, not very ragged, but without shoes and stockings. The hat of the elder was wreathed round with yellow flowers ; the younger, whose hat was only a rimless crown, had stuck it round with laurel leaves. They continued at play till I drew very near, and then they addressed me with the begging cant and the whining voice of sorrow. I said I served your mother this morning (the boys were so like the woman who had called at our door that I could not be mistaken). 'O!' says the elder, 'you could not serve my mother, for she's dead, and my father's on at the next town—he's a potter.' I persisted in my assertion, and that I would give them nothing. Says the elder, 'Let's away,' and away they flew like lightning." The woman's husband, who was only a side-figure in Dorothy's narrative, is wisely excluded from the poem.

This poem has been much rehandled; but until 1827 it underwent little alteration; 1807 and 1815 are identical; in 1820 lines 29, 30 assumed their present form, having been previously :

> " Two Brothers seem'd they, eight and ten years old ;
> And like that woman's face as gold is like to gold."

St. 1 stood originally thus :

> "She had a tall Man's height, or more ;
> No bonnet screen'd her from the heat ;
> A long drab-colour'd Cloak she wore,
> A Mantle reaching to her feet :
> What other dress she had I could not know ; [1]
> Only she wore a Cap that was as white as snow."

Altered thus in 1827 :

> " Before me as the Wanderer stood,
> No bonnet screened her from the heat ;
> Nor claimed she service from the hood [2]
> Of a blue mantle, to her feet
> Depending with a graceful flow ;
> Only she wore a cap pure as unsullied snow."

Altered again in 1832 :

> " Before my eyes a Wanderer stood ;
> Her face from summer's noon-day heat
> Nor [No 1836-43] bonnet shaded, nor the hood

---

[1] " A villainous line, one of the very worst in my whole writings."—Wordsworth to Barron Field.

[2] "Too pompous for the occasion."—Wordsworth to Barron Field.

Of that [the 1836-43] blue cloak, which to her feet
Depended with a graceful flow;
Only she wore a cap as white as new-fallen snow."

The final text was reached in 1845. Two other
versions are given from MS. in Prof. Knight's notes on
the poem. The second stanza assumed its present form
in 1827 with only one difference, "lead" (1836) in l. 11
having been "head" previous to 1836. The text of the
earlier lines, 1807-1820, was:

"In all my walks,[1] through field or town,
Such Figure had I never seen:
Her face was of Egyptian brown:
Fit person was she for a Queen."

St. 3 in its present form dates from 1845. The earlier
readings were :

"Before me begging did she stand,
Pouring out sorrows like a sea ;[2]
Grief after grief:—on English land
Such woes I knew could never be;" (1807.)

"Her suit no faltering scruples checked;
Forth did she pour, in current free,
Tales that could challenge no respect
But from a blind credulity ;" (1827.)

"She begged an alms; no scruple checked
The current of her ready plea
Words that could challenge," &c. (1832-43.)

Yet another version is given from MS. by Knight.
In l. 18, "a Weed of glorious feature," is in inverted
commas 1815-20.
The sixth stanza was added in 1827 with " Precursors
of [to, 1836]" in its fourth line.
L. 37 (1827) was previously: "They bolted on me
thus, and lo!" L. 42 (1827) was previously: "Nay but

---

[1] "Obtrusively personal."—Wordsworth to Barron
Field.
[2] "'Sea' clashes with 'was beautiful to see' below."—
Wordsworth to Barron Field.

I gave her pence, and she will buy you bread." L. 44 (1845) replaced two earlier readings :

"Sweet Boys, you're telling me a lie ;"
(1807-1820, and restored 1836-43.)

"Sweet Boys! Heaven hears that rash reply ;"[1]
(1827-32.)

The last line of the poem (1827) was in 1807-20 : "Off to some other play they both together flew."

Professor Knight ("Life of Wordsworth," iii. 150) prints a highly interesting letter of Wordsworth to Barron Field, in which he gives reasons in detail for the alterations introduced in 1827, and says generally that he aimed at giving "more eloquence and dignity to this poem, partly on its own account, and partly that it might harmonise better with the one appended to it." Some of Wordsworth's comments are embodied in the footnotes here given.—ED.

Sequel to the Foregoing (page 108).

Dated by Wordsworth 1817 ; first published 1827. Four lines, 32-35, were introduced in their present position in 1836, being taken from a passage following l. 13 in edd. 1827-32 :

"Spirits of beauty and of grace!
Associates in that eager chase ;
Ye, by a course to nature true,
The sterner judgment can subdue ;
And waken a relenting smile
When she encounters fraud or guile ;
And sometimes ye can charm away
The inward mischief, or allay,
Ye, who within the blameless mind,
Your favourite seat of empire find."

Ll. 27, 28 (1836); previously :

"   is still endeared
The faith"

L. 31 (1836); previously : "Or, if such thoughts."—ED.

---

[1] "Somewhat too refined."—Wordsworth to Barron Field.

Gipsies (*page* 109).

Composed at Coleorton. I had observed them, as here described, near Castle Donnington, on my way to and from Derby.—I. F.

Dated by Wordsworth 1807; first published 1807. In l. 1 a note of interrogation followed "here", 1807-20. In 1807-15 the poem closed thus:

> "Oh better wrong and strife,
> Better vain deeds or evil than such life !
> The silent Heavens have goings on;
> The stars have tasks—but these have none."

In 1820 an apology was added:

> "Oh, better wrong and strife,
> (By nature transient) than such [this, 1836] torpid life !
> The silent Heavens have goings-on;
> The stars have tasks—but these have none;
> Yet, witness all that stirs in heaven and [or, 1827] earth
> In scorn I speak not;—they are what their birth
> And breeding suffers [suffer, 1836] them to be ;
> Wild outcasts of society !"

In 1827 two of these lines (" The silent Heavens," &c.) were altered to the form in the text. Wordsworth promised Barron Field, and afterwards Sara Coleridge, that he would cancel the concluding apology, but did not fulfil the promise. "*Goings on*," he says, " is precisely the word wanted; but it makes a weak and apparently prosaic line so near the end of a poem." In manuscript fragments intended for " Michael," and printed in Knight's " Life of Wordsworth," i. 388, occurs the expression, " the goings on of earth and sky." (See Southey's use of *goings on* in Dowden's "Southey," 88.) Coleridge, in "Biog. Lit." (ed. 1847, ii. 156), instances this poem as affording an example of " thoughts and usages too great for the subject." The poet expresses his indignation roused by the Gipsies' rest " in a series of lines, the diction and imagery of which would have been rather above than below the mark, had they been applied to the immense empire of China unprogressive for thirty centuries." (Coleridge cites from the 1807 text.) See Mr. J. Dykes Campbell in the " Athenæum," Nov. 22, 1890, p. 700. —ED.

Ruth (*page* 110).

Written in Germany.   Suggested by an account I had
of a wanderer in Somersetshire.—I. F.

Dated by Wordsworth 1799 ; first published 1800.
Classed 1815-1820 among " Poems Founded on the Affec-
tions."   To understand what follows, the reader should
first number the stanzas as given in the text.   In March,
1802, as Dorothy Wordsworth's Journal shows, the poem
was rehandled.   Stanza 3 was added in ed. 1802, **and**
was retained in all subsequent editions ; its last two lines
(1827) stood thus in 1802-20 :

> " She passed her time ; and in this way
> She grew to woman's height."

Between stanza 10 and stanza 11 appeared seven stanzas
in 1802, of which four were new, and three were trans-
posed ; the three transposed stanzas are those now 22nd,
23rd, 24th.   Of the four stanzas which were new in 1802
two have been retained—now the 28th and 30th—and
two were omitted in all editions after 1805.   These
omitted stanzas appeared respectively as first and last of
the seven stanzas inserted in 1802 between the present
st. 10 and st. 11 ; they are as follows.—Stanza 11 of ed.
1802 :

> " Of march and ambush, siege and fight,
> Then did he tell ; and with delight
> The heart of Ruth would ache ;
> Wild histories they were, and dear :
> But 'twas a thing of heaven to hear
> When of himself he spake."

Stanza 17 of 1802 :

> " It is a purer, better mind :
> O Maiden innocent and kind
> What sights I might have seen !
> Even now upon my eyes they break !
> And he again began to speak
> Of lands where he had been."

The order of the seven inserted stanzas of 1802 was—
(1) " Of march," &c., (2) 28, (3) 22, (4) 23, (5) 24, (6) 30,
(7) " It is a purer," &c.   When shifting st. 22, 23, 24,
and changing them from narrative to dramatic, " he " and
" his " became " I " and " my " ; the other changes in
these stanzas will be noted presently.   We now come to

the treatment, in 1805, of the insertion between st. 10 and
st. 11. Stanzas 22, 23, 24 resumed the position which
they occupied in 1800, and now occupy; a new stanza,
now st. 29, was written; and the order in 1805 was—
(1) " Of march," &c., (2) 28, (3) 29, (4) 30, (5) " It is a
purer," &c. In 1815 the inserted five stanzas of 1805
disappear. In 1820, stanzas 28, 29, 30 reappear, and in
their present position.

Stanza 39 was added in 1802, with the following as its
first two lines:

> " The neighbours grieve for her, and say
> That she will, long before her day,"

The present reading is of 1805. Having now recorded
the insertion and omission of stanzas, I may note the total
number of stanzas in the poem in successive editions:
1800 contains 38 stanzas; 1802, 44; 1805, 45; 1815, 40;
1820-1849, 43.

Various readings may now be noted. Lines 3, 4 (1802)
were in 1800:

> " And so, not seven years old,
> The slighted child."

Ll. 8, 9 (1836); previously:

> " And from that oaten pipe could draw
> All sounds."

In l. 26 " But no ! " (1836) was previously " Ah no ! "
and in l. 27 " bore " (1805) replaced " bare."

Ll. 55-57 (1836); previously:

> " He spake of plants divine and strange
> That every hour [1802; " day," 1800] their blossoms
> change,
> Ten thousand lovely hues ! "

L. 73 (1836); previously " And then he said, ' How
sweet it were." Ll. 75-77 (1836, with " through shade ";
" in shade " 1845); previously:

> " A gardener in the shade,
> Still wandering with an easy mind
> To build."

L. 79, " bright years " (1836); previously " sweet
years."

L. 86, " Fond thoughts " (1832); previously " Dear
thoughts."

L. 98, "The wakeful Ruth" (1820); "Sweet Ruth alone" (1800-1815).

L. 133, "voluptuous" in all editions except 1802, where "unhallow'd." L. 135, "gorgeous," 1845; previously, "lovely." L. 138, "favoured bowers," 1845; "magic bowers,' 1800-1805; "gorgeous bowers," 1815-1843.

L. 140, "sometimes," 1805; "often," 1802; l. 142, "linked to," 1805; "amid," 1802; l. 143, "needs must have," 1805; "wanted not," 1802.

L. 145, "But ill he lived," all editions except 1802, where "Ill did he live."

Ll. 167, 168: ed. 1802 only has "thoughtlessness" for "confidence"; edd. 1820-36 read

> "When first, in confidence and pride,
> I crossed."

Ll. 169-171 (1843); previously:

> "It was a fresh and glorious world—
> A banner bright that was [shone, 1836] unfurled
> Before me suddenly;"

Ll. 175-180, stanza 30 assumed its present form in 1845. In 1802, when it first appeared, the stanza, then in a different position, stood thus :

> "So it was then, and so is now :
> For, Ruth! with thee I know not how
> I feel my spirit burn
> Even as the east when day comes forth ;
> And to the west, and south, and north,
> The morning doth return."

The first two lines became, in 1805 :

> "But wherefore speak of this?　For now
> Sweet [Dear, 1836] Ruth ! "

So amended, the first three lines of the stanza remained until 1843. The last three were altered to the present text in 1836.

L. 181, 1845; previously :

> "But now the pleasant dream was gone," (1800-1815)

> "Full soon the purer mind was gone," (1820-1843)

Ll. 196-198 (1836); in 1800-1815:

> " And there, exulting in her wrongs,
> Among the music of her songs,
> She fearfully carouz'd. "

In 1820-1832:

> " And there she sang tumultuous songs,
> By recollection of her wrongs,
> To fearful passion rouzed.[1]

L. 203, " clear brook," 1836 ; " wild brook," 1800-1832.
Ll. 214-215 (1802); in 1800 :

> " And to the pleasant banks of Tone
> She took her way, to dwell alone."

L. 217, "pain," 1802; " grief," 1800.
L. 226 (1805): " (And in this tale we all agree)," 1800.
—Ed.

Resolution and Independence (page 119).

Written at Town-end, Grasmere. This old man I met a few hundred yards from my cottage; and the account of him is taken from his own mouth. I was in the state of feeling described in the beginning of the poem, while crossing over Barton Fell from Mr. Clarkson's, at the foot of Ullswater, towards Askham. The image of the hare I then observed on the ridge of the Fell.—I. F.

Written May 3—July 4, 1802; first published 1807. On May 4th Dorothy Wordsworth " wrote out ' The Leech-Gatherer ' for William, which he had begun the night before." On May 7th " William . . . fell to work at ' The Leech-Gatherer '; he wrote hard at it till dinner-time; then he gave over, tired to death—he had finished the poem." Again on Sunday, May 9th, he " worked almost incessantly at ' The Leech-Gatherer' from morning till tea-time. . . . He wearied himself to death." On July 2 Dorothy " transcribed the alterations in ' The Leech-Gatherer,' " and on Sunday, July 4, " William finished ' The Leech-Gatherer.' " The incident on which the poem was founded is entered in Dorothy's Journal of

---

[1] The earlier reading was altered because Lamb observed that it was not English. " I liked it better myself; but certainly ' to carouse cups '—that is, to empty them— is the genuine English."—Wordsworth to Barron Field: Knight's " Life," iii. 152.

Oct. 3, 1800:—William and Dorothy—after a very rainy morning—met " an old man almost double," wearing an apron and night-cap, having an interesting face, " dark eyes and a long nose"; of Scotch parents; his children all dead but one, a sailor; " his trade was to gather leeches, but now leeches were scarce, and he had not strength for it; he lived by begging, and was making his way to Carlisle, where he should buy a few godly books to sell." (Dorothy's Journal in Knight's " Life of Words- worth," i., 272.) Mr. T. Hutchinson points out to me that the incident, as shown by references in the Journal to John Wordsworth and to Jones, must have occurred on or before Sept. 26, 1800, and probably on that day, when Jones, who returned to Grasmere on the 19th, took his departure.

In 1820 a stanza occurring between the present st. 8 and st. 9 was omitted, in consideration of reasons advanced by Coleridge in " Biographia Literaria ":

> " My course I stopped as soon as I espied
> The Old Man in that naked wilderness :
> Close by a Pond, upon the further side,
> He stood alone: a minute's space I guess
> I watch'd him, he continuing motionless :
> To the Pool's further margin then I drew ;
> He being all the while before me full in view."

In l. 29 the skylark " warbling " (1820) was previously "singing."   In l. 44 "his pride" (1815); " its pride" (1807); l. 46, " Following his plough " (1820); " Behind his plough " (1807-1815).

Ll. 53, 54 (1820); previously :

> " When up and down my fancy thus was driven,
> And I with these untoward thoughts had striven."

L. 67, " in life's pilgrimage " (1820); previously " in their pilgrimage."

L. 71, "limbs, body, and pale face " (1836); " his body, limbs, and face " (1807-1832).

L. 74, " Upon the margin of that " (1820); " Beside the little pond or " (1807-1815).

L. 82 (1820); previously " And now such freedom as I could I took;"

L. 88 (1820); previously " What kind of work is that which you pursue ? "

Ll. 90, 91 (1836); in 1807-1815:

" He answer'd me with pleasure and surprise,
And there was, while he spake, a fire about his eyes."

In 1820-1832, as now, except the first three words " He answered, while," Wordsworth perceived that the eyes would speak before the lips.

L. 99 (1827); in 1807-1820 (a heavily monosyllabic verse):

" He told me that he to this pond had come."

L. 112, " by apt admonishment " (1827); "and [" by," 1820] strong admonishment," 1807.

L. 114, " And hope" (1815); " The hope," 1807.

L. 117 (1820); in 1807: " And now, not knowing what the Old Man said "; in 1815: " But now, perplex'd by what the Old Man had said."

L. 123, " pools " (1827); previously " ponds."

On stanza 9 see Wordsworth's " Preface to the Edition of 1815." As to the poem generally, Wordsworth wrote to friends who received a copy in manuscript: " I will explain to you in prose my feelings in writing *that* poem. . . . I describe myself as having been exalted to the highest pitch of delight by the joyousness and beauty of nature ; and then as depressed, even in the midst of those beautiful objects, to the lowest dejection and despair. A young poet in the midst of the happiness of nature is described as overwhelmed by the thoughts of the miserable reverses which have befallen the happiest of all men, *viz.*, poets. I think of this till I am so deeply impressed with it, that I consider the manner in which I was rescued from my dejection and despair almost as an interposition of Providence. A person reading the poem with feelings like mine will have been awed and controlled, expecting something spiritual or supernatural. What is brought forward ? A lonely place, ' a pond by which an old man *was*, far from all house or home :' not *stood*, nor *sat*, but *was*—the figure presented in the most naked simplicity possible. This feeling of spirituality or supernaturalness is again referred to as being strong in my mind in this passage. How came he here ? thought I, or what can he be doing ? I then describe him, whether ill or well is not for me to judge with perfect confidence; but this I *can* confidently affirm, that though I believe God has given me a strong imagination, I cannot conceive a figure more impressive than that of an old man like this, the survivor

II.   X

of a wife and ten children, travelling alone among the mountains and all lonely places, carrying with him his own fortitude, and the necessities which an unjust state of society has laid upon him."—"Memoirs of Wordsworth," i. 172, 173. Was this the " letter to Mary and Sara about ' The Leech-Gatherer '" mentioned in Dorothy's Journal of June 14, 1802?—ED.

The Thorn (page 125).

Written at Alfoxden. Arose out of my observing, on the ridge of Quantock Hill, on a stormy day, a thorn which I had often passed, in calm and bright weather, without noticing it. I said to myself, " Cannot I by some invention do as much to make this Thorn permanently an impressive object as the storm has made it to my eyes at this moment ? " I began the poem accordingly, and composed it with great rapidity. Sir George Beaumont painted a picture from it which Wilkie thought his best. He gave it me; though when he saw it several times at Rydal Mount afterwards, he said, " I could make a better, and would like to paint the same subject over again." The sky in this picture is nobly done, but it reminds one too much of Wilson. The only fault, however, of any consequence is the female figure, which is too old and decrepit for one likely to frequent an eminence on such a call.—I. F.

Dated by Wordsworth 1798; first published 1798. In Dorothy Wordsworth's Journal, March 1, 1798, we read: " William wrote some lines describing a stunted thorn," and April 20: " Came home the Crookham way, by the thorn, and the little muddy pond." No note on this poem can be of equal interest with one which Wordsworth appended in edd. 1800-1805 : " This Poem ought to have been preceded by an introductory Poem, which I have been prevented from writing by never having felt myself in a mood when it was probable that I should write it well. The character which I have here introduced speaking is sufficiently common. The Reader will perhaps have a general notion of it, if he has ever known a man, a captain of a small trading vessel, for example, who being past the middle age of life, had retired upon an annuity or small independent income to some village or country town of which he was not a native, or in which he had not been accustomed to live. Such men, having little to do, become credulous and talkative from indolence;

and from the same cause, and other predisposing causes by which it is probable that such men may have been affected, they are prone to superstition. On which account it appeared to me proper to select a character like this to exhibit some of the general laws by which superstition acts upon the mind. Superstitious men are almost always men of slow faculties and deep feelings; their minds are not loose, but adhesive; they have a reasonable share of imagination, by which word I mean the faculty which produces impressive effects out of simple elements; but they are utterly destitute of fancy, the power by which pleasure and surprise are excited by sudden varieties of situation and by accumulated imagery.

" It was my wish in this poem to show the manner in which such men cleave to the same ideas; and to follow the turns of passion, always different, yet not palpably different, by which their conversation is swayed. I had two objects to attain; first, to represent a picture which should not be unimpressive, yet consistent with the character that should describe it; secondly, while I adhered to the style in which such persons describe, to take care that words, which in their minds are impregnated with passion, should likewise convey passion to Readers who are not accustomed to sympathize with men feeling in that manner or using such language. It seemed to me that this might be done by calling in the assistance of Lyrical and rapid Metre. It was necessary that the Poem, to be natural, should in reality move slowly; yet I hoped that, by the aid of the metre, to those who should at all enter into the spirit of the Poem, it would appear to move quickly. The Reader will have the kindness to excuse this note, as I am sensible that an introductory Poem is necessary to give the Poem its full effect.

" Upon this occasion I will request permission to add a few words closely connected with ' The Thorn ' and many other Poems in these volumes. There is a numerous class of readers who imagine that the same words cannot be repeated without tautology: this is a great error: virtual tautology is much oftener produced by using different words when the meaning is exactly the same. Words, a Poet's words more particularly, ought to be weighed in the balance of feeling, and not measured by the space which they occupy upon paper. For the Reader cannot be too often reminded that Poetry is passion: it is the history or science of feelings. Now every man must know that an attempt is rarely made to communicate

impassioned feelings without something of an accompany-
ing consciousness of the inadequateness of our own powers,
or the deficiencies of language.   During such efforts there
will be a craving in the mind, and as long as it is unsatis-
fied the speaker will cling to the same words, or words of
the same character.   There are also various other reasons
why repetition and apparent tautology are frequently
beauties of the highest kind.   Among the chief of these
reasons is the interest which the mind attaches to words,
not only as symbols of the passion, but as *things*, active
and efficient, which are of themselves part of the passion.
And further, from a spirit of fondness, exultation, and
gratitude, the mind luxuriates in the repetition of words
which appear successfully to communicate its feelings.
The truth of these remarks might be shown by innume-
rable passages from the Bible, and from the impassioned
poetry of every nation.   ' Awake, awake, Deborah ! ' &c.
Judges, chap. v., verses 12th, 27th, and part of 28th.
See also the whole of that tumultuous and wonderful
Poem."

Notwithstanding this note, Wordsworth in 1820 saw fit
to abbreviate the tautologies of the poem by omitting
these lines, which followed l. 4 of stanza 10 :

" Nay rack your brain—'tis all in vain,
I'll tell you every thing I know ;
But to the thorn and to the pond,
Which is a little step beyond,
I wish that you would go :
Perhaps when you are at the place
You something of her tale may trace.

XI.
I'll give you the best help I can ;
Before you up the mountain go,
Up to the dreary mountain-top,
I'll tell you all I know."

The lines remaining of stanzas 10 and 11 (1800-1815)
make up the present stanza 10.   At the same time (1820)
the last two lines of stanza 3 replaced the earlier :

" I've measured it from side to side,
'Tis three feet long, and two feet wide "—

lines of which, in 1815, Wordsworth said to Crabb Robin-
son, " They ought to be liked ; " and in st. 13 " grey-

haired Wilfred" became substitute for "old Farmer Simpson":

> "Last Christmas, when we talked of this,
> Old Farmer Simpson did maintain
> That in her womb the infant wrought" (1798-1815).

Stanza 12, ll. 5, 6, date from 1836; previously:

> "'Tis said a child was in her womb,
> As now to any eye was plain; (1798-1815.)

> "'Tis said ["Alas," 1827] her lamentable state
> Even to a careless eye was plain;" (1820.)

The close of st. 10 previous to 1820 was:

> "And she was happy, happy still,
> Whene'er she thought of Stephen Hill."

And the close of st. 12 :

> "Oh me ! ten thousand times I'd rather
> That he had died, that cruel father!"

In 1820 the period of Martha's suffering was shortened from twenty-two years to twenty, st. 10, l. 5, "'Tis now some two and twenty years," 1798-1815; "'Tis known that twenty years are passed," 1820; the present text is of 1845. In 1815 the present text in st. 11 was substituted for the earlier crude closing :

> "Poor Martha! on that woeful day
> A cruel, cruel fire, they say,
> Into her bones was sent ;
> It dried her body to a cinder,
> And almost turned her brain to tinder."

The tautologies of st. 14 in its earlier form were removed in 1827; ll. 1, 2 of the stanza (1798-1820):

> "No more I know; I wish I did,
> And I would tell it all to you";

followed by (l. 4) "There's none that ever knew"; ll. 5, 6:

> "And if a child was born or no,
> There's no one that could ever tell";

and again (last line of stanza), "There's no one knows, as I have said." Two slight changes made as early as 1800 may be noticed; st. 20, l. 1, then replaced "I've

heard the scarlet moss is red " (1798); and in st. 18, l. 2,
for " Her face " (1798) the 1800 text reads " In truth ";
the earlier reading was restored in 1815.   Line 5 of st. 21
gave Wordsworth poetic pains :

> " But then the beauteous hill of moss"
> (1800-1820, 1832).

> " It might not be—the hill of moss " (1827).

> " But then the speckled hill of moss " (1836).

The present text is of 1845.   In st. 1, l. 7, " prickly "
(1836) replaced " thorny; " in 1827, st. 9, l. 5, " The
hillock like " replaced " The heap that's like."   Several
slight verbal changes are here unnoticed.—Ed.

Hart Leap Well (*page* 133).

Written   at   Town-end,   Grasmere.   The   first   eight
stanzas were composed extempore one winter evening in
the cottage ; when, after having tired myself with labour-
ing at an awkward passage in " The Brothers," I started
with a sudden impulse to this to get rid of the other, and
finished it in a day or two.   My sister and I had past
the place a few weeks before in our wild winter journey
from Sockburn on the banks of the Tees to Grasmere.   A
peasant whom we met near the spot told us the story so
far as concerned the name of the Well, and the Hart, and
pointed out the Stones.   Both the Stones and the Well
are objects that may easily be missed ; the tradition by
this time may be extinct in the neighbourhood : the man
who related it to us was very old.—I. F.

Dated by Wordsworth 1800 ; first published 1800.
The Fenwick note shows that it was written early in that
year.   The alterations of text are all slight improvements
in detail.

Ll. 3, 4 (1836); previously :

> " He turned aside towards a Vassal's door,
> And ' Bring ' "

In l. 19 " Blanch " (1827) replaced " Brach," the name
of a kind of hunting dog (often a female), not of an indi-
vidual dog; in l. 20 the reading of 1800 (only) was:
" weary up the mountain."

L. 21 (1827); previously, " he chid and cheered "; a
good master would cheer before chiding.

L. 25, and l. 27 : in 1800 (only) the first of these lines ended with " chase," and " race " occurred twice in the second.

L. 35, " cracked his whip" (1820); previous, "smack'd."

L. 38, " glorious feat " (1820) ; previously, " glorious act," and l. 40, rhyming with this, was (1800-1815):

" And foaming like a mountain cataract."

L. 42, "nostril touched," 1820 ; " nose half-touched," 1800-1815.

L. 46 (1820); previously, " Was never man in such a joyful case "; and in l. 48, rhyming with this "place" (1800-1815).

L. 49, " climbing " (1802); " turning " (1800).

L. 50. The distance covered by the stag's three bounds was " nine roods " until 1845, when " four " was substituted.

L. 51, 1802; in 1800, " Three several marks which with his hoofs the Beast."

L. 52, " grassy " (1820) ; previously " verdant."

L. 54, " human eyes " (1836); previously " living eyes."

L. 65, " gallant stag " (1827) ; " gallant brute " (1800-1820).

Ll. 79, 80 (1815); previously :

" And soon the knight perform'd what he had said,
The fame whereof through many a land did ring."

L. 90 (1820); previously, "journey'd with his Paramour."

L. 98, " freeze " (1802); " curl " (1800).

L. 100, " for " (1815) ; " to " (1800-1805).

L. 113, " hill " (1815); " hills " (1800-1805).

L. 142 (1815) : " To this place from the stone " (1800); " From the stone upon the summit of the steep " (1802-1805).

L. 150, " the fountain " (1832); previously, " this fountain."

L. 153, " flowering thorn " (1836); previously, "scented thorn."

L. 157 (1827); previously, " But now here's neither grass."

L. 168 (1815) : " For them the quiet creatures " (1800-1805).—Ed.

Song at the Feast, &c. (page 140).

Henry Lord Clifford, etc., etc., who is the subject of this poem, was the son of John Lord Clifford, who was slain at Towton Field, which John Lord Clifford, as is known to the reader of English history, was the person who after the battle of Wakefield slew, in the pursuit, the young Earl of Rutland, son of the Duke of York, who had fallen in the battle, " in part of revenge " (say the Authors of the " History of Cumberland and Westmoreland "); " for the Earl's Father had slain his." A deed which worthily blemished the author (saith Speed); but who, as he adds, ''dare promise anything temperate of himself in the heat of martial fury ? chiefly, when it was resolved not to leave any branch of the York line standing ; for so one maketh this Lord to speak." This, no doubt, I would observe by the bye, was an action sufficiently in the vindictive spirit of the times, and yet not altogether so bad as represented ; " for the Earl was no child, as some writers would have him, but able to bear arms, being sixteen or seventeen years of age, as is evident from this, (say the Memoirs of the Countess of Pembroke, who was laudably anxious to wipe away, as far as could be, this stigma from the illustrious name to which she was born,) that he was the next child to King Edward the Fourth, which his mother had by Richard Duke of York, and that King was then eighteen years of age : and for the small distance betwixt her children, see Austin Vincent, in his 'Book of Nobility,' p. 622, where he writes of them all." It may further be observed, that Lord Clifford, who was then himself only twenty-five years of age, had been a leading man and commander two or three years together in the army of Lancaster, before this time ; and, therefore, would be less likely to think that the Earl of Rutland might be entitled to mercy from his youth.—But independent of this act, at best a cruel and savage one, the family of Clifford had done enough to draw upon them the vehement hatred of the House of York : so that after the Battle of Towton there was no hope for them but in flight and concealment. Henry, the subject of the poem, was deprived of his estate and honours during the space of twenty-four years ; all which time he lived as a shepherd in Yorkshire, or in Cumberland, where the estate of his father-in-law (Sir Lancelot Threlkeld) lay. He was restored to his estate and honours in the first year of Henry the Seventh. It is recorded that, " when called to

Parliament, he behaved nobly and wisely; but otherwise
came seldom to London or the Court; and rather de-
lighted to live in the country, where he repaired several of
his Castles, which had gone to decay during the late
troubles." Thus far is chiefly collected from Nicholson
and Burn; and I can add, from my own knowledge, that
there is a tradition current in the village of Threlkeld and
its neighbourhood, his principal retreat, that, in the
course of his shepherd-life, he had acquired great astro-
nomical knowledge. I cannot conclude this note without
adding a word upon the subject of those numerous and
noble feudal edifices, spoken of in the poem, the ruins of
some of which are, at this day, so great an ornament to
that interesting country. The Cliffords had always been
distinguished for an honourable pride in these Castles;
and we have seen that, after the wars of York and Lan-
caster, they were rebuilt; in the civil wars of Charles
the First they were again laid waste, and again restored
almost to their former magnificence by the celebrated
Lady Anne Clifford, Countess of Pembroke, etc., etc. Not
more than twenty-five years after this was done, when the
estates of Clifford had passed into the family of Tufton,
three of these Castles, namely, Brough, Brougham, and
Pendragon, were demolished, and the timber and other
materials sold by Thomas Earl of Thanet. We will
hope that, when this order was issued, the Earl had not
consulted the text of Isaiah, 58th chap. 12th verse, to
which the inscription placed over the gate of Pendragon
Castle, by the Countess of Pembroke (I believe his grand-
mother), at the time she repaired that structure, refers
the reader :—" *And they that shall be of thee shall build
the old waste places: thou shalt raise up the foundations of
many generations; and thou shalt be called the repairer of
the breach, the restorer of paths to dwell in.*" The Earl of
Thanet, the present possessor of the Estates, with a due
respect for the memory of his ancestors, and a proper sense
of the value and beauty of these remains of antiquity, has
(I am told) given orders that they shall be preserved from
all depredations.—W. W.

This poem was composed at Coleorton while I was
walking to and fro along the path that led from Sir
George Beaumont's Farm-house, where we resided, to the
Hall which was building at that time.—I. F.

Dated by Wordsworth 1807; first published 1807. The
change of text of perhaps chief interest is the introduction
in 1836 of greater metrical regularity, to the loss, I think,

of metrical beauty, in ll. 127-137. The earlier readings in this passage are:

   Ll. 126, 127—" They moved about in open sight,
              To and fro, for his delight."

   L. 129—" On the mountains visitant; "
   L. 131—" And the caves where Faeries sing."
   L. 135—" Face of thing that is to be."
   Ll. 136, 137 (1842); in 1807-1820:

     " And, if [if that, 1836] Men report him right,
     He can [could, 1827-1836] whisper words of might."

Perhaps it was also for metrical reasons that line 38 (1836) was altered from the earlier " Knight, squire, yeoman, page, or groom."

The other changes are few. L. 37 (1845) was previously " 'Though she is but a lonely Tower," altered perhaps because of the resemblance to l. 49. This l. 37 was followed in 1807-1820 by two lines:

    " Silent, deserted of her best,
    Without an Inmate or a Guest."

Altered (1820-1843) to:

    " To vacancy and silence left,
    Of all her guardian sons bereft,"

and omitted in 1845. In 1845, also, two lines were omitted which followed l. 117, and were connected with ll. 116, 117, then somewhat different in text:

    " Yet lacks not friends for solemn [simple, 1845] glee,
    And a chearful [spirit soothing, 1836-1843] company,
    That learn'd of him submissive ways;
    And comforted his private days" (1807-1843).

   Ll. 157-159 (1845) were previously:

    " Alas! the fervent Harper did not know
    That for a tranquil Soul the Lay was framed,
    Who, long compell'd in humble walks to go."

Is " royalty " (1815 only) for " loyalty " in l. 35 a misprint ?—ED.

   " Earth helped him with the cry of blood " (*page* 141).

   This line is from " The Battle of Bosworth Field," by Sir John Beaumont (brother to the Dramatist), whose poems are written with much spirit, elegance, and harmony; and have deservedly been reprinted lately in Chalmers' " Collection of English Poets."—W. W.

> " *And both the undying fish that swim*
> *Through Bowscale-tarn,*" etc. (*page* 143).

It is imagined by the people of the country that there are two immortal fish, inhabitants of this tarn, which lies in the mountains not far from Threlkeld.—Blencathara, mentioned before, is the old and proper name of the mountain vulgarly called Saddle-back.—W. W.

> " *Armour rusting in his Halls*
> *On the blood of Clifford calls* " (*page* 144).

The martial character of the Cliffords is well known to the readers of English history; but it may not be improper here to say, by way of comment on these lines and what follows, that besides several others who perished in the same manner, the four immediate progenitors of the person in whose hearing this is supposed to be spoken, all died in the field.—W. W.

Lines composed a few miles above Tintern Abbey (*page* 145).

No poem of mine was composed under circumstances more pleasant for me to remember than this. I began it upon leaving Tintern, after crossing the Wye, and concluded it just as I was entering Bristol in the evening, after a ramble of four or five days, with my sister. Not a line of it was altered, and not any part of it written down till I reached Bristol. It was published almost immediately after in the little volume of which so much has been said in these Notes.—I. F.

Written 1798; first published 1798. The earlier visit to the Wye, referred to in the opening lines, was in 1793, after Wordsworth's wanderings on Salisbury Plain. Changes of text are few. In l. 4 "soft inland murmur," 1845, replaced " sweet inland murmur."

Ll. 13-14 (1845) were previously:

> " Among the woods and copses lose themselves,
> Nor, with their green and simple hue, disturb
> The wild green landscape." (1798-1800.)

" Are clad in one green hue, and lose themselves
Among the woods and copses, nor disturb
The wild green landscape." (1802-1843.)

A line in the text of 1798, between l. 18 and l. 19—
" And the low copses—coming from the trees "—is can-
celled in the *errata* of that edition.

Ll. 22, 23 (1827); previously:

" Though absent long
These forms of beauty."

L. 32 (1820); previously, " As may have had no trivial
influence."—ED.

" *It is no Spirit who from heaven hath flown* " (*page* 150).

Written at Town-end, Grasmere.   I remember the
instant my sister, S. H., called me to the window of our
Cottage, saying, " Look how beautiful is yon star! It
has the sky all to itself."   I composed the verses im-
mediately.—I. F.

Dated by Wordsworth 1803; first published 1807.
Edd. 1836-1849 give the same text as 1807.   But in 1815
ll. 13-14 became :

" That even I beyond my natural race
Might step as thou dost now :—might one day trace."

In 1820-1832 this was abandoned, and ll. 9-14 became :

" O most ambitious Star! thy Presence brought
A startling recollection to my mind
Of the distinguished few among mankind,
Who dare to step beyond their natural race,
As thou seem'st now to do :—nor was a thought
Denied—that even I might one day trace
Some ground not mine ; "

Compare these lines with those prefixed to the entire
collection of Wordsworth's poetry—" If thou indeed de-
rive thy light from heaven."—ED.

French Revolution (*page* 151).

An extract from the long poem on my own poetical
education.   It was first published by Coleridge in his
" Friend," which is the reason of its having had a place in
every edition of my poems since.—I. F.

Dated by Wordsworth 1805, in which year " The

Prelude " was finished ; but the eleventh book containing this passage was probably written in Dec., 1804. I allow Wordsworth's date to stand; first published in " The Friend," No. 11, Oct. 26, 1809 ; first included in Wordsworth's Poems, 1815.

In l. 3, for " we " " The Prelude " has " us."

L. 11, " Enchantress " (1815); " Enchanter " (1809).

Ll. 15, 16 (1832); previously :

> " (To take an image which was felt no doubt
> Among the bowers of paradise itself.)"

The prosaic and self-conscious " to take an image " probably offended Wordsworth.

L. 24 (1815); in 1809, " Their ministers used to stir in lordly wise," and in l. 26, " deal."

L. 36, " subterranean " (1832); " subterraneous " (1809-1827).—ED.

" *Yes, it was the mountain echo* " (*page* 152).

Written at Town-end, Grasmere. The echo came from Nab-Scar, when I was walking on the opposite side of Rydal Mere. I will here mention, for my dear sister's sake, that, while she was sitting alone one day high up on this part of Loughrigg Fell, she was so affected by the voice of the Cuckoo heard from the crags at some distance that she could not suppress a wish to have a stone inscribed with her name among the rocks from which the sound proceeded. On my return from my walk I recited these verses to Mrs. Wordsworth.—I. F.

Dated by Wordsworth 1806; first published 1807. In ed. (1815) only this Poem is named " The Echo." In 1807 a stanza came between st. 1 and the present st. 2, which was omitted from all subsequent editions :

> " Whence the Voice ? from air or earth ?
> This the Cuckoo cannot tell;
> But a startling sound had birth,
> As the Bird must know full well."

There followed, in 1807 (only), as first two lines of the next stanza (*i.e.* the present st. 2):

> " Like the voice through earth and sky
> By the restless Cuckoo sent; "

The present text of these lines is of 1815.

In 1827 the first stanza was retouched; previously:

> " Yes! full surely 'twas the Echo,
> Solitary, clear, profound,
> Answering to thee, shouting Cuckoo!
> Giving to thee Sound for Sound."

The last stanza—now as in 1836—in 1807 stood thus:

> " Such within ourselves we hear
> Oft-times, ours though sent from far;
> Listen, ponder, hold them dear; "

In 1827 :

> " Such rebounds our inward ear
> Often catches from afar ;—
> Giddy Mortals hold them dear; "

In 1832 Wordsworth happily restored the third line as in 1807; the first two became:

> " Often as thy inward ear
> Catches such rebounds, beware—"

To Barron Field, who objected to the 1827 text, Wordsworth wrote : " The word 'rebounds' I wish much to introduce here; for the imaginative warning turns upon the echo, which ought to be revived as near the conclusion as possible."—Knight's " Life," iii. 155.—Ed.

To a Skylark (page 153).

Written at Rydal Mount.—I. F.

Dated by Wordsworth 1825; first published 1827. In 1845 Wordsworth transferred a stanza, coming second, from this poem to that named " A Morning Exercise." In the Fenwick note to this latter poem Wordsworth expresses a wish that its last five stanzas—interpreting the spirit of the skylark—should be read with the present poem.

In l. 10 "instinct" (1832) replaced " rapture " (1827).—Ed.

Laodamia (page 154).

Written at Rydal Mount. The incident of the trees growing and withering put the subject into my thoughts, and I wrote with the hope of giving it a loftier tone than, so far as I know, has been given to it by any of the Ancients who have treated of it. It cost me more trouble than almost anything of equal length I have ever written.—I. F.

Dated by Wordsworth 1814; first published 1815. Classed, 1815-1820, among " Poems Founded on the Affections," and according to Crabb Robinson (" Diary," May 9, 1815), "not much esteemed" by its author, as belonging to this " inferior " class. Yet to Mrs. Alaric Watts the poet spoke of " Lycidas " and " Laodamia " as " twin immortals."—" Alaric Watts," i. 240.

Of several changes of text, by far the most important is that which concerns the fate of Laodamia after death, ll. 158-163; the several forms of this stanza are the following:

> " Ah, judge her gently who so deeply loved!
> Her, who, in reason's spite, yet without crime,
> Was in a trance of passion thus removed;
> Delivered from the galling yoke of time
> And these frail elements—to gather flowers
> Of blissful quiet 'mid unfading bowers." (1815-1820.)

In 1827 she was found guilty of crime, and punished accordingly:

> " By no weak pity might the Gods be moved;
> She who thus perished not without the crime
> Of Lovers that in Reason's spite have loved,
> Was doomed to wander in a grosser clime,
> Apart from happy Ghosts—that gather flowers," etc.

In 1832 her punishment was less cruel; for "to wander in a grosser clime " we have, " to wear out her appointed time." In 1843 the present text of the stanza was reached, except in its first two lines, which stood:

> " She—who though warned, exhorted, and reproved,
> Thus died, from passion desperate to a crime—"

Finally, in 1845, these lines assumed the form in the text. Two MS. experiments are given in Professor Knight's notes.

Ll. 1-4 (1827) were previously:

> " With sacrifice before the rising morn
> Performed, my slaughtered Lord have I required;
> And in thick darkness, amid shades forlorn,
> Him of the infernal Gods have I desired: "

Landor in 1824 (" Imag. Conversations," Southey and

Porson) objected to the rhyme "required"—"desired.".
Wordsworth, in a letter to Landor, Jan. 21, 1824 (Knight's
"Life," iii. 95), admits the objection, and says that he had
tried to alter the words. Another objection of Landor—
that to ll. 101, 102 in the earlier form (1815-1820)—

> "Spake, as a witness, of a second birth
> For all that is most perfect upon earth;"

—the objection that "witness" and "second birth" come
"stinking and reeking to us from the conventicle,"
Wordsworth repels; but in 1827 the present reading was
substituted. One other change is significant: l. 76, "A
fervent, not ungovernable love" (1820) was in 1815,
"The fervor—not the impotence of love." The remaining
changes are slight: l. 45 "could" (1820), "did" (1815);
l. 51 "Which" (1820), "That" (1815); l. 58 "Thou
should'st elude" (1842), previously "That thou should'st
cheat"; l. 68 (1836), previously "Know, virtue were not
virtue if the joys"; l. 82 "vernal" (1827), "beauty's"
(1815-1820); l. 122 "The oracle" (1820), "Our future
course" (1815); l. 146 "Seeking" (1836), previously
"Towards"; l. 147 "that" (1827), previously "this."

Professor Knight ("Poet. Works," vi. Appendix, p.
357) gives from MS. two stanzas at one time intended to
follow the present st. 2:

"That rapture failing, the distracted Queen
Knelt and embraced the Statue of the God:
'Mighty the boon I ask, but Earth has seen
Effects as awful from thy gracious nod;
All-ruling Jove, unbind the mortal chain,
Nor let the force of prayer be spent in vain!'

Round the high-scaled [? high-seated] Temple a soft breeze
Along the column [s ?] sighed—all else was still—
Mute, vacant as the face of summer seas,
No sign accorded of a favouring will.
Dejected she withdraws—her palace-gate
Enters—and, traversing a room of state,

O terror!" etc. See also additional note on page 344.—
ED.

Dion (page 161).

This poem began with the following stanza, which has
been displaced on account of its detaining the reader too
long from the subject, and as rather precluding, than

preparing for the due effect of the allusion to the genius of Plato :

> " Fair is the Swan, whose majesty, prevailing
> O'er breezeless water, on Locarno's lake,
> Bears him on while proudly sailing
> He leaves behind a moon-illumined wake :
> Behold! the mantling spirit of reserve
> Fashions his neck into a goodly curve ;
> An arch thrown back between luxuriant wings
> Of whitest garniture, like fir-tree boughs
> To which, on some unruffled morning, clings
> A flaky weight of winter's purest snows!
> —Behold!—as with a gushing impulse heaves
> That downy prow, and softly cleaves
> The mirror of the crystal flood,
> Vanish inverted hill, and shadowy wood,
> And pendent rocks, where'er, in gliding state,
> Winds the mute Creature without visible Mate
> Or Rival, save the Queen of night
> Showering down a silver light,
> From heaven, upon her chosen Favourite! "—W. W.

This poem was first introduced by a stanza that I have since transferred to the Notes, for reasons there given, and I cannot comply with the request expressed by some of my friends that the rejected stanza should be restored. I hope they will be content if it be, hereafter, immediately attached to the poem, instead of its being degraded to a place in the Notes.—I. F.

Dated by Wordsworth 1816; first published 1820. Classed 1820-1843 among " Poems of Sentiment and Reflection." Professor Knight dates this poem 1814, because in one of the notes dictated to Miss Fenwick in 1843 (as given in " Memoirs," ii. 75) Wordsworth says of " Laodamia " that it was " written at the same time as ' Dion ' and ' Artegal and Elidure.' " But against this vague statement there are the facts; (1) that Wordsworth in 1837 dated ' Dion ' 1816 ; (2) that it was not printed in ed. 1815 ; (3) that " Artegal and Elidure " is dated by Wordsworth 1815. The most interesting fact about the text is the excision, in 1837, of the opening passage which describes the swan, now given by Wordsworth in his note. In the Fenwick note to " The Evening Walk " Wordsworth says that the swan in " Dion " came from his youthful recollection of the swans on Esthwaite lake.

Ll. 1, 2 (1837); previously :

"So pure, so bright, so fitted to embrace,
Where'er he turned, a natural grace."

Ll. 7, 8 (1837); previously :

"Nor less the homage that was seen to wait
On Dion's virtues, when the lunar beam."

Ll. 35-37 (1827); in 1820 :

"And, wheresoe'er the great Deliverer passed,
Fruits were strewn before his eye,
And flowers upon his person cast."

L. 39, "doth" (1827); "did" (1820).

L. 52, "sublime delight" (1837); previously "delight,"
and in l. 53 ed. 1837 has "Now hath he"; edd. 1843-
1849, identical in l. 53 with 1820-1832.

L. 82, "Exclaimed the Chieftain" (1827); "Intrusive
Presence!" (1820).

L. 110, "shuddered" (1832); "shudder" (1820-1827).

An interesting comparison of the poem with its source
in "Plutarch," by Mr. Heard, is given in Prof. Knight's
edition. The Fury, in "Plutarch," appears sweeping the
house with a brush, "simply ominous of coming evil . . .
the moral significance assigned to it in the poem is Words-
worth's own interpretation."—ED.

The Pass of Kirkstone (*page* 165).

Written at Rydal Mount. Thoughts and feelings of
many walks in all weathers, by day and night, over this
Pass, alone and with beloved friends.—I. F.

Dated by Wordsworth 1817; first published 1820.
Prof. Knight mentions that a MS. copy sent to the
Beaumonts is prefaced with the words "Composed chiefly
in a walk from the top of Kirkstone to Patterdale, by W.
Wordsworth, 1817," and is endorsed "Mr. Wordsworth's
Verses, June 27, 1817." Some slight variations of the
MS. are recorded by Knight. The printed text of 1820
differs from the final text only in l. 48, "the" (1820),
"this" (1836); l. 53, "as often we" (1820), "as all men
may" (1836); and l. 55, "we" (1820), "they" (1836).—
ED.

To Enterprise (*page* 168).

Written probably 1820; first published 1822, in

"Memorials of a Tour on the Continent, 1820." In this volume Wordsworth notes that "The Italian Itinerant" led to the train of thought which produced "To Enterprise." From 1827 to 1843 the poem remained connected with the poems of the Tour of 1820; in 1845 it was placed in its present position.

The third section of this poem ("If there be movements," etc.) was added in 1827, with the reading in l. 102, "an abject Nation"; "a prostrate," 1832. The other changes of text are the following:

L. 3, "that" (1837); previously "a." L. 26, "And" (1845); previously "or."

Ll. 29-32 (1837):

> "And thou (if rightly I rehearse
> What wondering Shepherds told in verse)
> From rocky fortress in mid air
> (The food which pleased thee best to win)
> Didst off the flame-eyed Eagle scare
> With infant shout,—as often sweep," (1822.)

> "And thou, whose earliest thoughts held dear
> Allurements that were edged with fear,
> (The food that pleased thee best, to win)
> From rocky fortress in mid air
> The flame-eyed Eagle oft wouldst scare
> With infant shout,—as often sweep," (1827.)

1832 identical in first three lines with 1827; then it proceeds:

> "With infant shout wouldst often scare
> From her rock-fortress in mid air
> The flame-eyed Eagle—often sweep,"

L. 34, "Or" (1837); previously "And."
Ll. 62-64 (1837); previously:

> "and a couch of rest;
> Thou to his dangers dost enchain,
> 'Mid the blank world of snow and ice." (1822.)

Ed. 1832 reverses the order of the two lines here given from ed. 1822. Ed. 1843 removes the semicolon after "rest", thus altering the sense; ed. 1845 restores the semicolon.

Ll. 68, 69 (1837); previously:

> "glide serene
> From cloud to cloud,"

L. 71, " How they, in bells " (1832); previously " Or,
in their bells."

Ll. 77-82. These lines about the steamship were added
in 1832 ; cf. Coleridge's lines on the steamship in " Youth
and Age."

L. 113, " caught amid a whirl " (1837) ; previously
" stifled under weight."

Ll. 115, 116 (1845); previously:

> " Heaving with convulsive throes,—
> It quivers—and is still." (1822-1832.)

> " Raised in a moment; with convulsive throes
> It heaved—and all is still;" (1837.)

Ll. 128-132.   The present text is identical with that of
1832, and in ll. 128-130 with 1822, except that in these
editions " while " stood for " when," and in 1832 " tall
pine's " for " pine tree's."   In 1832 ll. 131, 132 were
added.   In 1837 the text became :

> " Clothing a tall pine's northern side,
> In rough November days when winds have tried
> Their force on all things else—left naked far and wide."

Ed. 1843 reverts to 1832, with " while " altered to
" when."

L. 160, " his name " (1837); " the name " (1822).—ED.

" *Living hill* " (*page* 171).

————————— " awhile the living hill
Heaved with convulsive throes, and all was still."
DR. DARWIN.—W.W.

" *Inmate of a mountain dwelling* " (*page* 173).

Written at Rydal Mount. The lady was Miss Blackett,
then residing with Mr. Montagu Burgoyne at Fox-Ghyll.
We were tempted to remain too long upon the mountain ;
and I, imprudently, with the hope of shortening the way,
led her among the crags and down a steep slope, which
entangled us in difficulties that were met by her with
much spirit and courage.—I. F.

Dated by Wordsworth 1816; first published 1820.
The most interesting textual point concerns the word
" choral " in l. 25.   In both edd. of 1820, and in 1827, the

word is "choral"; in 1832 and subsequent edd. it is
"coral." Did Wordsworth alter the text, or is this a
misprint? I have ventured in this instance to print the
earlier reading.

Ll. 6, 7 (1827); the reading of edd. 1820 looks like an
oversight:

> " In the moment of dismay,
>   While," etc.,

" dismay " in the second line of the stanza rhyming with
" dismay " in the fourth.

L. 17 (1845); previously:

> " —Take thy flight; possess, inherit " (1820).
>
> " Now—take flight; possess, inherit " (1836).

L. 21, " their " (1836); previously " the."—ED.

To a Young Lady (page 174).

Composed at the same time and on the same view as " I
met Louisa in the shade : " indeed they were designed to
make one piece.—I. F.

Dated by Wordsworth 1803; first published 1807.
Wordsworth dates " Louisa," which he says was written
at the same time as this poem, 1805. It is impossible to
say whether both should be dated 1803, or 1805. They
are perhaps more in accord with the poetic spirit of the
year of Dorothy's expedition with her brother to Scotland
than with that of the sad year of John Wordsworth's death.
But the mountain excursion of " Louisa " (i.e., Dorothy ?)
may have been suggested by the expedition of William
and Dorothy to Patterdale in the autumn of 1805. This
poem was classed 1815-1832 among " Poems proceeding
from Sentiment and Reflection."

L. 5, " heart-stirring " (1837); previously " delightful."
Ll. 8, 9 (1827, with " That " for " Which " (1836) in
l. 9); previously:

> " As if thy heritage were joy,
>   And pleasure were thy trade."

L. 16, " serene " (1815); " alive " (1807).—ED.

Water-Fowl (page 175).

Observed frequently over the lakes of Rydal and Gras-
mere.—I. F.

In the text I dated this fragment from " The Recluse,'

(Part I, B. 1,) 1804, but I fear erroneously. Wordsworth himself dates the fragment 1812. Professor Knight dates the First Book of "The Recluse" 1805, but it is certainly written as if in 1800, a few months after the poet's removal to Dove Cottage. Perhaps it was not actually completed until 1812, or possibly this passage was added in that year. The extract appeared in "A Description of the Scenery of the Lakes," 1823 (perhaps also in ed. 1822); it does not appear in the earliest form of "A Description" —that prefixed to the Rev. Joseph Wilkinson's "Select Views in Cumberland, Westmoreland, and Lancashire," 1810, nor in 1820; it was first included in Wordsworth's Poetical Works in 1827. The present text is identical with that of 1823 and 1827; but "The Recluse" shows the following variations:

Lines 1-3:

> " Behold how with a grace
> Of ceaseless motion, that might scarcely seem
> Inferior to angelical, they prolong "

L. 12, " upwards and downwards "; l. 15, " Ten times and more "; l. 20, " among their plumes "; l. 21:

> " Tempt the smooth water or the gleaming ice."—ED.

View from the Top of Black Comb (*page* 176).

Mrs. Wordsworth and I, as mentioned in the "Epistle to Sir G. Beaumont," lived some time under its shadow. —I. F.

Dated by Wordsworth 1813; first published 1815. In l. 21, " Her " (1827) replaced " Its " (1815-1820); in l. 25 "line" (1832) replaced "frame" (1815-1827). Compare the Inscription " Written with a Slate Pencil on a Stone, on the Side of the Mountain of Black Comb."—ED.

The Haunted Tree (*page* 178).

This tree grew in the park of Rydal, and I have often listened to its creaking as described.—I. F.

Dated by Wordsworth 1819; first published 1820. Named in the Duddon Volume of 1820 " To —— "; named as now in the collected " Miscellaneous Poems " of that year. Line 34, " O lovely Wanderer of the trackless hills," was added in 1827. An instance of Wordsworth's fastidiousness is seen in l. 15 : " wearied with the chase "

(1836) was in 1820 " weary of," in 1827 " wearied of," in 1832 " wearied by." In l. 7 " the" (1827) was " that " (1820); in l. 29 " the" (1836) was previously " this "; in l. 37 " the while " (1849) was previously " the whilst." Line 10 (1827) displaced the earlier " As beautiful a couch as e'er on earth."—ED.

The Triad (page 179).

Written at Rydal Mount. The girls, Edith Southey, my daughter Dora, and Sara Coleridge.—I. F.

Dated by Wordsworth 1828; first published in "The Keepsake," 1829; first included in Wordsworth's Poetical Works, 1832. The girls are described in the order in which the names are given in the Fenwick note. The allusion in l. 40 is perhaps to St. Herbert's Island, Derwentwater, near the home of Edith Southey. In l. 137 there is, says Sara Coleridge (" Memoir and Letters of Sara Coleridge,") an allusion to a supposed likeness between Dora Wordsworth's contour of face and the great Memnon head in the British Museum. " There is," Sara Coleridge (one of the triad) writes, "no truth in the Poem as a whole, although bits of truth, glazed and magnified, are embodied in it."

Lines 19-21 (1836); previously :

" And not the boldest tongue of envious pride
In you those interweavings could reprove
Which they, the progeny of Jove,"

L. 24, " sing " (1836); previously " speak."
Ll. 34, 35 (1836); previously :

" Fear not this constraining measure !
Drawn by a poetic spell."

L. 42, " snow-white sail!" (1845); previously " silver sail."
Ll. 59, 60 (1845); previously :

" That its fair flowers may brush from off his cheek
The too, too happy tear ! "

Ll. 88-93 (1836); previously :

" While to these shades a Nymph I call,
The youngest of the lovely Three.—
' Come if the notes thine ear may pierce,
Submissive to the might of verse,
By none more deeply felt than Thee ! ' "

L. 98, "But" (1829) changed to "And" (1832); "But" restored (1836).

L. 104 (1836); previously "How light her air, how delicate her glee!"

L. 112, "flowers" (1832); "flower" (1829).

L. 118, "Yet more" (1836); "Yet is it more" (1829-1832).

Lines 123-126 (1836); previously only two lines:

"Though where she is beloved and loves, as free
As bird that rifles blossoms on a tree,"

L. 147, "lowly" (1832); "lowliest" (1829).

Lines 155-162 (1832), with the reading in 157, 158, "there ensue Aught untoward," altered to present reading 1845). In 1836, l. 155, the reading "the genuine law!" looks like a misprint. The passage in 1829 ran thus:

"O the charm that manners draw,
Nature, from thy genuine law!
Through benign affections—pure,
In the slight of self—secure,
If, from what her hand would do,
Or tongue utter, there ensue
Aught untoward or unfit,
Transient mischief, vague mischance,
Shunn'd by guarded elegance," [comma, and no break in sense.]

L. 170 (1832); "Oberon the fairy" (1829).

L. 185 "peaceful" (1832); "fearless," (1829).—ED.

The Wishing-Gate (page 186).

Written at Rydal Mount. See also "Wishing-gate Destroyed."—I. F.

Dated by Wordsworth 1828; first published in "The Keepsake," 1829; first included in Wordsworth's Poetical Works, 1832, where it appears among "Poems of Sentiment and Reflection"; placed among "Poems of the Imagination," 1836. The only changes of text from that of 1829 are in l. 31, "Yea!" (1832) for "Yes," and in l. 64, "thirst" (1836) for "yearn" (1829-1832).—ED.

The Wishing-Gate Destroyed (page 189).

"In the Vale of Grasmere, by the side of the old highway leading to Ambleside, is a gate which, time out of mind, has been called the Wishing-gate."

Having been told, upon what I thought good authority, that this gate had been destroyed, and the opening, where it hung, walled up, I gave vent immediately to my feelings in these stanzas. But going to the place some time after, I found, with much delight, my old favourite unmolested.—W.W.

Date uncertain; probably after 1836-1837, since it is not included in that edition, and certainly not later than 1842, in which year it was first published in " Poems, chiefly of Early and Late Years." Text unchanged.—ED.

The Primrose of the Rock (page 191).

Written at Rydal Mount. The rock stands on the right hand a little way leading up the middle road from Rydal to Grasmere. We have been in the habit of calling it the Glow-worm Rock from the number of glow-worms we have often seen hanging on it as described. The tuft of primrose has, I fear, been washed away by the heavy rains.—I. F.

Dated by Wordsworth 1831; first published, 1835. In Dorothy Wordsworth's Journal, April 24, 1802, we read: " We walked in the evening to Rydal. Coleridge and I lingered behind. . . . We all stood to look at Glow-worm Rock—a primrose that grew there, and just looked out on the road from its own sheltered bower." (Knight's " Life of Wordsworth," i. 310.) Text unchanged.—ED.

Presentiments (page 193).

Written at Rydal Mount.—I. F.

Dated by Wordsworth 1830; first published 1835. Text unchanged.—ED.

Vernal Ode (page 196).

Composed at Rydal Mount, to place in view the immortality of succession where immortality is denied, as far as we know, to the individual creature.—I. F.

Dated by Wordsworth 1817; first published 1820; named (in the Duddon volume) " Ode.—1817 "; in the Miscellaneous Poems, " Ode," but has the page-heading " Vernal Ode "; placed among " Poems of the Imagination," 1820, 1836-1849; among " Poems of Sentiment and Reflection," 1827-1832. In 1820 and 1827 this Ode consisted of five stanzas or sections; in 1832 the second and third were run into one; in 1836 the first eight lines of the third stanza (" What if those bright fires") were added (with the word " image " instead of the 1845-1849 " vision "), and the present arrangement in five stanzas was adopted. Two other changes of importance were made in the original ode : first, lines 37-39 replaced (1827) the one line of 1820 (Miscellaneous Poems), " So wills eternal Love, with power divine "; in the *Duddon* volume of 1820 (the earlier of the two texts), the line is, " So wills eternal Love and Power divine." The second change of importance is in the original opening of stanza 3 (now lines 48-51), which was in 1820 :

> " And what if his presiding breath
> Impart a sympathetic motion
> Unto the gates of life and death,
> Throughout the bounds of earth and ocean."

The present text of these lines is of 1827.

L. 3, " the " (1836); previously " that."

L. 9 (1827); in 1820, " Poised in the middle region of the air."

L. 12 (1827); in 1820, " Until he reached a rock, of summit bare."

L. 13, " noontide " (1827); " summer " (1820).

Ll. 29, 30 (1836); in 1820-1832 :

> " and [but, 1827-1832] imaged to his hope
> (Alas, how faintly !) in the hue."

L. 34, " star " (1827); " orb " (1820).

L. 68, " subtle " (1827); " joyous " (1820).

L. 69, " breezes " (1849); " zephyrs " in all previous editions.

L. 71, " Mortals, rejoice," (1827); " Rejoice, O men ! " (1820).

L. 102, " common weal " (1845); previously " public weal."—ED.

Devotional Incitements (page 200).

Written at Rydal Mount.—I. F.

Dated by Wordsworth 1832; first published 1835. The two couplets, ll. 50-54, appeared in a reverse order

in 1835 with the reading " The solemn rites, the " etc. ;
the transposition was made in 1836. In l. 69, " eternal
Will" (1836) replaced " almighty Will " (1835). Line
71 (1845) replaced the earlier readings :

" Her admonitions Nature yields " (1835).

" Divine admonishment She yields " (1836).—ED.

The Cuckoo Clock (page 203).

Of this clock I have nothing further to say than what
the poem expresses, except that it must be here recorded
that it was a present from the dear friend for whose sake
these Notes were chiefly undertaken, and who has written
them from my dictation.—I. F.

Date uncertain; probably after 1836-1837, in the edition
of which date it is not found, and certainly not later than
1842, when it was first published in " Poems chiefly of
Early and Late Years." Text unchanged. The last
line of stanza 3 refers to the " wandering Voice " of
Wordsworth's poem " To the Cuckoo." In connection
with this stanza it may be noted that the cuckoo clock
was not stopped during Wordsworth's last illness. He
died " just," Mrs. Cookson said, " when the cuckoo clock
was singing noon."—Knight's " Life," iii. 439.—ED.

To the Clouds (page 205).

These verses were suggested while I was walking on
the foot-road between Rydal Mount and Grasmere. The
clouds were driving over the top of Nab-Scar across the
vale : they set my thoughts agoing, and the rest followed
almost immediately.—I. F.

Date uncertain ; probably after 1836-1837, in the edition
of which date it is not found, and certainly not later than
1842, when it was first published (with the title " Address
to the Clouds ") in " Poems, chiefly of Early and Late
Years." Printed text unchanged ; but Professor Knight
in notes to the poem gives some variations from MS.—ED.

Suggested by a Picture of the Bird of Paradise (page 208).

This subject has been treated of in another Note. I
will here only by way of comment direct attention to the
fact that pictures of animals and other productions of

nature as seen in conservatories, menageries, museums, etc., would do little for the national mind, nay they would be rather injurious to it, if the imagination were excluded by the presence of the object, more or less out of a state of nature. If it were not that we learn to talk and think of the lion and the eagle, the palm-tree and even the cedar, from the impassioned introduction of them so frequently into Holy Scripture and by great poets, and divines who write as poets, the spiritual part of our nature, and therefore the higher part of it, would derive no benefit from such intercourse with such objects.—I. F.

Date uncertain; probably between 1836-1837 and 1842 (for same reason as last two poems; see preceding notes); first published 1842, in " Poems, chiefly of Early and Late Years." Text unchanged.—Ed.

A Jewish Family (page 209).

Coleridge, my daughter, and I, in 1828, passed a fortnight upon the banks of the Rhine, principally under the hospitable roof of Mr. Aders of Gotesburg, but two days of the time we spent at St. Goar in rambles among the neighbouring valleys. It was at St. Goar that I saw the Jewish family here described. Though exceedingly poor, and in rags, they were not less beautiful than I have endeavoured to make them appear. We had taken a little dinner with us in a basket, and invited them to partake of it, which the mother refused to do, both for herself and children, saying it was with them a fast-day; adding diffidently, that whether such observances were right or wrong, she felt it her duty to keep them strictly. The Jews, who are numerous on this part of the Rhine, greatly surpass the German peasantry in the beauty of their features and in the intelligence of their countenances. But the lower classes of the German peasantry have, here at least, the air of people grievously opprest. Nursing mothers, at the age of seven or eight and twenty often look haggard and far more decayed and withered than women of Cumberland and Westmoreland twice their age. This comes from being underfed and overworked in their vineyards in a hot and glaring sun.—I. F.

Dated by Wordsworth 1828; first published 1835. Text unchanged, but a few different readings from a MS. copy sent by Dorothy Wordsworth to Lady Beaumont are given in notes to the poem by Prof. Knight.—Ed.

On the Power of Sound (page 211).

Written at Rydal Mount. I have often regretted that
my tour in Ireland, chiefly performed in the short days of
October in a Carriage-and-four (I was with Mr. Mar-
shall), supplied my memory with so few images that were
new, and with so little motive to write. The lines how-
ever in this poem, " Thou too be heard, lone eagle! "
were suggested near the Giant's Causeway, or rather at
the promontory of Fairhead, where a pair of eagles
wheeled above our heads and darted off as if to hide
themselves in a blaze of sky made by the setting sun.
—I. F.

Dated by Wordsworth 1828; first published 1835.
In stanza 11, the three lines beginning " Ye wandering
utterances " replaced in 1836 the following of 1835 :

> " O for some soul-affecting scheme
> Of *moral* music, to unite
> Wanderers whose portion is the faintest dream."

Prof. Knight gives a different opening of stanza 12 from
a MS. copy by Dorothy Wordsworth. He also happily
compares with the lines in stanza 14 :

> " O Silence ! are Man's noisy years
> No more than moments of thy life ? "

the similar lines in " Ode on Intimations of Immortality,
&c.":

> " Our noisy years seem moments in the being
> Of the eternal Silence."—ED.

Peter Bell (page 219).

Written at Alfoxden. Founded upon an anecdote,
which I read in a newspaper, of an ass being found hang-
ing his head over a canal in a wretched posture. Upon
examination a dead body was found in the water and
proved to be the body of its master. The countenance,
gait, and figure of Peter, were taken from a wild rover
with whom I walked from Builth, on the river Wye,
downwards nearly as far as the town of Hay. He told
me strange stories. It has always been a pleasure to me
through life to catch at every opportunity that has
occurred in my rambles of becoming acquainted with this

class of people. The number of Peter's wives was taken
from the trespasses in this way of a lawless creature who
lived in the county of Durham, and used to be attended by
many women, sometimes not less than half a dozen, as
disorderly as himself. Benoni, or the child of sorrow, I
knew when I was a school-boy. His mother had been
deserted by a gentleman in the neighbourhood, she her-
self being a gentlewoman by birth. The circumstances
of her story were told me by my dear old Dame, Anne
Tyson, who was her confidante. The lady died broken-
hearted.—In the woods of Alfoxden I used to take great
delight in noticing the habits, tricks, and physiognomy of
asses ; and I have no doubt that I was thus put upon
writing the poem out of liking for the creature that is
so often dreadfully abused.—The crescent-moon, which
makes such a figure in the prologue, assumed this
character one evening while I was watching its beauty in
front of Alfoxden House. I intended this poem for the
volume before spoken of, but it was not published for
more than twenty years afterwards.—The worship of the
Methodists or Ranters is often heard during the stillness
of the summer evening in the country with affecting
accompaniments of rural beauty. In both the psalmody
and the voice of the preacher there is, not unfrequently,
much solemnity likely to impress the feelings of the
rudest characters under favourable circumstances.—I. F.

Dated by Wordsworth 1798 ; first published 1819. In
Dorothy Wordsworth's Journal we find "April 20,
[1798] . . . The moon crescent. 'Peter Bell' begun."
When Hazlitt visited Alfoxden in 1798 Wordsworth
"read us the story of 'Peter Bell' in the open air . . . .
and he announced the fate of his hero in prophetic tones."
When the publication of "Lyrical Ballads" was under
consideration Coleridge wrote to Joseph Cottle : "Words-
worth would not object to the publishing of 'Peter Bell'
or the 'Salisbury Plain' [i e., 'Guilt and Sorrow']
singly : but to the publishing of his poems in two volumes
he is decisively repugnant and oppugnant." (Cottle's
"Reminiscences, &c." ed. 1847, p. 179). Additions were
made in 1802 ; we read in Dorothy's Journal, Feb.
17th . . "I copied the second part of 'Peter Bell.'" Feb.
18th . . . "I copied new part of 'Peter Bell' in William's
absence." . . Feb. 20th, "I wrote the first part of 'Peter
Bell.'" Feb. 21 . . . "I wrote the second prologue to
'Peter Bell.' . . After dinner I wrote the first prologue."
In 1812 (June 6th), Crabb Robinson lent the MS. of

" Peter Bell " to C. Lamb, who did not value the poem highly.

On satires and parodies connected with " Peter Bell " see " Peter Bell and his Tormentors ' in Gosse's " Gossip in a Library." John Hamilton Reynolds' " Peter Bell: A Lyrical Ballad " (1819), appeared before the original. The authorship of " The Dead Asses : A Lyrical Ballad," 1819, is unknown. " Benjamin the Waggoner," 1819, also anonymous, is a much more elaborate attack on Wordsworth, and is largely concerned with " Peter Bell." Shelley's " Peter Bell the Third " deals less with style than with Wordsworth's decay of imagination, as connected with a decay of his ardour for political freedom. Peter is the hero of a blank verse parody in " Warreniana," 1824.

In 1820, Wordsworth, yielding to the representations of friends, removed or altered some of the stanzas which had excited ridicule. See Crabb Robinson's " Diary " for June 2 of that year. The stanza beginning " It is a party in a parlour," was omitted, Wordsworth says, " though one of the most imaginative in the whole piece— not to offend the pious." (Wordsworth to Barron Field, in Knight's " Life," iii. 155). In 1827 and 1836 Wordsworth made considerable changes in " Peter Bell," and even so late as 1849 it was retouched; thus, as the Poem stands, it is the result of fifty years' consideration.

L. 2, " There's " (1827); previously " And."

L. 5 (1849); " Whose shape is like the crescent moon " (1819-1843); " For shape just like " (1845).

L. 13, " danger's in " (1845); previously " danger fills."

L. 16, " untroubled I admire " (1827); " I from the helm admire " (1819-1820).

L. 24 (1827); " Or deep into the Heavens we dive " (1819); " Or into massy clouds we dive " (1820).

L. 31 " among " (1820); " between " (1819).

Ll. 41, 42 (1827); previously :

> " The towns in Saturn are ill-built,
> But proud let *him* be who has seen them ;"

L. 45, " among them " (1827); previously " between them."

L. 50, " little Earth " (1827); previously " darling speck."

L. 56, " she is " (1836); previously " it is."

L. 77, " homesick Loon " (1827); previously " heart-sick loon."

After l. 80, came in 1819-1820 the following stanza (omitted 1827):

> " Out—out—and like a brooding hen,
> Beside your sooty hearth-stone cower;
> Go, creep along the dirt, and pick
> Your way with your good walking-stick,
> Just three good miles an hour!"

L. 98, " that land " (1827); previously " the land."

L. 119 (1845); previously " My radiant pinnace you forget."

L. 129 (1827); previously " For, I myself, in very truth."

Ll. 171, 172 (1845); in 1819:

> " Off flew my sparkling Boat in scorn,
> Yea, in a trance of indignation ! "

The second line became in 1820: " Spurning her freight with indignation."

Ll. 174, 175 (1845); in 1819 " to " for " toward " (1827) and " some vexation " (1819-1843).

L. 184, " quickly " (1827), " promptly " (1819-1820).

The last stanza of Prologue dates from 1827; previously:

> " Breath failed me as I spake—but soon
> With lips, no doubt, and visage pale,
> And sore too from a slight contusion,
> Did I, to cover my confusion,
> Begin the *promised* Tale."

PART FIRST (p. 226).—The first stanza dates from 1820. That which it replaced was objected to by Crabb Robinson, and Wordsworth yielded:

> " All by the moonlight river side
> It gave three miserable groans;
> ' 'Tis come then to a pretty pass,'
> Said Peter to the groaning Ass,
> ' But I will *bang* your bones ! ' "   (1819.)

Then the 1819 text proceeded:

> " ' Good Sir ! ' the Vicar's voice exclaim'd,
> ' You rush at once into the middle;'
> And little Bess, with accent sweeter,
> Cried, ' O dear Sir ! but who is Peter ? '
> Said Stephen,—' 'Tis a downright riddle ! '

"The Squire said, ' Sure as paradise
' Was lost to man by Adam's sinning,
' This leap is for us all too bold ;
' Who Peter was, let that be told,
' And start from the beginning.' "

The earlier stanza was omitted in 1820, and in the second the following change was made :

" ' Like winds that lash the waves, or smite
The woods the [" the " omitted 1827] autumnal
        foliage thinning—
' Hold ! ' said the Squire, ' I pray you, hold !
Who Peter was, &c.' "

The second stanza in the text dates from 1836. Lamb's opinion perhaps induced these changes. (See Lamb's letters, ed. Ainger, ii. 20.)

Ll. 214, 215, " that [" its " 1819, " his " 1836] ponderous knell " (1843) ; " A [" its " 1819, " his " 1843] far-renowned alarum " (1845).

Ll. 271, 272 (1820) ; in 1819 :

" With Peter Bell, I need not tell
That this had never been the case ;—"

L. 342, " cheerily " (1836) ; " cheerfully " (1819-1832).

L. 354 (1827) ; previously " Till he is brought to an old quarry.—"

After l. 355 came in 1819 a stanza omitted in 1820 :

" ' What ! would'st thou daunt me grisly den ?
' Back must I, having come so far ?
' Stretch as thou wilt thy gloomy jaws,
' I'll on, nor would I give two straws
' For lantern or for star ! ' "

Then followed in the next stanza, 1819 (altered 1820 to present text) :

" And so where on the huge rough stones
The black and massy shadows lay,
And through, &c."

After l. 375, ed. 1819 had the following stanza, omitted 1820 :

" Now you'll suppose that Peter Bell
Felt small temptation here to tarry,
And so it was,—but I must add,

His heart was not a little glad
When he was out of the old quarry."

L. 381, "the deep" (1827); previously "that deep."
L. 383 (1836); previously "And now he is among the trees."
In 1819 l. 385 was followed by these stanzas :

"'No doubt I'm founder'd in these woods—
'For once,' quoth he, 'I will be wise,
'With better speed I'll back again—
'And lest the journey should prove vain,
'Will take yon Ass, my lawful prize!'

"Off Peter hied,—'A comely beast!
'Though not so plump as he might be ;
'My honest friend, with such a platter,
'You should have been a little fatter,
'But come, Sir, come with me!'

"But first doth Peter deem it fit
To spy about him far and near ;
There 's not a single house in sight,
No woodman's hut, no cottage light—
Peter you need not fear!"

Then came the present stanza, "There 's nothing to be seen but woods," and that which immediately follows ("His head is with a halter bound") having "Ass's" for "Creature's" (1827), and "With ready heel ["heels" 1836] the creature's ["his shaggy" 1827] side." There followed next, in 1819, a stanza omitted in 1836 :

"'What 's this!' cried Peter, brandishing
A new-peel'd sapling white as cream ;
The Ass knew well what Peter said,
But, as before, hung down his head
Over the silent stream."

This stanza was altered in 1820 in its second line :

"A new-peeled sapling ;—though, I deem,"

and in its fourth line had "He" for "But"; and again altered 1827 thus :

"though, I deem,
This threat was understood full well,
Firm, as before, the Sentinel
Stood by the silent stream."

The present text of this entire passage is of 1836.

Ll. 421-425 (1827); previously " I'll cure you of these desperate tricks," with " And " for " Yet " in l. 422, and " Ass's hide " in l. 424 for " sounding hide."

Ll. 426, 427 (1836); previously:

> " What followed ?—yielding to the shock
> The Ass, as if, &c."

L. 431 (1836); previously " And then upon his side he fell."

L. 433, " And while " (1843); previously " And as."

Ll. 434, 435, now as in 1819-1820 and 1836-1849; but in 1827-1832:

> " The Beast on his tormentor turned
> A [" His " 1832] shining hazel eye."

L. 440 (1836); previously " Towards the river deep and clear."

L. 442 (1832); previously " Heaved his lank sides."

After line 447 came, in ed. 1819:

> " ' 'Tis come now to a pretty pass '
> Said Peter to the groaning Ass,
> ' But I will *bang* your bones.'
>
> " And Peter halts to gather breath,
> And now full clearly was it shown.
> (What he before in part had seen)
> How gaunt was the poor Ass and lean,
> Yea wasted to a skeleton ! "

In 1820 this last stanza was retained; and the entire preceding stanza omitted; so too in 1827-1832, but with the new readings " And while he halts, was clearly shown," and " How gaunt the Creature was." The present text, giving the sense of the two stanzas, is of 1836.

L. 462 (1836); replacing the earlier:

> " But, while upon the ground he lay" (1819)
>
> " That instant, while outstretched he lay " (1827).

L. 465 (1836); previously " A loud and piteous bray !"

Ll. 479, 480 (1836); previously " an endless shout, The long dry see-saw."

L. 492 (1836); previously " And Peter now uplifts his

eyes." ᵼThe remaining lines of the stanza 1819-1832 were :

> " Steady the moon doth look and clear,
> And like themselves the rocks appear,
> And tranquil [" quiet " 1827-1832] are the skies."

L. 496 (1836); previously " Whereat, in resolute mood, once more "; and l. 498, " Foul purpose, quickly put to flight "; and l. 500, " beneath the shadowy trees " (present text of 1836).

L. 503; in 1832 (only) " the gallows."

Ll. 508, 509 (1836); previously " Or a gay ring,' and " brisk vagaries."

After line 515 occurred the stanza (prefixed by Shelley to his " Peter Bell ") omitted by Wordsworth after 1819 :

> " Is it a party in a parlour ?
> Cramm'd just as they on earth were cramm'd—
> Some sipping punch, some sipping tea,
> But, as you by their faces see,
> All silent and all damn'd ! "

In Crabb Robinson's Diary, June 6, 1812 (Knight's "Life of Wordsworth," ii. 200) we find : " Mrs. Basil Montagu told me she had no doubt she had suggested this image to Wordsworth by relating to him an anecdote. A person, walking in a friend's garden, looking in at a window, saw a company of ladies at a table near the window with countenances *fixed*. In an instant he was aware of their condition, and broke the window. He saved them from incipient suffocation.

Ll. 516, 517 (1827); previously :

> " A throbbing pulse the Gazer hath—
> Puzzled he was, and now is daunted ; "

L. 519 (1836); previously " Like one intent upon a book."

L. 530 (1836); previously " And drops, a senseless weight, as if his life were flown."

Ll. 536-540 (1827); previously " A happy respite !— but he wakes ;—And feels." L. 538 " And to stretch forth his hands is trying ; " l. 539 " Sure when he knows where, &c. ;" l. 540 " He'll sink into, &c."

L. 549 " Glassy " ᵼ1827); previously " Placid."

Ll. 553-555 (1827); in 1819:

> "So, faltering not in *this* intent,
> He makes his staff an instrument
> The river's depth to sound.—"

In 1820:

> "So toward the stream his head he bent,
> And downward thrust his staff, intent
> To reach the Man who there lay drowned.—"

L. 572. The words "resigned to" mean "absorbed in," a use found in the Lake District, and occurring in Dorothy Wordsworth's Journal. See Knight's "Life," p. 311, and footnote.

Ll. 586, 587 (1836); previously:

> "The meagre Shadow all this while—
> What aim is his?"

Ll. 591-595 (1836); in 1819:

> "That Peter on his back should mount
> He shows a wish, well as he can,
> 'I'll go, I'll go, whate'er betide—
> 'He to his home my way will guide,
> 'The cottage of the drowned man.'"

In 1820:

> "But no—his purpose and his wish
> The Suppliant shows, well as he can,
> Thought Peter whatsoe'er betide
> I'll go, and he my way, &c. (as in 1819).

L. 596 (1836); "This uttered ["hoping" 1820] Peter mounts forthwith" (1819); "Encouraged by this hope, he mounts" (1827); "This hoping, Peter boldly mounts" (1832).

L. 599 "That" (1827); "The" (1819-1820).

L. 610 (1836); previously "And takes his way towards the south."

L. 636 "Grasping" (1843); previously "Holding."

L. 640 (1843); "What seeks the boy?—the silent dead!" (1819-1832); "Seeking for whom?—the silent dead" (1836).

L. 652 (1820); "The listening Ass doth rightly spell" (1819).

L. 659 "cry" (1836); previously "noise."

L. 666 (1820); "Meanwhile the Ass to gain his end" (1819).

L. 673 " footsteps " (1845) ; previously " footstep."

L. 676 " the " (1836) ; previously " a."

After l. 695 in edd. 1819-1820 came a stanza omitted 1827 :

> " The verdant pathway, in and out,
> Winds upwards like a straggling chain ;
> And, when two toilsome miles are past,
> Up through the rocks it leads at last
> Into a high and open plain."

L. 700 " A " (1832) ; previously " The."

Ll. 701-703 (1836) ; in 1819 :

> " How blank !—but whence this rustling sound
> Which, all too long, the pair hath chased !
> —A dancing leaf is close behind,"

In 1820 the first line became " But whence that faintly-rustling sound."

Ll. 706, 707 (1836) ; previously :

> " When Peter spies the withered leaf,
> It yields no cure to his distress—"

L. 723 (1836) ; previously " Ha ! why this comfortless despair ? "

Ll. 733-735 (1836) ; previously :

>   " darting pains,
> As meteors shoot through heaven's wide plains,
> Pass through his bosom—and repass ! "

Ll. 741, 742 (1827) ; previously :

> " Reading as you or I might read
> At night in any pious book."

L. 748 " lonely taper " (1836) ; previously " good man's taper."

L. 756 " thus plainly seen " (1836) ; " which thus was framed " 1819-1820) ; " full plainly seen " (1827-1832).

L. 761 " to confound the meek " (1836) ; previously " to torment the good."

Ll. 766-768 (1836) a significant alteration of sense as well as words ; previously :

> " I know you, potent Spirits ! well,
> How, with the feeling and the sense
> Playing, ye govern foes or friends,
> Yok'd to your will, for fearful ends."

L. 791 (1836) ; previously " and danced."

L. 803 " snugly " (1836) ; previously " clearly."

L. 812 " has " (1836) ; previously " hath."

L. 833 " upset " (1836) ; previously " confound."
Ll. 851, 852 (1836) ; in 1819 :

> " But now [" Meanwhile " 1820] the pair have
> reach'd a spot
> Where, shelter'd by a rocky cove."

L. 858 (1836) ; previously "The building seems, wall,
roof, and tower."
Ll. 861-864 (1836) ; previously :

> " Deep-sighing as he passed along,
> Quoth Peter, ' In the shire of Fife,
> ' ' Mid such a ruin, following still
> ' From land to land a lawless will,"

L. 869 " That make " (1827) ; "making " 1819-1820.
L. 874 (1836) " As if ["And a," 1832] confusing dark-
ness came."
L. 891 (1836) ; previously " A lonely house her dwell-
ing was."
Ll. 918-920 (1820) ; in 1819 :

> " Distraction reigns in soul and sense,
> And reason drops in impotence
> From her deserted pinnacle."

L. 939 " ear " 1820 ; " ears " 1819.
Ll. 941-943 (1836) : in 1819-1832 :

> " Though clamorous as a hunter's horn
> Re-echoed from a naked rock
> 'Tis [" Is " 1832] from that tabernacle—List "

Ll. 971-980.   These stanzas, which speak of the entry
of Jesus unto Jerusalem on an ass were omitted 1827 ;
restored 1832.   In 1819-1832 l. 971 was " 'Tis said, that
through prevailing grace ; " in l. 973 " shoulders ; " l.
974 " Meek beast! in memory of the Lord ; " l. 976 "In
memory of that solemn day."
Ll. 982, 983 (1836) ; previously :

> " Towards a gate in open view
> Turns up a narrow lane ; his chest."

Ll. 992-995 (1836); previously :

> " Had gone two hundred yards, not more ;
> When to a lonely house he came ;
> He turn'd aside towards the same
> And stopp'd before the door."

L. 1002 " In hopes " (1836) previously " In hope."

L. 1013 " to " (1827); " at " (1819-1820).

L. 1016 (1832); previously " What could he do ?—The woman lay."

L. 1041 " Widow " (1836); previously " sufferer."

L. 1085 (1836); previously " And to the pillow gives her burning head."

L. 1090 " His elbows " (1827); " And resting on " (1819-1820).

L. 1096 " Lifts " (1827); " turns " (1819-1820).

L. 1104 (1836); previously " Of night his inward grief and fear."

L. 1109 " hath " (1827); previously " had."

L. 1111 " Forth to ' (1836); previously " Towards."

L. 1133 " Renounced " (1832); previously " repressed." —ED.

Additional Note on Laodamia.

The stanza of Laodamia beginning " And while my youthful peers " was added while the poem was in the printer's hands (Wordsworth to De Quincey, Feb. 8, 1815); and at the same time Wordsworth altered " the oracle " of his MS. in the next stanza (l. 122) to " our future course," lest the words " should seem to allude to the other answer of the Oracle which commanded the sacrifice of Iphigenia." In defence of the alteration at the close of the poem Wordsworth wrote to his nephew, John Wordsworth, in 1831 : " As first written, the heroine was dismissed to happiness in Elysium. To what purpose then the mission of Protesilaus ? He exhorts her to moderate her passion; the exhortation is fruitless, and no punishment follows. So it stood : at present she is placed among unhappy ghosts for disregard of the exhortation. Virgil also places her there, but compare the two passages and give me *your* opinion." (Quoted in " William Wordsworth," by Elizabeth Wordsworth, p. 131)—ED.

END OF VOL. II.

CHISWICK PRESS :—C. WHITTINGHAM AND CO., TOOKS COURT, CHANCERY LANE.

Lightning Source UK Ltd.
Milton Keynes UK
UKHW020606170219
337398UK00013B/1009/P